Virilio Now

D0887950

Theory Now

Series Editor: Ryan Bishop

Virilio Now

Current Perspectives in Virilio Studies

EDITED BY
JOHN ARMITAGE

polity

Copyright this collection © Polity Press 2011

Copyright chapter 7 © Nigel Thrift 2005. Originally published in *Cultural Politics: An International Journal*, Volume 1, Number 3, November 2005

Chapter 11 originally published as 'Etudes d'impact' in *Événementiel Vs Action Culturelle, Internationale de L'imaginaire*, n.s. 22, 2007 © Paul Virilio 2007. This English edition © Polity Press 2011

Copyright Introduction, chapters 1,2,3,4,5,6,8,9,10 © Polity Press 2011

The right of the authors to be identified as Author of this Work has been asserted in accordance with the UK Copyright, Designs and Patents Act 1988.

First published in 2011 by Polity Press

Polity Press
65 Bridge Street
Cambridge CB2 1UR, UK

Polity Press
350 Main Street
Malden, MA 02148, USA

All rights reserved. Except for the quotation of short passages for the purpose of criticism and review, no part of this publication may be reproduced, stored in a retrieval system, or transmitted, in any form or by any means, electronic, mechanical, photocopying, recording or otherwise, without the prior permission of the publisher.

ISBN-13: 978-0-7456-4877-4
ISBN-13: 978-0-7456-4878-1(pb)

A catalogue record for this book is available from the British Library.

Typeset in 11 on 13 pt Bembo
by Servis Filmsetting Ltd, Stockport, Cheshire
Printed and bound in Great Britain by MPG Books Group Limited, Bodmin, Cornwall

The publisher has used its best endeavours to ensure that the URLs for external websites referred to in this book are correct and active at the time of going to press. However, the publisher has no responsibility for the websites and can make no guarantee that a site will remain live or that the content is or will remain appropriate.

Every effort has been made to trace all copyright holders, but if any have been inadvertently overlooked the publisher will be pleased to include any necessary credits in any subsequent reprint or edition.

For further information on Polity, visit our website: www.politybooks.com

Contents

For Zygmunt Bauman

Notes on Contributors

JOHN ARMITAGE is Associate Dean and Head of Department of Media at Northumbria University. He is co-editor, with Ryan Bishop and Douglas Kellner, of the Berg journal *Cultural Politics*.

PAUL CROSTHWAITE is Lecturer in English Literature at Cardiff University. His publications include *Trauma, Postmodernism, and the Aftermath of World War II* (Palgrave Macmillan, 2009), articles in *Angelaki*, *Cultural Politics*, and *Textual Practice*, and, as editor, *Criticism, Crisis, and Contemporary Narrative: Textual Horizons in an Age of Global Risk* (Routledge, 2011). He is currently writing a book entitled *Reading the Markets: Finance, Feeling, and Representation in Contemporary Literature and Culture*.

SEAN CUBITT is Professor of Global Media and Communication at Winchester School of Art, University of Southampton; Professional Fellow in Media and Communications at the University of Melbourne; and Honorary Professor of the University of Dundee. His publications include *Timeshift: On Video Culture*, *Videography: Video Media as Art and Culture*, *Digital Aesthetics*, *Simulation and Social Theory*, *The Cinema Effect* and *EcoMedia*. He is the series editor for Leonardo Books at MIT Press.

JOY GARNETT is a painter who lives and works in New York. Her work has been exhibited widely at venues that include P.S.1-MoMA Contemporary Art Center and the Whitney Museum of American Art (both in New York). She is a recipient of a grant from Anonymous Was a Woman, and serves as Arts Editor for the scholarly journal *Cultural Politics*. She is represented by Winkleman Gallery, New York.

ARTHUR KROKER is Canada Research Chair in Technology, Culture and Theory, Professor of Political Science, and Director of the Pacific Center for Technology and Culture at the University of Victoria, Canada. His most recent projects include the monograph *Born Again Ideology: Religion, Technology and Terrorism* (New World Perspectives, 2008), and *Critical Digital Studies: A Reader*, co-edited with Marilouise Kroker (University of Toronto, 2008). Among others, his books include *The Will to Technology and the Culture of Nihilism: Heidegger, Nietzsche, and Marx* (University of Toronto Press, 2004). With Marilouise Kroker, he is the co-editor of the *Digital Futures* book series for the University of Toronto Press, as well as the peer-reviewed, electronic journal *CTheory*. www. krokers.net; www.ctheory.net

SCOTT MCQUIRE is Associate Professor and Reader in the Media and Communication Program at the University of Melbourne. His most recent books are *The Media City: Media, Architecture and Urban Space* (2008), which won the Urban Communication Foundation's 2009 Jane Jacobs Publication Award and the *Urban Screens Reader* (2009) which he co-edited with Meredith Martin and Sabine Niederer.

ADAM SHARR is Professor of Architecture at the University of Newcastle upon Tyne, principal of Adam Sharr Architects, editor of *arq: Architectural Research Quarterly* (Cambridge University Press), with Richard Weston, and series editor of *Thinkers for Architects* (Routledge).

ELIN O'HARA SLAVICK is a Distinguished Professor of Studio Art, Theory and Practice at the University of North Carolina at Chapel Hill. She is the author of *Bomb After Bomb: A Violent Cartography* (CHARTA, 2007). Her work has been exhibited internationally.

NIGEL THRIFT is Vice-Chancellor of the University of Warwick, an Emeritus Professor of the University of Bristol and a Visiting Professor at the University of Oxford. He is the author of *Non-Representational Theory: Space, Politics, Affect* (2007) and (with Paul Glennie) *Shaping the Day: A History of Timekeeping in England and Wales, 1300-1800* (2009).

PAUL VIRILIO is former Director of the École Spéciale d'Architecture in Paris. He is the author of many books on war and cinema, perception, architecture, art, militarism, and technology, including, most recently, *The University of Disaster* (2010) and *The Futurism of the Instant* (2010), both published by Polity.

Acknowledgements

I would like to thank several people for their help in preparing *Virilio Now: Current Perspectives in Virilio Studies* for publication: Ryan Bishop, my American friend, who initially suggested the book and who acted above and beyond the call of duty as an anonymous referee on every chapter in this volume; Andrea Drugan, my editor at Polity, whose enthusiasm for *Virilio Now* never seemed to waver, even when mine did; Professor Lynn Dobbs, Dean of the School of Arts and Social Sciences at Northumbria University, whose 'wizzy' (her favourite buzzword) financial acumen gave rise to a generous sabbatical in 2009, during which I undertook much of the work that you, dear reader, are now holding in your hands; Professor Rosie Cunningham, Associate Dean of Academic Development in the School of Arts and Social Sciences at Northumbria University, who has always supported my efforts to continue reading, writing, and publishing, despite the black hole that is university administration, and inside which, contrary to all known astronomical laws, the gravitational force is still not strong enough to prevent books like this one escaping; Joy Garnett, my other American friend, whose magnificent painting adorns the cover of this volume and whose knowledge of contemporary art I have to come value much more than she knows; all the contributors to *Virilio Now*, many of whom are less academic colleagues than good friends; Paul Virilio, for his own contributions to this book and for enduring no less than three major interview sessions with me in Paris (1997, 1999) and La Rochelle (2009); Julia Hall at Berg Publishers, for allowing Polity to publish Nigel Thrift's 'Panicsville: Paul Virilio and the Esthetic of Disaster' from *Cultural Politics* in this volume; Zygmunt Bauman, whose sociology seminars at his and his wife Janina's home I shall never forget because they both awakened and challenged me whilst I was an undergraduate in politics at the University of Leeds between 1979–82; my friends at *Cultural Politics* and, in particular, Douglas Kellner and John Beck, Sean Cubitt, Mark Featherstone, Patrice Riemens, Kevin Robins, and Chris Turner; my mirror twin, Joanne Roberts, always fond, sometimes fragile, she reciprocally rights our schooner's course, regulates our sails, on our own private ocean, over ten thousand kisses deep; and, finally, I would like to thank my mother and father, Barbara and Jeffrey Armitage, for that most precious of all gifts, the gift of life itself.

John Armitage
Newcastle upon Tyne, August 2010

1

Paul Virilio: A Critical Overview

John Armitage

Introducing Paul Virilio

Born in Paris in 1932, Paul Virilio started his professional life as a painter and exceptional maker of stained-glass imagery, working with Henri Matisse and Georges Braque. Such artistic beginnings also augured the birth of an unusual academic career. Virilio established an architectural practice in 1963 with the architect Claude Parent before taking part in the *événements* of May 1968 and subsequently went on to teach architecture at the *École Spéciale d'Architecture* in Paris-Montparnasse in 1968. His initial writings in the 1960s comprised articles on city planning and the militarization of public space for *Architecture Principe* (Virilio and Parent 1996a), the architectural practice and journal of the same title he set up with Parent, as well as reflections on the organization of territory and military fortifications, and contributions to the journals *Esprit*, *Cause Commune* and *Traverses*. In 1975, Virilio published *Bunker Archeology* (1994a), the culmination of his research, begun in 1958, on the Atlantic Wall, the massive system of coastal fortifications constructed by the Nazis during the Second World War (1942–4) along the western shores of Europe to protect against an expected

Image 1.1: Paul Virilio, following the 'Third War' interview, L'Argoat Bar and Restaurant, La Rochelle, France (John Armitage, 2009).

Allied invasion of the mainland from the United Kingdom. He retired in 1997 and today dedicates his time to writing, being a reluctant traveller, and living in La Rochelle, a city and seaport in south-western France on the Atlantic Ocean's Bay of Biscay.

Virilio describes himself as a French 'critic of the art of technology' (Virilio and Armitage 2009: 101–2) and has favoured architecture, art, and technology as important areas of critique, and from his first works he has used these as arenas within which to exemplify his cultural theory and philosophy. Latterly, as Virilio explains in Chapter 2 of *Virilio Now: Current Perspectives in Virilio Studies*, 'The Third War: Cities, Conflict, and Contemporary Art', the interview with me that was conducted in 2009 (Image 1.1)

where he discusses his extant thinking on the concept of the postmodern and the birth of the city, the philosophy of war, aesthetic
resistance, temporal compression, technoscience and 'progress', he
has developed an intense concern with 'the problem of the end
of geography', and has had his ideas and images about 'the end of
the fullness or the wholeness of the Earth' published and exhibited
alongside the French photojournalist and documentary filmmaker
Raymond Depardon at the *Fondation Cartier pour l'art contemporain*
(Virilio and Depardon 2008).

The most important academic conference on Virilio's writings
thus far, which took place in Germany in 2006, was held at the
Zentrum für Kunst und Medientechnologie (ZKM) and concentrated
on his involvement with architecture, art and technology (Gente
2008). However, Virilio's work on these three important areas
has frequently been misconstrued by cultural theorists, architects,
artists and other critics of technology.

To be clear, the key philosophical influences on Virilio are
Edmund Husserl (1970) and Maurice Merleau-Ponty (1962).
However, Virilio's own radical approach to critique ensues
from his formation in architectural, aesthetic and technological
critique focusing first of all on the theory of the 'oblique function' (Virilio and Parent 1996b), an architectural method I have
described elsewhere, along with Joanne Roberts (2007: 428), as
one that appropriates city space by way of 'the *Gestalt* psychology
of form, the endorsement of incessantly flowing movement and
gravitational bodies in flux on slanting planes', and which led to
the construction of his and Parent's main architectural work: the
Church of Sainte-Bernadette-du-Banlay in Nevers in 1966 (Images 1.2
and 1.3):

Concentrating on the cultural theory of architecture, art and,
increasingly, technologized spaces following the advent of 'new
Brutalism', an architectural term created in the UK in 1954 to
describe the style of Le Corbusier at the time of Marseilles and
Chandigarh, the Smithsons, Archigram, Paul Rudolph and Kenzo
Tange, Virilio began specializing in the critique of modern architecture. The nature of Virilio's critique is opinionated, review-like
and unceremonious, involved, at least in the 1960s and 1970s,
mostly with architecture and notions of 'critical space', but crucially

Image 1.2: Church of Sainte-Bernadette-du-Banlay, west elevation (John Armitage, 2006).

Image 1.3: Church of Sainte-Bernadette-du-Banlay, east elevation (John Armitage, 2006).

shaped by Georges Perec's (1997) *Species of Space and Other Pieces* and a variety of architectural yet, significantly, militarily inflected philosophers and commentators ranging from Martin Heidegger (1977) to Ernst Jünger (2004), Albert Speer (1995), Sun Tzu (1993) and Carl von Clausewitz (1976).

Understanding Virilio

Perhaps the key to understanding the importance of Virilio's work on architecture, art and technology lies in the connections he makes between architecture, the organization of territory, and an idiosyncratic 'archaeology' of military fortifications, such as military bunkers, and the structure he creates for building these connections with art and technology (Virilio 1994a). Virilio explains this structure as an 'archaeology' of military configurations, and it works less as a chronology of Western military fortifications and more as an aesthetic foundation for interdisciplinary cultural research into the increasingly technologized history of peace, war and strategic studies in the humanities and the arts. It can therefore be interpreted as a reworking of familiar cultural and particularly aesthetic critiques of the technological effects of technology on the organization of social life and space from the First World War to the present day (see, e.g., Ellul 1973). For instance, Virilio (1994a: 7) commences his *Bunker Archeology* with a quotation – Heidegger's important critique of 'combat' and 'combatants' – which proposes that, with the emergence within any military assault of the 'unheard of' (in addition to the 'unsaid' and the 'unthought'), the link between combat and the world is considerably changed, and as much by poets and thinkers as generals and statesmen. From the First World War, Virilio argues, there have been what, given the absence of any other concept, I shall call various diverse and intersecting *regimes of combat*. These regimes of combat can be critiqued by way of Virilio's theorization of military architecture, which opposes the idea that, when combat ceases, that which it has brought about disappears. This is fundamental because the 'reality' of combat is assigned a connotation of precise importance. For Virilio, the reality of combat never ceases to exist or to reappear within contemporary cultures. Thus the reality of combat never disappears but, rather, and, while the world attempts to avert its gaze, makes its reappearance felt after the beginning of the very modern First and Second World Wars, and architecture, art, and technology have favoured positions in such developments. Virilio's thoughts are consequently more similar to a military theory rather than to traditional cultural theories of architecture, art and technology.

In much the same manner, Chapter 3, Adam Sharr's 'Burning Bruder Klaus: Towards an Architecture of Slipstream', engages with Virilio's conceptions about buildings and aggression, theorizations of the end of art, and the architecture of annihilation to question not merely technologies of combat in the conventional sense but also Virilio's cultural theory of architecture, art and technology in the unconventional sense of a building, the Bruder Klaus *Feldkapelle* near the village of Wachendorf, Germany (architect Peter Zumthor, 2007), dedicated to the fifteenth century Swiss saint Niklaus von Flüe, known usually as Bruder Klaus, that, uncommonly, met a fiery inauguration. 'The violence of this small building's origins', argues Sharr, 'and the speeds of its construction and use', can not only be associated with Virilio's philosophy of architecture but also open it to question and especially to the question of architectural deceleration.

While Virilio's philosophy of architecture may well be problematic with regard to questions of deceleration, it is obvious, nonetheless, that his approach to architecture, art and technology acknowledges them as crucial sites of insecurity. Moreover, Virilio observes that, as part of a world where, when combat ceases, that which it had brought about does not disappear, architecture, art, and technology operate as territories of insecurity founded on the reality of combat. In Virilio's (1976) early work, he described this culture as one rooted in the idea that, when combat ceases, that which has brought it about reappears as contemporary geopolitics. The world speeds up and the political participates in an ever more 'dromological' (Virilio 1986) or accelerated realm which did not previously exist, an area which is generated by the military and political repercussions of the revolution in transport and transmission. Gathering speed whilst becoming more and more politicized, militarized, transferred and broadcast on cinema and television screens, architecture, art and technology thus turn into the focal points of Virilio's (re)consideration of 'popular defence' as 'ecological struggles' (Virilio 1990). Naturally, everything alters with the appearance of the 'unheard of' of 'Pure Power', with the previously 'unsaid' of 'Revolutionary Resistance' understood with reference to the, until that time, 'unthought' of 'the problem of speed and its vectors, of the expansion of its area' (Virilio 1990: 89). At the outset, such an 'unheard of' of pure power remains no more than an outline for a programme of revolutionary resistance, for territorial defence, or, put differently, for the beginnings of popular struggle against the 'enemy' of *'physical or mechanical acceleration*, the acceleration of particles, of vehicles'(Virilio 1990: 89; original emphases). In terms of the structure of Virilio's writings on territorial defence, the culture develops into one where works of architecture, art and technology come to territorialize our insecurities, which are themselves derived from the reality of combat, and this procedure is more and more rationalized through practices of seizure, through the reality of combat, and through an 'aesthetics of disappearance', Virilio's (2009a) conception of a socio-cultural regime all the time more activated by the technological effects of cinematics. For Virilio, the aesthetics of disappearance refers to the mediated technological effects typical of the contemporary arts. Whereas the ancient aesthetics of appearance was based on lasting material supports (wood/canvas in the case of paintings; marble in the case of statues, etc.) the present-day aesthetics of disappearance is founded on temporary immaterial supports (plastic/digital storage in the case of films, etc.). Contemporary images therefore do not so much appear (except as a function of human cognition) as continually disappear. Modern-day images thus apparently move across but actually and repeatedly vanish from the fundamentally immaterial support of the screen as part of a cinematic sequence. In the case of film, such images disappear at twenty-four frames per second or, in the case of special effects, at sixty frames per second and above.

In Chapter 4, 'Vector Politics and the Aesthetics of Disappearance', Sean Cubitt similarly envisages Virilio's reaction not to film as such but to the *YouTube* phenomenon, to the cultural phenomenon that has us all becoming images. Certainly, for Cubitt, the works of architecture or art that appear and disappear on the vision technology that is *YouTube* now accelerate all the 'felt materialities of existence, of life', and so our increasingly deterritorialized insecurities reach out not for reality but for the reality substitutes that are special effects. Involved in daily battles with the 'immaterial immediacy of filmic representations' and their hyperrationalized systems of confinement at work everywhere today in our global cities, the reality of the 'vector' (a term meaning a quantity having direction and scale, particularly as establishing the place of one point in space compared with another) in Cubitt's view can be located in the discourses of biology, mathematics and, most importantly, contemporary media theory. As ontology and as politics, Cubitt nevertheless argues that Virilio's combative relationship to the vector fails to spot that there are 'vectorial' 'behaviors that are significant, even if they do not appear so from the biopolitical vantage where they are merely statistical anomalies'. Thus, from Cubitt's standpoint, Virilio's aesthetics of disappearance does not fully encapsulate our contemporary socio-cultural regime gradually more set in motion by the technoscientific effects and cinematics of *YouTube* or the possibly optimistic 'vector politics' that will continue in the 'wide field of computerized information governance', electronic struggles 'over the soul of change', and the 'intellectual, creative, and political fight for openness'.

Yet, for Virilio (1991) at any rate, such struggles, fights or combat should be understood as struggles over territories of insecurity or as related to the innovative philosophical premises that he sets up, particularly in his texts of the early 1980s, such as *The Lost Dimension*. And so there continues within this regime of architectural, artistic and technological relationships the idea that, when combat ceases, that which it has brought about reappears as 'critical space', which means that physical or real space suddenly finds itself in a perilous condition. This regime of territorialized insecurity Virilio imagines as a contemporary regime of combat whereby real space comes under threat, because, in the present period, territorialization is no longer based on substance but on cybernetics or the separation of the world of real space and its form of territorialization from the world of cybernetic space and its mode of virtualization. The 'unity of space', Virilio suggests, 'which served as a basis for Le Corbusier, for the Archigram group, for all of us in a sense', is, then, 'in the process of being broken up' by way of the accelerated appearance of the 'unheard of' of cybernetic or virtual space (Virilio and Armitage 2001: 24). In other words, revolutionary resistance is now crucially concerned with the 'unsaid' of virtualized speed-space, whether that is the 'unheard of' of the development of ideas related to the pure power of technology, the popular defence of real space or ecological struggles against cyberspace or the disappearance of whole dimensions.

Entering the regime of virtualized speed-space, the processes and growth of the pure power of technology, the popular defence of real space, and ecological struggles against cyberspace, ultimately establishes the possibility of Virilio's deliberation on the militarized production of architectural, artistic and technologized cinematics, and a popular defence not so much of real space as of real, human, or embodied perception, particularly given our increasingly deterritorialized insecurities. In *War and Cinema: The Logistics of Perception,* the 'sight machine' is the basis of Virilio's (1989: 1) study of 'the systematic use of camera techniques in the conflicts of the twentieth century', of armed photography, video surveillance of the front line, aerial reconnaissance, the organization of combat, indirect sighting devices, and the emergent 'derealization' of military encounter. In industrialized conflict, Virilio argues, the depiction of events surpasses the production of facts, as images gradually begin to exceed objects and real time starts to shift beyond real space. 'Soon', Virilio writes, 'a conflict of strategic and political interpretation would ensue, with radio and then radar completing the picture', thus preparing the way for a *'logistics of military perception,* in which a supply of images would become the equivalent of an ammunition supply' (Virilio 1989: 1; original emphases).

Perception, imagery and weaponry are also the characteristic terrain of Virilio's (2005a) Sun Tzu-like theorization of the *Negative Horizon,* of 'dromoscopy', or his conception of acceleration and its essentially devastating function within postmodern global culture and society. Theorizing Western political and

military history, Virilio uncovers its craving for acceleration and
the resulting appearance of a 'chrono' or speed politics over a
'spatio' or territorial politics. Traversing human history, architecture and art, primitive hunter-gatherer societies, the taming
of animals, the construction of highways, covert military technologies, and present-day combat, Virilio demonstrates how the
pure power of technological acceleration has virtually eradicated
real space to gratify the West's need for speed. In revealing what
he considers to be the global effects of this relentless and highly
politicized acceleration for human visual perception in particular, Virilio presents a unique if disconcerting image of political
history.

Virilio's theories, I argue, are at their best when they focus not
on the processes and development of the pure power of technology as such but, rather, when such processes are *in transition*, when
architecture, art and technology no longer remain connected to
their ostensible purposes, but, instead, become more and more
concerned with issues related to, for example, *The Vision Machine*
(1994b), which is a stimulating examination of the technologies
of human visual perception, their manufacture and their distribution of representations throughout human history. Reviewing art
history, technologies of combat and the development of the city,
Virilio's (1994b: 63) *The Vision Machine* introduces a new 'logistics
of the image', which has advanced through distinct eras of proliferation. From 'the age of painting, engraving, and etching', ending
'with the eighteenth century', Virilio's history of visual regimes
changes with 'the age of photography and film' in the nineteenth
century (1994b: 63). The postmodern epoch begins 'with the
invention of video recording, holography, and computer graphics . . . as though, at the close of the twentieth century, the end of
modernity were itself marked by the end of a logic of public representation' (Virilio 1994b: 63). *The Vision Machine* thus presents
an invigorating explanation of the history of vision and transforms
both the conventional periodization of art history and our knowledge of postmodern culture. Once the vision machine is examined
by Virilio, its analytical value and function are revealed as aids to
understanding the technologization of human visual perception in
and of the world. The vision machine is thus a cinematic or sight

machine in a gradually more cinematic visual system, a machine and a system that is also linked to the newly developing technologies of environmental control that bring about what Virilio (2000a) calls *Polar Inertia*.

An important text and a critical investigation into the associations between real space, real time and technology, *Polar Inertia* looks at how notions of 'here' and 'now', territorialization, and the human body are being restructured by new information and communications technologies, such as the Internet, on a global scale. In a characteristic offensive that contemplates everything from ships to spaceships, cinema and a technoscience that functions more and more without a conscience, Virilio proposes that the new technologies have produced a generalized inertia or inactivity that has become the distinctive order of postmodernity, a contention which argues that 'the "real time" of interactivity' has overtaken 'the real space of customary activity', whereby 'we are moving towards home activity on earth analogous to the activity of astronauts moving around in high orbit' (Virilio 2000a: 69). Accordingly, as real time replaces the real space and ancient dominion of our earthly territory, everything occurs *now* and, crucially, with no obligation on the part of the human body to move. The supremacy of real time, of speed-space, denotes not just the generalized arrival of the pure power of technologized screens in public as well as private spaces, but also the assimilation of international relations and politics into vision machines as global conflict combines with the pace of today's vision technologies. Virilio's (2002a) predictions in *Desert Screen: War at the Speed of Light*, for instance, equate the Gulf War of 1991 between the United States and its allies and Saddam Hussein's Iraq with a decisive moment in the history and future of combat, as the final industrialized and the first informationalized war:

> *The desert is a screen* where all is exposed to the searching eye of an adversary employing the full array of object-acquisition systems: advanced alert satellites, AWACS and aerial reconnaissance devices, piloted or automatic, such as the tele-commanded drones employed extensively by the Israelis in the region (2002a: 26–7; original emphases)

Virilio (2002a: 21; original emphases) offers his reports on the desert as a screen as the deliberations of a '*hostage of the televisual interface*', of a 'tele-spectator' who has become 'directly involved in an uncertainty principle dependent upon the very rhythm of "communiqués", in the manner of embassy officials'. Claiming that we now exist in an era of worldwide confrontation witnessed in real time, of geopolitical and chronological disintegration, Virilio portrays the current conjuncture as one that is depleted by Cold War geopolitics, as an epoch wherein everything is revealed to the penetrating gaze of political opponents using an extensive range of militarized and mediated technological systems, which, of course, from here on in, prevent any opportunity for non-technologized geopolitical cooperation or international relations.

Virilio (1995) critiques this present conjuncture as a shift from cinematics and the vision machine to the architecture, art and technoculture of *The Art of the Motor*. Technoculture is a culture that alters how we comprehend the world of architecture and art, and develops into a culture flooded with politicized and accelerated information that puts an end to the continuation of human-centred time. Virilio offers his most extreme interpretation in *Open Sky* (1997): technoculture is a culture that is no longer rooted in the production of the territorialized security of architecture, art and technology, but in the deterritorialized insecurity of an 'architecture' and 'art' shaped by the wholly destructive technologies of mediated communication and surveillance. So, for example, the Kosovo War of 1999 between the North Atlantic Treaty Organization (NATO) and Slobodan Milošević's Serbia was decided not by any concerns about the production of ter-ritorialized security, but by the 'unsaid' of strategic rather than moral factors and a menacing 'advance' in the techniques of combat: that of territorial space being substituted by an 'orbital' or 'aero-electro-magnetic space' where practices of worldwide 'telesurveillance' are connected to the devastating force of air-power and Cruise Missiles as territorialized states, the increasingly deterritorialized military and the media, become components of a near-perfect yet ethically questionable development associated with newly militarized information and communications tech-nologies (Virilio 2000b; Virilio and Armitage 2000). This new regime of combat is no longer anchored in any obvious differences between territory and insecurity, between the 'landscape' and the 'reality' of the world of 'events' (Virilio 2000c). Without doubt, for Virilio, the new 'reality' of the world of events has in fact ingested everyday life through a kind of accelerated cultural pandemonium. The dominance and repetitive bouts of this accelerated cultural chaos, of mass mediated brutality, is such that the urban public sphere in particular cannot be experienced except as an ever more deterritorialized form of bewilderment, with war machines and the speeding-up of events in postmodern everyday life now becoming clearly continuing if problematic technologies and temporal concerns for Virilio. The realm of the 'landscape of events' is thus more politicized and militarized as well as progressively derived from the 'reality' of media reporting. Virilio (2000d) makes use of the expression 'information bomb' from Albert Einstein's physics and laws of relativity to hypothesize this switch into the real time of media networks. Simultaneously, the border between the civilian-political field and the military field collapses in a development which Virilio (2000d: 1) describes as the 'militarization of science' whereby 'the extent of progress achieved' can now only be gauged by 'the scale of technical catastrophes occasioned'.

By focusing on Virilio's (2000d) *The Information Bomb* and interrelated issues of real time, Scott McQuire's 'Virilio's Media as Philosophy', which forms Chapter 5, considers Virilio's understanding of media networks by means of an investigation into his conception of the media as 'complex transformers' of 'human modes of being in the modern world'. Yet, as McQuire argues, Virilio's 'technological determinism', a possibly reductionist theoretical idea that assumes that technology alone powers the growth of cultural structures and social values, contains its own dangers, even if it does generate stimulating critiques of the media seldom equalled today. From McQuire's perspective, therefore, Virilio's media philosophy, whilst broaching important questions involving the political and the military, ignores, to a significant extent, key problems relating to the specificities of any alternative media strategy or varieties of cultural cohesion in the era of technoscience, 'progress' and disaster.

All the same, far-reaching inferences can be extracted from Virilio's philosophical critique of contemporary media and technoculture. One is that it becomes feasible for architecture, art and technology to double as analytical vehicles; meanwhile, inside technoculture itself critical groupings and theory become fundamental to understanding that the '11 September 2001 attack' was *an act of total war*, remarkably conceived and executed, with a minimum of resources' or that the destruction wrought on Washington DC's Pentagon Building and New York City's World Trade Center, left 'America out for the count', and the Manhattan skyline as both 'the front of the new war' and the prototype of a new 'temporary authoritarian zone' (Virilio 2002b: 82; original emphases; Armitage 2010: 18–19). The chief dilemmas of technoculture are no longer those of economy and politics, but ones of art, fear, and a culture driven by technoscience, where the upper limits of aesthetics are discarded and genetic engineering and the Human Genome Project expand inexorably (Virilio 2003a). According to Virilio, these developments are powered by new and disrespectful principles of reasoning, anti-human stratagems, hideous varieties of existence and torment and systems of thinking founded on disappearance such as Abstract Expressionism and the slaughter of men and women who were merely cannon fodder in the dugouts of the First and Second World Wars, all of which come to substitute 'pitiful' (in the sense of deserving of or arousing pity or compassion) architecture, art and technology. In architecture, art and technology these modes of analysis that Virilio (2003b) calls the *Unknown Quantity* are of various types. However, one significant logic is towards 'the accumulation of excesses of all kinds, including two World Wars, forty years of the balance of terror, and an unprecedented proliferation of major accidents', with another logic towards 'chance events' (Virilio 2003b: frontispiece). But these logics entail not the end of war, accidents and death but the beginning of 'a spirit in which excess wins out over moderation and unreason over the wisdom of nations' (Virilio 2003b: frontispiece). Architecture, art and technology all combine with demolition and combat, with 'progress' *as* catastrophe, and also fragment into the continually splintering 'unsaid' of contemporary temporalities, and as such 'liberate' or 'emancipate' the customary laws of architecture, art and technology from the 'earth's gravity' by increasingly creating, deterritorializing, and obtaining progressively more 'escape velocity' from non-technological and 'simple' reality (Virilio 2003b: frontispiece). Thus architecture, art and technology are 'liberated' or 'emancipated' and, as forms of combat that reappear, let loose carnage on the world and promote the very rapid evolution of major disasters, such as Bhopal in 1984, Chernobyl in 1986, or, in the present period, the 2010 Deepwater Horizon oil spill in the Gulf of Mexico that is the largest offshore oil spill in the history of the United States.

Bringing into play Virilio's notions of architecture, art and technology, above all in *Art and Fear* (2003a) and *Unknown Quantity* (2003b), Elin O'Hara Slavick's 'Empathetic Vision: Aesthetics of Power and Loss', which comprises Chapter 6, interrogates his disparagement of many contemporary artists as tainted by aggression and tyrannical power systems. Arguing and demonstrating through her presentation of a collection of outstanding artists and their compelling images that many in the postmodern art world intentionally work in opposition to violence and the abuse of power, O'Hara Slavick writes fervently about these artists and their work, from Leah Bailis' 'Fence' (2007) and O'Hara Slavick's own 'Hiroshima Mask' (2008) to Lisa Ross' 'Mauthausen' (2003), the latter of which is a series of photographs of showerheads at the Nazi Mauthausen concentration camp in Austria. Following Susan Sontag (2003), O'Hara Slavick invites us to contemplate what Virilio means by objecting to anguish, as distinct from recognizing it. Disputing what some might see as Virilio's bleak aesthetic theories, O'Hara Slavick refuses to accept that either she or the extremely impressive group of contemporary artists that she has gathered together here are associated with or participate in that bleakness.

Nonetheless, Virilio insists that his sometimes gloomy conjectures on contemporary architecture, art and technology can no longer overlook the *City of Panic* (2005b), no longer ignore a critical investigation into the postmodern city. Architecture, art and technology combine with the guiding principles of contemporary urban culture in such a way that they conspire with its basic procedures of panic (the narrative of all postmodern cities according to Virilio). Furthermore, in his recent work, Virilio has sketched out a theoretical model of a new regime of combat as cities the world over are rebuilt by means of the promotion of terror. This is the regime of combat founded upon the fundamental propagation of gated 'communities', including strictly controlled entrances, closed perimeter walls and fences, and security-led patrolled shopping malls representing safety-conscious retailers and consumers, interconnecting internal walkways, and parking areas, way beyond the dominance of previously modern practices of architecture, art and technology, and where only the ever-expanding web of surveillance that monitors our behaviour and activities and a media constantly engineering the empire of fear survive. The theoretical transformations in Virilio's contemporary work are extraordinary, and are governed by the idea of the 'city of panic' as modern urban centres are demolished and substituted by postmodern metropolitan decentred homogeneities and we come to acknowledge that the contemporary city – Tijuana and London, Baghdad, Tehran, Kabul and Mumbai – if truth be told, is a battleground. To critique contemporary urban culture, Virilio has contended, it is essential to centre our thoughts on dread and alarm as images become ubiquitous: images do not any longer occur in a mental and cerebral time and space; instead the 'instrumental image is instantly provided for us by television' (Virilio 2005b: 85). Postmodern architecture, art and technology, for instance, he proposes, could be described as the recurring forms of the near-incomprehensible city of panic:

> '. . . *the image loop has become the signature of contemporary disasters'*. And so, the incessant round of satellites doing the vast ring road of the City-World is now doubled with the *looping* of terrorizing images in a 'state of siege' of the viewer's mind. The most obvious result is this raging mass psychosis of the BESIEGED affecting people throughout the world in the age of globalization. (Virilio 2005b: 85; original emphases)

Despite the above, in 'Panicsville: Paul Virilio and the Aesthetic of Disaster', which is Chapter 7 of this book, Nigel Thrift critically appraises Virilio's *City of Panic*. Identifying what Thrift understands as the difficulties with the portents of widespread devastation and ultimate doom contained in both the substance and tenor of Virilio's work on the postmodern city, Thrift turns to current social science urban research to build an alternative and rather more cautious explanation of the present-day metropolis because, for him, careful accounts of the postmodern city are nearer to the truth of existing urban culture. Perhaps, therefore, as Thrift argues, what is required is a reinvigorated resumption of friendly relations between cultural theory and urban practice that will be beneficial to real architectural and artistic, technological and, importantly, political 'progress', even if the era is as threatening as Virilio portrays it.

In almost total contrast to Thrift's 'Panicsville', Chapter 8, 'Three Theses on Virilio Now', Arthur Kroker's contribution, engages with Virilio's *City of Panic* as the 'City of Transformation' in US President Barack Obama's America in addition to numerous other 'Minor Simulations', 'Major Disturbances', and Walter Benjamin's (1968: 257) 'Angel of History', an angel whose 'face is turned toward the past'. Benjamin:

> Where we perceive a chain of events, he sees one single catastrophe which keeps piling wreckage upon wreckage and hurls it in front of his feet. The angel would like to stay, awaken the dead, and make whole what has been smashed. But a storm is blowing from Paradise; it has got caught in his wings with such violence that the angel can no longer close them. This storm irresistibly propels him into the future to which his back is turned, while the pile of debris before him grows skyward. This storm is what we call progress.(Benjamin 1968: 257–8)

In company with Benjamin's angel of history, with his face directed to days gone by, Kroker understands that it is not a sequence of events or a solitary disaster but the destiny of all cultural theorists, inclusive of Virilio, to be wrecked by the deadweight of a history that they imagined they were making whole. But, and counter to Thrift, Kroker claims that Virilio's work encapsulates magnificently the long nightmare that is the city of panic. In fact, Kroker is not merely unworried by Virilio's occasionally eccentric writings and accelerated style but also sees him both as a tempest-inducing sage calling into the world the hell of the violence of speed which marks

out postmodern culture and as a clairvoyant regarding the future of
technoculture. However, even for Kroker, Virilio's work, whilst
forever precisely depicting the facts of the techno-zeitgeist in the
city of transformation, rather too frequently reads as the work of
someone whose back is turned to the future. Mourning as the
heap of wreckage before him destroys the atmospheric environment, Virilio, from Kroker's perspective, consequently weeps for
all those things rendered outmoded by the hurricane of networked
culture, by the 'progress' that necessitates the disappearance of all
ethical possibilities instantaneously shut out by the syntax of new
information and communications technologies.

On the other hand, Virilio does not simply register a series
of regimes of combat such as the city of panic through a veil of
crocodile tears brought on by the vanishing of all moral principles.
Rather, his is a critique of the destiny of the idea and reality of
'the future' in contemporary culture, which, in previous centuries,
assured us of an ever-improving existence but which, today, is
alive with insecurity, hazards and terror. Virilio thus opposes these
regimes of combat because, for him, our everyday lives are more
and more encircled by dangers, terror campaigns, 'natural' disasters, and man-made tragedies. As a result, Virilio's work launches a
cultural politics of *The Original Accident* (2007a):

> From the arsenal of Venice in the age of Galileo right up to the secret
> laboratories of the post-Cold War, via the Manhattan Project of Los
> Alamos, science has become the arsenal of major accidents, the great
> catastrophe factory toiling away in anticipation of the cataclysms of
> hyperterrorism. (Virilio 2007a: 76)

Exhorting us to confront the costs of our new information and communications technologies allied with science, Virilio (2007a: 23–30)
petitions for the construction of 'The Accident Museum' to combat
our increasingly 'normalized' familiarization with revulsion and
carnage, with our day-by-day experience of fear. Yet he (2007a: 7;
original emphases) does so for the sake of a '*preventive intelligence*' that
can assist us in managing both 'natural' and non-natural calamities
such as terrorism. Hence Virilio (2007a: 7) 'aims first and foremost
to take a stand against the collapse of ethical and aesthetic landmarks,

that loss of meaning we so often witness now as victims much more than as actors. . .'. The Accident Museum accordingly:

> hopes to act as a counterpoint to the outrages of all stripes that we are swamped with on a daily basis by the major media outlets, that museum of horrors that no one seems to realize precedes and accompanies the escalation of even bigger disasters. (Virilio 2007a: 7–8)

So it would be an error to believe that Virilio's opposition to the innumerable regimes of combat at work in contemporary culture is one of absolute refusal of the path of the future of postmodernity, even if that future is constantly put in the shade for him by the nightmare vision of an obsolete humankind engulfed by a cataclysm of its own invention: the original accident. Following a short period of endorsement for a sort of Paris Commune style anarcho-syndicalism during the *évènements* of May 1968 (Virilio and Armitage 2001: 19–20), Virilio has thus at last embraced a standpoint on postmodern culture that is a critical consideration of technoscientific 'progress', a 'progress' at any price, with no boundaries, a 'progress' that amalgamates postindustrial science with hyperterrorism and which endangers the very foundations of human civilization. Hostile to the existing contemporary cultural politics of the future of the world and to the discovery of the original accident, Virilio castigates the abuse of our mounting collection of technoscientific developments and lobbies for the building of the Accident Museum.

Likewise, in Chapter 9, 'The Accident of Finance', Paul Crosthwaite engages with Virilio's stance on postmodern cultural politics and the prospects for civilization. Yet Crosthwaite's investigation is a meditation on the technoscientifically generated breakdown of stock markets around the globe, from 1987's 'Black Monday' to 2010's 'Flash Crash', when a disastrous collapse of US corporate market stocks transpired, followed by a more or less instant bounce-back. Here, the accident is interpreted by Crosthwaite as a variant of economic descent and deterioration, of deficit, and due to the ever more pervasive use of 'program trading' computer software that, from time to time, brings into being a frighteningly 'efficient' and wholly automated transaction machine whose commands jeopardize the very underpinnings of even the most neoliberal market conditions. Reorienting Virilio's writings on the vulnerability inherent within human 'progress' given its present financial systems, Crosthwaite analyses both the way in which Cold War nuclear fears have recently been overshadowed by post-Cold War financial angst in contemporary awareness and the depiction of this financial anguish in modern-day creative writing such as James Harland's (2002) *The Month of the Leopard* and Sebastian Faulks' (2009) *A Week in December*. Contrasting the analogous theoretical advances enunciated by Virilio and Jean Baudrillard (2002) in particular, Crosthwaite evaluates the scenarios for preventing 'the accident of finance' and for ameliorating the financial system that is nowadays seemingly endemic to our array of technoscientific creations in the age of international business, 'dromoeconomics' or the political economy of speed, and hypermodern organization (Virilio 1986; Armitage 2006: 339–53).

Virilio now: a conclusion and a perspective on Virilio's current studies

In Virilio's (2007b; 2009b: 57–82) current studies and interviews, his ideas about a number of the topics I have been discussing have turned to contemporary art, to a regime of combat based on varieties of perception and blindness. Virilio's cultural theory is at all times a kind of art, concerned of late with the destructive nature of technology and the connections between perception, artists and their materials. Indeed, in Virilio's opinion, contemporary art and perception are presently undergoing a transition that will only intensify our already considerable territorial insecurities as we enter the world of supposed 'new media' in art (Rush 2005), a world Virilio interprets as one that is emptied by dematerialization, by the loss of the apparent physical substance of art, and by an immaterial cultural politics that is coming into being through the damage done by new information and communications technologies. Virilio's cultural politics are an effort to reveal this widespread socio-cultural change as the radical experience of twenty-first century speed aligned with politics and mass culture. The field of postmodern cultural politics, in Virilio's judgement, is replete with attempts to characterize this sphere of radicalized new media art as mass culture by way of possession of an extreme or blind panic. Consequently, Virilio's urgency alters somewhat in postmodern culture away from reflections on war and peace towards induced panic and especially to the reality of our increasing dependence on the latest all-seeing communications technologies of the information bomb and so forth. Significantly, the continuing systems of reasoning at work within postmodern culture and politics tend to eradicate our very human reaction to architecture, art and technology. For Virilio, contemporary reality is bound up with regimes of combat, with the information bomb, so that the present reality of humanity is one of the loss of what Aldous Huxley (1943) once called, in one of Virilio's favourite books, *The Art of Seeing*, and with it one person's unhurried and imaginative engagement with the politics and aesthetics of another. Virilio understands the contemporary work of new media art in particular as signifying the instant when the postmodern regime of combat abolished our previously territorialized and secure feeling for the aesthetic (the reality of the twentieth century and, by comparison, it's rather decelerated modern artists) and became a new regime of combat, which is a regime of combat anchored in new modes of cultural politics and perception or new media art as light in opposition to 'old media' art as matter. Similar to Friedrich A. Kittler's (2010: 229) recently translated Berlin lectures on *Optical Media*, Virilio's (2007b) *Art as Far as the Eye Can See*, for example, gazes into the future of optical media and sees the emergence of a wholly dematerialized art, of what Kittler explains as 'a system that not only transmits but also stores and processes light as light'. 'In a last dramatic peripeteia of its deeds and sufferings', Kittler comments,

> this light will thus cease to be continuous electromagnetic waves. On the contrary, to adapt Newton freely, it will again function in its twin nature as particles in order to be equally as universal, equally as discrete, and equally as manipulable as today's computers. (Kittler 2010: 229)

Nevertheless, when, in 'Expect the Unexpected', Virilio (2007b: 1–33) expands on these ideas, he submits, I argue, a problematic mode or regime of combat. The 'postmodern period', he writes,

has seen a gradual shift away from an art once substantial, marked
by architecture, music, sculpture, and painting, and towards a purely
accidental art that the crisis in international architecture flagged at
practically the same time as the crisis in symphonic music.

This drift away from substantial art has been part and parcel of the
boom in film and radio and, in particular, television, the medium that
has ended up finally flattening all forms of representation, thanks to its
abrupt use of presentation, whereby real time definitely outclasses the
real space of major artworks, whether of literature or the visual arts.
(Virilio 2007b: 2–3)

As a result of the above, I maintain, Virilio has a cultural politics not so much of the original accident as a cultural politics of
the tragedy of an accidental art that denounces the postmodern
period for cultural and political reasons on top of particular types
of filmic, radiophonic and televisual projects. This case in point
demonstrates his unmistakable refusal of the regime of combat that
is insubstantial art, and compressed modes of representation, which
do not develop a substantial instant of representation but merely
develop a cultural politics derived from the sudden use of presentation which, for Virilio, is a kind of blindness. As Virilio puts it in
'The Third War' interview:

It is this tragic element in contemporary art that I consider in *Art as
Far as the Eye Can See*, where I wanted to convey both a sense of
our current blindness as well as a sense of immensity. Moreover, the
tragedy of contemporary art is also a global tragedy because, being a
part of our world of instantaneity, contemporary art has literally been
lost sight of. (Virilio 2011: 38)

The contemporary state of affairs of architecture, art and technology, in Virilio's estimation, then, is to have arrived at a condition
of real time that absolutely surpasses the real space of important
works in the visual arts and elsewhere.

Virilio's relationship to the current situation of the visual arts
and technology is investigated in Chapter 10, 'Virilio and Visual
Culture: On the American Apocalyptic Sublime', by Joy Garnett
and John Armitage. Presenting an analysis of Virilio's position

as articulated primarily in his *Art as Far as the Eye Can See* and Virilio and Raymond Depardon's (2008) *Native Land: Stop-Eject*, Garnett and Armitage take issue with Virilio's assumption that real time definitely, always and everywhere today, exceeds the real space of significant visual artworks. Opening with a reflection on Virilio's association with visual culture as embodied in *Art as Far as the Eye Can See*, Garnett and Armitage proceed by introducing and then developing the concept of the 'apocalyptic sublime', a '"Virilian"-like state that might happen anywhere there is an abrupt disconnection between what is anticipated and what is observed' (Garnett and Armitage 2011: 59–78). Additionally, Garnett and Armitage propose that a noteworthy and important further problem with Virilio's recent work on visual culture is a surprising lack of engagement with contemporary painters and particularly American painters of the apocalyptic sublime, as demonstrated by their continued absence in both his own *Unknown Quantity* (2003b) exhibition and his and Depardon's *Native Land: Stop-Eject* joint exhibition at the *Fondation Cartier pour l'art contemporain* (Virilio and Depardon 2008). Thus, in this chapter, Garnett and Armitage make a contribution to the emerging sub-discipline of postmodern Virilian visual cultural studies through a consideration of three American painters – the late Canadian performance artist and filmmaker Jack Goldstein (1945–2003), Sarah Trigg (1973–) and the American painter Marc Handelman (1975–) – whose work is particularly involved with what we identify as the 'American apocalyptic sublime'. Goldstein, Trigg and Handelman are therefore painters for the twenty-first century whose works not only manifest the American apocalyptic sublime but also complicate Virilio's notion that real time has gone beyond the real space of contemporary visual artworks.

However, as Virilio shows in 'Impact Studies', which constitutes Chapter 11, and which is, in fact, the concluding chapter of *Virilio Now*, postmodern visual culture is not simply about painters, artists and filmmakers but also about 'impact makers', about the construction of near-apocalyptic events and a transcendent fashioning of misinformation that, for Virilio, is the most important kind of propaganda or 'ethological pollution' at work today. Hence, from Virilio's perspective, the contemporary 'globalization of affects' entails the triggering of an accident and a 'present' wherein real time governs history as well as a future in which the event loses out to the 'impact strategy' of advertising, to the contemporary art and cultural politics of globalized networks.

Interestingly, and regardless of his recent concentration on impact makers, Virilio's attention to postmodern architecture, art and technology is at present assuming a newly escalated and worldwide form, predominantly in his most recent texts, such as *The University of Disaster* (2010a), *The Future of the Instant: Stop-Eject* (2010b), and, in French, *L'Administration de la peur* (*The Administration of Fear*) (2010c). It is, I argue, an intensified and globalized form of the city of panic, a *world of panic* where it is 'urban displacement' (Virilio 2010a: 98–9), the rising number of upcoming environmental migrants, calculated at one billion by Christian Aid, that becomes 'incomparably more serious than the immigration of the industrial age, and which is already being called the migration offensive of the third millennium' (Virilio 2010b: 1). The vital question of postmodern architecture, art, and technology is therefore how they respond to one billion environmental migrants within the confines of an urbanization of the contemporary world that is currently destroying the traditional difference between 'sedentariness' and nomadism by way of the ascendancy of real time over real space. Architecture, art, and technology thus continue to perform the most important explicatory functions in Virilio's philosophy. For Virilio, postmodern culture is increasingly typified by 'habitable human traffic', by a 'transpolitical delocalization that is now overturning the Geopolitics of settlement in the age of globalization', or, in other words, by the development of a new regime of combat that is coming into existence 'at the precise moment that the teletechnologies of information are ensuring that sedentary man is everywhere at home, and the nomad, nowhere, beyond the provisional accommodation offered by a now pointless transhumance'(Virilio 2010b: 2–3). In this world of panic there is a new and very important place for the problem of the end of geography as a focal point beyond the cultural politics of dislocation and homelessness, beyond the deterritorialization that comprises Virilio's (2010b: 32–70) 'Ultracity' of refugee camps, ex-urbanization, and the newly formed deterritorialized global 'nations' of enforced deportees.

In conclusion, the chapters that follow consider Virilio's main ideas now. Their current perspectives both by and on Virilio are organized generally along the lines of Virilio's own intellectual chronology and studies to provide a clear understanding and awareness of how he and the additional contributors to this book are advancing and enlarging Virilian cultural theory. The chapters by contributors other than Virilio should not be appreciated as essays that just tag along at the rear of Virilio's work but as chapters that delve into the influence he has had on the field of cultural theory and is having on the fields of critical theory and war studies, cultural geography, contemporary art, architecture, political studies, media philosophy, visual culture, aesthetics, the political economy of international business, literature, art theory and propaganda analysis right now. Throughout the book, the contributors, inclusive of Virilio, turn to his writings and make use of contemporary viewpoints, for instance, Virilio's (2011: 29; original emphasis) assertion in 'The Third War' interview that we are 'only *now* entering the era of the postmodern'. A further inventory of these contemporary positions is unnecessary here, as is any additional explanation of Virilio's own works.

Either reading Virilio or reading about Virilio is always invigorating, and at his finest he is one of the most thrilling and insightful cultural theorists writing today, which is also why he draws a growing number of well-regarded commentators on his work, such as the contributors to *Virilio Now*. Virilio's are, without doubt, some of the most inspired contributions to postmodern critical cultural theory, and his analyses of contemporary cultural everyday life are nothing other than first-rate.

References

Armitage, John (2006) 'Paul Virilio: A Critic of International Business?. From Dromoeconomics to Hypermodern Organization and Beyond', *Critical Perspectives on International Business*, 2, 4: 339–53.
— (2010) 'Temporary Authoritarian Zone', in Monica Narula et al.

(eds.), *Sarai Reader 08: Fear*. New Delhi: Center for the Study of Developing Societies, pp. 18–19.

Armitage, John, and Joanne Roberts (2007) 'On the Eventuality of Total Destruction', *City*, 11, 3: 428–32.

Baudrillard, Jean (2002) *Screened Out*. London: Verso.

Benjamin, Walter (1968) 'Theses on the Philosophy of History' in his *Illuminations*. New York: Schocken Books, pp. 253–64.

Clausewitz, Carl von (1976) *Clausewitz On War*. Princeton: Princeton University Press.

Ellul, Jacques (1973) *The Technological Society*. New York: Random House.

Faulks, Sebastian (2009) A *Week in December*. London: Hutchinson.

Garnett, Joy, and Armitage, John (2011) 'Apocalypse Now: An Interview with Joy Garnett', *Cultural Politics*, 7, 1: 59–78.

Gente, Peter (ed.) (2008) *Paul Virilio und die Künste*. Berlin: Merve Verlag.

Harland, James (2002) *The Month of the Leopard*. London: Simon and Schuster.

Heidegger, Martin (1977) *The Question Concerning Technology and Other Essays*. New York: Harper Perennial.

Husserl, Edmund (1970) *The Crisis of European Sciences and Transcendental Phenomenology*. Evanston: Northwestern University Press.

Huxley, Aldous (1943) *The Art of Seeing*. London: Chatto and Windus.

Jünger, Ernst (2004) *Storm of Steel*. London: Penguin.

Kittler, Friedrich A. (2010) *Optical Media: Berlin Lectures 1999*. Cambridge: Polity.

Merleau-Ponty, Maurice (1962) *Phenomenology of Perception*. London: Routledge.

Perec, Georges (1997) *Species of Space and Other Pieces*. London: Penguin.

Rush, Michael (2005) *New Media in Art*. London: Thames and Hudson.

Sontag, Susan (2003) *Regarding the Pain of Others*. New York: Picador.

Speer, Albert (1995) *Inside the Third Reich*. London: Phoenix.

Sun Tzu (1993) *The Art of War*. Ware: Wordsworth Editions.

Virilio, Paul (1976) *L'Insécurité du territoire*. Paris: Stock.

— (1986) *Speed & Politics: An Essay on Dromology*. New York: Semiotext(e).

— (1989) *War and Cinema: The Logistics of Perception*. London: Verso.

— (1990) *Popular Defense & Ecological Struggles*. New York: Semiotext(e).

—(1991) *The Lost Dimension*. New York: Semiotext(e).

—(1994a) *Bunker Archeology*. Princeton: Princeton Architectural Press.

—(1994b) *The Vision Machine*. London: British Film Institute.

—(1995) *The Art of the Motor*. Minneapolis: University of Minnesota Press.

—(1997) *Open Sky*. London: Verso.

—(2000a) *Polar Inertia*. London: Sage.

—(2000b) *Strategy of Deception*. London: Verso.

—(2000c) *A Landscape of Events*. Princeton: Princeton Architectural Press.

—(2000d) *The Information Bomb*. London: Verso.

—(2002a) *Desert Screen: War at the Speed of Light*. London: Continuum.

—(2002b) *Ground Zero*. London: Verso.

—(2003a) *Art and Fear*. London: Continuum.

—(2003b) *Unknown Quantity*. London: Thames and Hudson.

—(2005a) *Negative Horizon*. London: Continuum.

—(2005b) *City of Panic*. Oxford: Berg.

—(2007a) *The Original Accident*. Cambridge: Polity.

—(2007b) *Art as Far as the Eye Can See*. Oxford: Berg.

—(2009a) *The Aesthetics of Disappearance*. New York: Semiotext(e).

—(2009b) *Grey Ecology*. New York: Atropos.

—(2010a) *The University of Disaster*. Cambridge: Polity.

—(2010b) *The Future of the Instant: Stop-Eject*. Cambridge: Polity.

—(2010c) *L'Administration de la peur*. Paris: Textuel.

—with John Armitage (2000) 'Ctheory Interview With Paul Virilio: The Kosovo War Took Place In Orbital Space', in Arthur and Marilouise Kroker (eds.), *CTHEORY*, pp. 1–4. www.ctheory.net/articles.aspx?id=132

—with John Armitage (2001) 'From Modernism to Hypermodernism and Beyond', in John Armitage (ed.), *Virilio Live: Selected Interviews*. London: Sage, pp. 15–47.

—with John Armitage (2009) 'In the Cities of the Beyond: An Interview with Paul Virilio', in the Dutch Cahier on Art and the Public Domain *OPEN 18: 2030: War Zone Amsterdam: Imagining the Unimaginable*, edited by Brigitte van der Sande. NAi Publishers, SKOR, Amsterdam, pp. 100–11.

—with Raymond Depardon (2008) *Native Land: Stop-Eject*. Paris: Fondation Cartier pour l'art contemporain.

—with Claude Parent (1996a) *Architecture Principe 1966 and 1996*. Besançon: Les Éditions de L'Imprimeur.

—with Claude Parent (1996b) *The Function of the Oblique*. London: Architectural Association.

2

The Third War: Cities, Conflict and Contemporary Art

Interview with Paul Virilio

John Armitage

John Armitage: *Professor Virilio, as a philosopher of the city, war and contemporary art, to what extent can today's cities still be described in terms of postmodern theory? Does the time and space of the city remain that of the postmodern city? In what ways is your conceptualization of the city influenced by other French theorists?*

Paul Virilio: We are only *now* entering the era of the postmodern. When Jean-François Lyotard, Jean Baudrillard and Jacques Derrida all wrote about the postmodern in the 1980s and 1990s, I argued against their use of this term since I preferred the term 'hypermodern'.[1] But now I think that we have truly entered into the postmodern age. And we have left the era of the hypermodern for that of the postmodern first and foremost due to acceleration, due to the fact that, currently, it is *the instant that dominates*. It is the '*Kairos*' of the real time of immediacy and ubiquity which today governs the real space of geography, thereby putting duration, temporality and human history into a profound crisis derived from the sudden emergence of interactivity.[2] What distinguishes my thinking from someone like Lyotard, consequently, is that his work never took the end of geography into account. And neither do the writings of many others today! In fact, no one has really taken the end of geography seriously except me! The only person who showed any interest in my work in this area was Gilles Deleuze, who, in his book *Foucault*, demonstrated that he understood the geographical dimension of 'control societies'.[3] It was my work that inspired Deleuze in this area, given that we had meetings where I introduced him to the concept of 'control societies', an idea that is still very powerful because it encapsulates the replacement of walls by electronic turnstiles and, increasingly, as in today's large airports, the substitution of electronic turnstiles by electronic corridors. In the end, though, what separates me from Lyotard and Baudrillard in particular is that their writings are linked to a Marxist and psychoanalytic culture that is simply not mine. My culture is a military one, which is why many people call me a defence intellectual.

JA: *Does the fact that you share common cultural ground more with military personnel and other defence intellectuals than with cultural theorists mean that, for you, the birth of the city was a military rather than a cultural development?*

PV: For me, but for many historians also, the birth of the city is the result of an army that has come to a standstill. The city is then an agglomeration that is defined and determined by war. The beginnings of the city, of agglomeration, are thus post-tribal since tribal peoples, by their very nature, do not constitute a mass. From the moment of our sedentariness, therefore, agglomeration comes to dominate tribal movement. But, today, it is acceleration that dominates agglomeration. You see, tribes and their horses did not amount to much in terms of their ability to move. Hence, agglomeration began to dominate the movement of tribal peoples. And it is here also that the 'right of blood' gives way to the 'right of the soil' or the right of agglomeration and accumulation in a given place. Yet, even in our day, in Germany for example, citizenship is still legally or at least formally recognized through the 'right of blood'. The origins of the city are thus the outcome of the founding and development of fortified enclosures all over the world, of the massification and agglomeration of armies that have stopped. Gradually enclosed by their own demography, cities have slowly moved towards the contemporary megalopolis, a movement that we are witnessing everywhere and in all directions.

JA: *In several of your main works, such as City of Panic (2005), you stress the relationship between the city and war. Which writers and texts on the city and war should we bear in mind in the era of the privatization of war and global terrorism?*

PV: We must consider the city and war in relation to the logic of the trajectory, which today prevails over both the object and the subject. For me, Sun Tzu's ancient writings on war are still of paramount importance because, being Chinese, his thought is based on the trajectory of movement much more than is the case with, for instance, Vauban, the French seventeenth-century military engineer, or the German nineteenth-century philosopher of war, Carl von Clausewitz.[4] These military thinkers, and especially Vauban, thought in a particularly structured way, a form of thought that I call *rigidified*. Vauban, for example, was the inventor of statistical thinking, of rigidified thought concerning the military and fortifications. Clausewitz, on the other hand, brought the political dimension to the study of warfare. Indeed, I would say that Clausewitz brought the *totalitarian* aspect to the examination of war. Here, of course, Clausewitz is still relevant.

Yet, today, we have passed beyond both Vauban and Clausewitz by way of the acceleration of absolute movement, of the momentum of absolute speed. The *Blitzkrieg* or 'lightning war' and the onslaught that was the dropping of the atomic bomb on Hiroshima by the Americans during the Second World War put an end to the inertia of war. For war no longer takes place primarily in real time and space but in *delocalized* time and space. Certainly, war has now not only extended to space as a whole, with the advent of air war and satellite warfare and so forth, but also to a new kind of delocalization. Consider the lack of confrontation between regular armies in Africa or in Iraq where American corporations, such as *Blackwater*, become the local focal point of the ongoing privatization of war.[5] War has moved away from the conventional battlefield. It is no longer a conflict between regular armies or even nation states but, rather, a war between privatized yet wholly post-industrialized corporations like *Blackwater*. Similarly, terrorism is increasingly reduced not merely to gangs but to lone individuals. In a certain sense, then, it is the city that has become the enclosure or the arena of confrontation. Historically, during the First and Second World Wars, for example, war was a geostrategic activity involving battles for Verdun, Stalingrad or Okinawa. Yet, nowadays, the large set-piece battles of the past focused on the city have given way to the *anti-city strategy*. Think about Hiroshima where the invention of the atomic bomb made the city the target of destruction and, crucially, *dissuasion*.

These days, however, purely military dissuasion, for instance the Americans threatening the Russians with rockets or the Russians threatening the Americans with other rockets, has been replaced by terrorism. Let me remind you that the small band of individuals who destroyed New York City's *World Trade Center* caused the same number of deaths, three thousand to be precise, as the Japanese attack on Pearl Harbor during the Second World War. However, where the Japanese used torpedoes carried by airplanes and warships to accomplish their attack, the destruction of the *World Trade Center* required only two hijacked airplanes and about twelve men. Accordingly, we have entered a logic that has nothing in common any more with the destruction of the city or of putting the city under siege but, instead, a logic of pure or individualized terrorism.

JA: *How does the logic of terrorism alter the character of postmodern warfare?*

PV: We are currently witnessing an extremely important moment regarding the changes that are taking place in the nature of war. For we have just invented what I call the *Third War*. The *First War* is the civil war, which can take many forms, such as a localized affray. Before the *First War* became the *Second War* or a national and international phenomenon, then, it was simply a civil war, a scuffle, or, put differently, a war without a structure. But, eventually, war became a structured activity at the national and the international level, with, for example, wars between cities involving standing armies, forts and the like. Civil wars have, of course, continued to this day, as we saw in the 1930s with the Spanish Civil War, or the war over the former Yugoslavia during the 1990s. At the same time, we have seen national and international wars where not only cities but nations have been pitted against each other. And, finally, we have observed the emergence in the twentieth century of the phenomenon of world war.

Nevertheless, we are now entering the *Third War* or what might be described as the last stage of war, by which I mean the *war on civilians*. The *Third War* is not concerned with regular armies but with authorized and unauthorized gangs ranging from *Blackwater* mercenaries to religion-inspired terrorists waging war on civilians. In fact, what such gangs have declared war on is the *innocence of population*, on the population as inhabitants, as people of the city. For me, as for any right-minded person, *a civilian is innocent by definition*, not that the terrorists will agree obviously. This is because, for the terrorists, civilians are guilty because they participate in political activity by voting. So, we are at present entering a war without precedent. The *Third War* is not a civil war but a war against civilians that does not include regular armies but only privatized armies, war lords, gangs in the suburbs, and terrorists.

Thus the question that arises, and which is absolutely monstrous, is the question of *the passage from military dissuasion to civil dissuasion*. For, in our day, war no longer concerns military dissuasion but, rather, the dissuasion of civilians. And civil dissuasion includes *everyone*. Everyone must be dissuaded. Such shifts also help to explain the ongoing global transition from the concept of the armed forces per se to the idea of the armed forces *as a police force*. Without doubt, what we are witnessing here is a transition from a globalizing military rhetoric of dissuasion towards a *globalitarian* civilian language of dissuasion, a civilian dissuasion that is not even totalitarian any longer but *globalitarian*.[6] Indeed, globalitarian civilian dissuasion calls into question fundamental rights of civilians, of citizenship, and even our basic human rights. What is under siege today, then, is our right to be human. Moreover, globalitarian civilian dissuasion is a threat of such magnitude that many of us are, in effect, *immobilized*. We can no longer *move* anymore. Unlike the threat of nuclear dissuasion, therefore, which prevented the Russian and American armies from 'moving' during the Cold War, globalitarian civilian dissuasion prevents everyone from moving.

And yet, at the same time, contemporary societies are becoming *hyper-mobile*! Hence the importance of the trajectory, of trajec-tography, and, significantly, what I have labelled *traceability*.[7] For human beings in the present period are becoming trajectories or pathways controlled through their portable objects, such as their computers, cellphones and their GPS-monitored movements. As a result, concepts like national identity become increasingly unimportant because our lives are more and more kept in check through our tagged and tracked movements. This is why the idea of national identity is disappearing for many people: as the accel-eration of technological movement increases, national identity is replaced by technologized monitoring and traceability, by the 'Just in Time, Zero Stocks' society in which accelerated technological flows win out over the once private citizen.

JA: *Given the emergence of the Third War, globalitarianism, and traceability, how might we conceive of a philosophy of war in the current climate?*

PV: There is no such thing as a philosophy of war at the moment, even if there may well be one again in the future. This is because, as yet, there is no *chronostrategist* or strategist of time. We have geostrategists, for sure, and geostrategy, but no chronostrategists or chronostrategy. But, if we do consider the handiwork of contem-porary geostrategists, what do we find? Let us take Sri Lanka, Israel and Gaza as our examples because I think that the situation in these countries and territories in the Far and Middle East exemplifies the *Third War* I have just described. The proof of the existence of the *Third War* lies in the fact that, in these instances, we see not only the invention but also the execution of this extraordinary *Third War*, which, as I have emphasized, is a war on civilians. However, the key point about the *Third War* is that it is a *failed war*. Before, *First* and *Second Wars* were won or lost. Nowadays, though, in the era of *Third War*, everyone loses, with the result that failed wars, failed states, and pyrrhic victories are everywhere, and at the spatial scale of whole nations! For this reason, we are no longer sure what a philosophy of war would actually mean today, especially given that the structures of the *Second War* have collapsed and are being replaced by something that looks very much like the *Third War* on civilians or some kind of accident. For wars today are neither won nor lost but failed. And this, naturally, only highlights the current crisis in the philosophy of war. Yet this crisis in the philosophy of war is also a crisis of the political, which, in its turn, throws the philosophy of a military thinker like Clausewitz into crisis too! At the moment, therefore, the situation we find ourselves in is the situation where the war against civilians is increasingly the most common form of war.

Let me remind you of the absurdity of what has been happening recently in Sri Lanka between the Tamil Tigers, who were waging an aggressive secessionist struggle that sought to establish an independent Tamil state in the north east of the country, and the Sinhalese majority government. It was not the government's armed forces but its *civilian population that was slaughtered in battle*. You may say that the Sri Lankan government troops have won against the Tigers. But what have these troops lost? They have lost their rapport, their connection and their basic relationship with the entire civilian population of Sri Lanka.

Likewise, Israel's war on Gaza was a war that was at odds with the very principles of war itself in that there were no actual war gains. The aim of war has always been that there is something to gain, in the sense that war is a kind of 'profitable' trade or business. But what we saw in Gaza was a war without any benefit to Israel. No territorial benefit. No economic benefit. Not even any media benefit. Israel's war on Gaza consequently backfired. To be sure, in the end, Israel's final attacks on Gaza were counter-productive, not only at the level of territory or international politics, but also at the level of domestic Israeli politics. For me, Israel's attacks on Gaza are analogous to Germany's bombing of Guernica during the Spanish Civil War, a war which essentially ushered in the Second World War, as well as the idea of bombing civilians, an idea that, as we all know, culminated in the dropping of atomic bombs on Hiroshima and Nagasaki by the Americans. Furthermore, in a certain way, what took place in Gaza was just as serious and just as bad as what took place in Guernica if not in Hiroshima or

Nagasaki. For what happened in Gaza was the very opposite of
what a war should be. Israel's war on Gaza was thus a *Third War* or
a failed war in which the Israelis neither managed to dissuade the
Palestinian civilian population of Gaza nor Hamas 'terrorists' and
their supporters from blowing themselves up as suicide bombers.
Whatever the aim of Israel's war on Gaza was, then, it was not
achieved. There was no 'profit' in its efforts, not even civilian
dissuasion, which is what makes the situation in the Middle East
so serious. The Palestinians, for example, have not turned against
Hamas. Israel's war on Gaza was, from my point of view, a *Third*
or failed war. Yet I am not against the state of Israel, even if I am
against its war on Gaza. Equally, I am in favour of a Palestinian
state. In sum, what we can say about the philosophy of war today is
that there is as yet not only no chronostrategist but also *no strategist
of the crisis of the strategic!*

JA: *For you, then, because we lack a coherent philosophy of war at present,
over and above the requisite chronostrategists, strategic thinking itself has
entered a kind of crisis. How does the absence of a philosophy of war and
chronostrategists reveal itself in everyday life?*

PV: It shows itself through the fact that war has been replaced by
the integral accident! The ecological, economic and political or
integral accident has thus become an element that rises above and
beyond war. War or politics become facets of the integral accident,
of our catastrophes and disasters. I remind you that, in Latin, 'disaster' contains 'aster' or the word for a heavenly body. This means
that it is the Earth, our own heavenly body, which is becoming
an integral accident. At the level of our globalizing world, then,
war is increasingly superseded by disaster, by ecological, economic
and political collapse. Why? Because the Earth is too small for
so-called 'progress' and too small for the conflicts that arise as a
result of 'progress'. One encounters here the problem of the end
of geography, which, in our world of accelerated instantaneity, is
also the end of the fullness or the wholeness of the Earth. We have
to come to terms with the finiteness of the Earth, with the fact that
the Earth is too small and yet also round or complete. Hence our
task is to take care of both the limits and the richness of the Earth.

Obviously, this is not a typical political vision. But, for me, this is the key metaphysical dimension and question that arises from the disaster of technical 'progress' today.

JA: *Beyond the broader metaphysical aspects of the current catastrophe that is technoscientific 'progress', how might we theorize or enhance our understanding of the contemporary city as a war zone? Which are the most important cities and issues?*

PV: The city is the last or ultimate war zone because it is the place of the concentration of the innocents. Yet we know that, in cities today, terroristic individuals can cause just as much damage with their 'dirty bombs' as the armed forces. Let us take Brazil and India, and especially Sao Paolo and Mumbai, as our examples. In Sao Paolo, for instance, according to a Brazilian friend of mine, no day passes by where one does not hear the sound of heavy weapons fire. And I mean heavy weapons! Helicopters flying over and firing upon the *favelas*, firing upon whole neighbourhoods! In Mumbai, temporarily at any rate, following the departure of the police, the army too is effectively vacating the unruly neighbourhoods.

But often missed by commentators concerning terrorist attacks on cities is the important fact that such massive assaults, like the one that was launched against Mumbai, also generate, in part, the current huge movements of whole populations. Such is the ongoing exodus that, in the next forty or fifty years, experts predict that there will be up to *one billion people* on the move because of terroristic dislocation, climatic change, ecological catastrophe, and the outsourcing of economic production by multinational corporations.[8] Just like the 'cities of the beyond' that we have talked about, it follows that there is also a 'world of the beyond', a world of the migrant, of the exile.[9] As I have said many times before, the sedentary person is the person who is at home everywhere whilst the nomad is the person who is nowhere at home. However, nowadays, the sedentary person is also a person who, thanks not only to displacement by terrorism and so on but also by the teletechnologies of information, of mobile and portable technologies, has been set adrift from his or her previous moorings in the city.

JA: *One of the most remarkable features of your work is the way in which you consistently attend to contemporary art and its relationship to warfare. What is the importance of the link between war and contemporary art in your writings?*

PV: First of all, we must return to the concept of contemporary art. And I insist that we talk of *contemporary* art and not *modern* art because contemporary art is a victim of war. Let me give you some very stark twentieth-century evidence for this claim about art and war. Think, for instance, of French Surrealism. Both Louis Aragon and André Breton took their friends to see the battlefields of the First World War. But, now, of course, no one wants to talk about such events. Surrealism, then, just like Dada, sprang from the First World War whereas Viennese Actionism arose from the Second World War. So, contemporary art is as much about the fantasies of war as it is about anything else. One cannot understand contemporary art without accounting for its 'war wounds', without considering the fact that contemporary art has been *disabled* by war.

For me, therefore, art lost something of itself during the war-torn twentieth century, which means that there is a tragic dimension to contemporary art. It does not matter whether we are discussing film, television, or exhibitions in art galleries, there is today a tragic aspect to art that is exemplified by 'artists' such as Günther Von Hagens, who, as we all know, exhibits real human corpses! It is this tragic element in contemporary art that I consider in *Art as Far as the Eye Can See*, where I wanted to convey both a sense of our current blindness as well as a sense of immensity.[10] Moreover, the tragedy of contemporary art is also a global tragedy because, being a part of our world of instantaneity, contemporary art has literally been lost of sight of. What is contemporary about contemporary art is that art no longer has a *place*, just like those ancient uninhabited cities no longer have a place. Furthermore, contemporary art does not really *belong* to our epoch because it is so technologically dispersed, distributed, discharged and transmitted by way of the continuing acceleration of history and reality towards *tele-reality*, immediacy, ubiquity and instantaneity. This is a major event since, at the present time, film, television and contemporary art are concerned only with forms of propaganda, with the globalization of affects, and the force of the emotional states they can bring about in their viewers.[11]

JA: *How might contemporary artists counter such misinformation, influences and powers, and, instead, contribute to a more critical comprehension of the feelings and conditions wrought by war?*

PV: Artists can play a part in our understanding of the world of war for sure. But the tragic dimension of art is unavoidable. Let me give you an example, which is a quotation from the work of Octavio Paz: 'When poetry ends, the great massacres begin'. The world of Louis Aragon, of the genius-artist, has been replaced by the world of Sarkozy, a world where poetry is no more but where the great massacres have already begun! Yet my concern with the great massacres, with the disappearance of poetry, is not primarily a concern with truth and falsehood but with the apocalypse, with my stance as a *revelationary*! I am not a *revolutionary* but a *revelationary*! This is very important! Ancient and modern societies were revolutionary and brought into being revolutionaries. But I am a revelationary. For *what is revealed forces itself above what is past and forces itself upon our situation as a revelation*, as in the case of the integral accident and finitude. Revelationary thought is a new type of thought.

JA: *As you have suggested in your many interviews, cultural conceptions of resistance are vital for you. But how should artists interpret and resist our contemporary condition? What specific kinds of critical theoretical and/or practical contributions can they make to today's world?*

PV: Artists must resist that temporal compression that reduces to nothing the magnitude of the world! They must resist what can only be described as an *occupation*. For we are *living under an occupation*. And I know what this term means, because I lived under the German occupation of France during the Second World War when I was young. But what is important is that I have the feeling that I am under occupation again, not by a military power but by a temporal compression that alters *all* relations between people, such as their sexual relations, or their relations with politics. Temporal compression impacts upon all human domains today and it is a phenomenon that we should resist. In this sense, I am completely against so-called 'progress' because temporal compression is one of the delirious results of this 'progress'! Indeed, temporal compression *is* progress today and it is also the reason why the political situation has become impossible! Let me explain: the man of politics used to be a mediator, an inter-mediary if you will. But, today, we have shifted from the concept and reality of political *representation* to the idea and reality of *'live' presentation* and *performance*. I am of course completely against this situation, which is both abhorrent and one which we need to think about very deeply because I have not seen anything in the art world that gives me hope in the present period. If there is resistance in this area, then I have not seen it yet! I see many *collaborators* but no artists who might be considered to be doing 'the right thing'. Yet, as I say, the term that interests me most of all is the term *under occupation* because *we are under occupation*. More importantly, this term helps to explain the current situation much better than terms such as 'resistance' or 'collaboration'. Why? Because, whilst the resister is actually under occupation, the collaborator refuses the occupation by denying its existence. For my part, I do the opposite: I proclaim the occupation! I am a resister who speaks about the occupation rather than a resister who blows the system up. And it is in this sense, as I said earlier, that I am a defence intellectual.

JA: *I would like to begin concluding our interview with a focus on your recent critical evaluation of the militarization of science in* The University of Disaster *(2010). Why, when we are trying to grasp the postmodern development of technology, should we concentrate on what you call 'the military-industrial and scientific complex'?*

PV: Because scientists have themselves become victims of war! As J. Robert Oppenheimer said after the Trinity test of Los Alamos during the 1940s: 'perhaps we have committed a sin?' But what Oppenheimer was talking about was a 'scientific' sin. Yet we have now gone far beyond 'science'. Let me give you an example: today, what makes the sciences 'exact sciences' has nothing to do with magic and everything to do with the scientific procedure involving the establishment of proof by way of the experimental having now reached beyond its limits. When Oppenheimer was at Los Alamos, for example, and his team of scientists pushed the nuclear button, they had no idea whether space itself would survive or disintegrate. That is, if space *had* perished or fallen to pieces, the scientists themselves would have been *captured in a disintegration of their own design!* What is of the utmost importance here is that this was the first time in history that a break up of this kind had ever taken place, where the scientists themselves *did not know what the outcome of the disintegration of space would entail after detonating a nuclear bomb.* At that juncture, then, even the scientists realized that experimental scientific procedures had now gone beyond their limits. This is fundamental because it meant, and still means today, that *scientists cannot continue experimenting without risking the end of the world!* Scientists are thus not only risking their own end but also that of the entire world! Here, of course, we are caught up in a scientific logic that is the equivalent of *total war!* What is necessary, therefore, is not a war against a *military enemy* but a war against the *militarization of science.*

Equally importantly, the militarization of science has more recently become the militarization of knowledge! This is because the militarization of science no longer involves merely the physical sciences of biology, chemistry and so on, the sciences traditionally associated with the military-industrial complex, but the *entirety of knowledge itself!* On that day at Los Alamos, when Oppenheimer set off the atomic bomb, he and his team also wrecked the entirety of knowledge. Nowadays, needless to say, we city-dwellers also find ourselves in a situation where we are constantly faced with the militarization of *political* knowledge, with the militarization of the knowledge of our own *communities*, both of which are threats to democracy.

And this is what I mean when, in *The University of Disaster*, I write of the 'accident of knowledge'.[12] In fact, I argue that there are three kinds of accidents: accidents of *substance*, accidents of *distances* and accidents of *knowledge*. Thus, whilst accidents of substance are absolute, necessary, relative and haphazard and accidents of distances are the result of speed-polluting distances and the proportions of nature, the accident of knowledge derives from the militarization of all knowledge. And it is from the last of these three accidents that stems the urgency of the need to institute *The*

University of Disaster. The University of Disaster is necessary in order for us to be able to study our current situation wherein substances, distances, and knowledge are all under threat.

JA: *Finally, your theoretical work on The Museum of Accidents has less prominence in your most recent writings than it had previously. Have you changed your assessment of the potential impact of your idea of The Museum of Accidents? How, for example, does The Museum of Accidents relate to The University of Disaster?*

PV: Well, first of all, I had the idea of *The Museum of Accidents*.[13] *The Museum of Accidents* went from a concept to a very real proposal for a museum about the accidents at Chernobyl. But *The Museum of Accidents* has become less interesting to me over the years and now I prefer to think in terms of a *Conservatory of Catastrophe*, a *Conservatory* not exclusively concerned with the arts but with *Catastrophe*, with the idea of preserving the excess, of protecting the memory of the unexpected, and of the surprise. In other words, the *Conservatory of Catastrophe* asks the question: what is at stake in the moment of the accident? The *Conservatory of Catastrophe* is an important idea because the university system is in crisis everywhere and not only in France. What we are witnessing is a disaster at the very foundation of the idea of the university. As you know, the university was first created in medieval times in cities such as Bologna, following the 'Great Fear of the Millennium', or the year 1000, which itself followed on from a great many barbarities of the age. For these reasons, various religious, ethnic and linguistic groups united to create the *university* that led us to our current *universality*. But, of course, today, the terror and barbarity of the epoch is called progress! We cannot escape the damage done by progress. Progress *is* the catastrophe!

For me, we are currently living with *the consequences of progress*, and especially as scientific procedures have reached beyond all previous experimental limits. Consider the example of the Hadron Collider at CERN in Geneva, Switzerland, where the scientists risked the entirety of humanity heading into a black hole! No wonder that there have been at least two court cases against CERN. And, importantly, these court cases were started by two

American scientists, two physicists actually, who argued that CERN did not have the right to potentially cause a black hole. Who has allowed the people at CERN to take such risks? Otto Roessler, a chaos theorist, also began a court case against CERN. However, the important point, as I have been saying all along in this interview, is that *scientific procedures and the establishment of proof through the experimental method have now reached beyond their prior limits!* So, despite the fact that the Hadron collider broke down for some considerable time, we still need to consider *The University of Disaster* as an exceptionally *positive* idea, and one that runs counter to current received scientific ideas. This is because, in the realm of scientific knowledge, *there is no such thing as a university that 'crash tests' the accident of knowledge!* The questions that we need to ask, then, are: what is the damage done by progress? What are the *limits* of experimentation? These are the questions that must be the basis of our future. We must confront the *objective*, not the *ideological* crisis of knowledge. For the prospect of us all being thrown into a black hole, much like the Americans' detonation of the atom bomb at Hiroshima, has nothing at all to do with ideology.

Translated by Patrice Riemens

Notes

'The Third War: Cities, Conflict and Contemporary Art: Interview with Paul Virilio' was conducted by John Armitage at *L'Argoat Bar and Restaurant*, La Rochelle, France, on 22 May 2009. The interview is the second part of a single dialogue with Paul Virilio. The first part of the interview was published in Dutch and English as 'In the Cities of the Beyond: An Interview with Paul Virilio' in the Dutch Cahier on Art and the Public Domain *OPEN 18: 2030: War Zone Amsterdam: Imagining the Unimaginable*, edited by Brigitte van der Sande, NAi Publishers, SKOR, Amsterdam, pp. 100–11. John Armitage would like to thank Paul Virilio for agreeing to be interviewed, for a splendid lunch at *Grande Brasserie de Poissons*, and Patrice Riemens for his continuing friendship and for translating the interview from French into English.

1. On the term 'hypermodern' see 'From Modernism to Hypermodernism and Beyond' in John Armitage (ed.) (2001), *Virilio Live: Selected Interviews*. London: Sage, pp. 15–47.

2. On the '*Kairos*' see Paul Virilio (2009), *Le Futurisme de l'instant: Stop-Eject*. Paris: Galilée.

3. See Gilles Deleuze (2006), *Foucault*. London: Continuum. Also relevant is Deleuze's 'Postscript on Control Societies', published in his (1995) *Negotiations 1972–1990*. New York: Columbia University Press, pp. 177–82.

4. See Sun Tzu (2009), *The Art of War*. London: Penguin; Anne Blanchard (2007), *Vauban*. Paris: Fayard; and Carl von Clausewitz (2008), *On War*. Oxford: Oxford University Press.

5. See Peter W. Singer (2007), *Corporate Warriors: The Rise of the Privatized Military Industry*. Cornell: Cornell University Press.

6. On the term 'globalitarianism' see 'From Modernism to Hypermodernism and Beyond', in Armitage (2001), *Virilio Live*, pp. 15–47 where Virilio (2001: 29–30) defines globalitarianism as 'what transcends totalitarianism' by way of globalization and the 'convergence of time towards a single world time'.

7. On 'traceability' see Paul Virilio (2009), *Le Futurisme de l'instant: Stop-Eject*. Paris: Galilée.

8. For Virilio's perspective on contemporary nomadism see his (2009) *Le Futurisme de l'instant: Stop-Eject*.

9. See 'In the Cities of the Beyond'

10. See Paul Virilio (2007) *Art as Far as the Eye Can See*. Oxford: Berg.

11. On these and related issues see Paul Virilio's contribution to this volume entitled 'Impact Studies'.

12. See Paul Virilio (2010), *The University of Disaster*. Cambridge: Polity.

13. See Paul Virilio (2003) 'The Museum of Accidents', in his *Unknown Quantity*. London: Thames and Hudson, pp 58–83.

References

Blanchard, Anne (2007) *Vauban*. Paris: Fayard.
Clausewitz, Carl von (2008) *On War*. Oxford: Oxford University Press.

Deleuze, Gilles (1995) 'Postscript on Control Societies', in his *Negotiations 1972–1990*. New York: Columbia University Press, pp. 177–82.

Deleuze, Gilles (2006) *Foucault*. London: Continuum.

Singer, Peter W. (2007) *Corporate Warriors: The Rise of the Privatized Military Industry*. Cornell: Cornell University Press.

Tzu, Sun (2009) *The Art of War*. London: Penguin.

Virilio, Paul (2003) 'The Museum of Accidents' in his *Unknown Quantity*. London: Thames and Hudson, pp. 58–83.

— (2005) *City of Panic*. Oxford: Berg.

— (2007) *Art as Far as the Eye Can See*. Oxford: Berg.

— (2009) *Le Futurisme de l'instant: Stop-Eject*. Paris: Galilée.

— (2010) *The University of Disaster*. Cambridge: Polity.

Virilo, Paul and Armitage, John (2001) 'From Modernism to Hypermodernism and Beyond', in John Armitage (ed.), *Virilio Live: Selected Interviews*. London: Sage, pp. 15–47.

— (2009) 'In the Cities of the Beyond: An Interview with Paul Virilio', in *OPEN 18: 2030: War Zone Amsterdam: Imagining the Unimaginable*, ed. Brigitte van der Sande. NAi Publishers, SKOR, Amsterdam: 100–11.

3

Burning Bruder Klaus: Towards an Architecture of Slipstream

Adam Sharr

Most buildings meet a violent end – through the demolition ball or the destructions of war (Bevan 2006).This chapter is about a building that, unusually, met a violent beginning (Image 3.1). Its trials were orchestrated by its architect, Peter Zumthor, in 2007. 120 pine trees were felled and sawn into logs still bearing their bark. Dragged to a hilltop, they were tilted together and roughly fixed to form a timber wigwam, open to the sky. This was used as formwork around which twenty-four successive pours of concrete were packed (Image 3.2). When the concrete had cured, numerous small circular holes were diamond-drilled through the solid mass. The logs were then set on fire. Fed by air drawn through the holes, the conflagration reached an extraordinary temperature, burning for three weeks and billowing clouds of black smoke over the horizon. When the blaze finally subsided, a concrete monolith was left containing a stinking blackened void which bore the shape of the logs and the imprint of their bark.

Molten lead was then dripped laboriously onto the floor of this space forming a weirdly striated surface, a miniaturised un-shifting dune landscape. Glass spheres were fixed to the insides of the draw holes; their smooth, luminous geometric perfection in stark

Image 3.1: The Bruder Klaus Chapel sat on its hilltop (Adam Sharr).

Image 3.2: *The concrete walls display*   Image 3.3: *The interior surface is shaped*
the poured layers of their construction.   *by the logs that were burnt away. Glass*
The holes which once fed the fire with   *baubles are fitted to the inside of the*
air now provide an enigmatic light to   *draw holes (Adam Sharr).*
the interior (Adam Sharr).

contrast to the rough blackened concrete surfaces surrounding
them (Image 3.3). Small furniture elements were fitted: a tray for
votive candles, a seat, a small sculpture and a cogwheel figure both
in bronze. The burnt-out block was left open to the sky, and rain
and snow gathers on the floor which falls towards the centre of the
space to collect it. Finally, a heavy triangular steel door was fixed
to the outside, its spherical handle a stainless steel imitation of the
glass balls. The door shuts with a clang which reverberates around
the soot-stained echo chamber within. This concrete mass was

dedicated, in a Catholic mass, to the fifteenth-century Swiss saint Niklaus von Flüe, known commonly as Bruder Klaus. It surveys the village of Wachendorf, located in the rolling landscape of the Eifel between Cologne and Bonn, and it is open to visitors for a few hours each week.

Architecture manifests the ideas informing its procurement, inhabitation and design. After recounting the circumstances of its construction, I will examine the artefact of the Bruder Klaus *Feldkapelle* here to ascertain what it stands for.[1] The violence of this small building's origins, and the speeds of its construction and use, are related to Paul Virilio's thinking about architecture. The chapel opens his thinking to question. I will explore what it contributes to an appreciation of Virilio's ideas about architecture now.

1.

Bruder Klaus is patron saint of the *Katholische Landvolkbewegung*, the Catholic Rural People's Movement, in Germany.[2] Brought up on a farm, von Flüe is reported to have served in the military and had a family before receiving divine inspiration and leaving home for a life as a hermit (Glazier and Hellwig 2004). Establishing himself in the Ranft, in what is now the Swiss canton of Obwalden, he reputedly lived a life of denial without taking (bodily) food or drink for twenty years, living an ascetic life in a hut in close connection with the land and the seasons. When a family of farmers in Wachendorf chose to build themselves a chapel, they wished to dedicate it to their patron saint. And they persuaded Peter Zumthor – the famous Swiss architect known for his Thermal Bath at Vals and Art Museum in Bregenz – to design it for them. In interview, Zumthor has spoken of his personal connection with the saint:

> Bruder Klaus is everybody's favourite saint in Switzerland. Half of the population is Catholic . . . For me he represents an upright figure who does not make any wrong compromises; any compromise. And also he is staying himself. He is a positive figure for me also in his opposition

to the church at that time. The other thing is the emotional thing. My mother visits him in a church in Basel . . . A little shy she says, 'he has always helped me' . . . This is something very emotional that I like: this figure is so important to her and to others. (Lynch 2009)

The architect continued by describing how he conceived the design to reflect the spirit of the saint:

The main thing was that there is no altar, so it is not a space for the church. To seek to make a new, a tiny little space in a field that in the end expresses hopes about human existence. Sorry, this is a little bit pathetic. Can you do this? I asked that this should be completely contemporary, so at the beginning there was all sorts of stuff about solar cells and stuff like that. And it boiled down over the years to the pure essential. All of these things fell off. At the end it was the chapel and the material and the rain and the water and whatever . . . I wanted to take this commission to make something really contemporary. It has this abstract goal. (Lynch 2009)

The architect's rhetoric is about stripping form back to basics, peeling layers away, in order to find what he considers the most raw, the most abstract expression. This architectural asceticism is apparent in the chapel's iconographies. Zumthor emphasized the lack of altar. Its absence is highlighted by a triptych of architectural elements, spare in their shape and layout. First is the bronze cogwheel fixed to the concrete on a single central spike, representing a figure drawn by the saint to describe how he contemplated the nature of God, with the undivided Godhead at the centre. Second is the votive candle tray, similarly centred, standing on a single column. Third is a bust of von Flüe, extruded from a small square bronze upright. Zumthor's rhetoric for describing this spare space with its sparse iconography – emphasizing the abstract, the centred, the essential and the uncompromising – outlines a particular match of client, architect and ethic (Harries 1997). But this rhetoric of timelessness seems to deny the world which Virilio has described: where any possibility for raw architectural essentials has been subsumed into an accelerating, militarizing culture that has become the lens through which we appreciate our vectors of existence.

2.

Virilio has charted a vector of speed gathering force from the 'technocultures' of the military-industrial complex.[3] Logistics, armaments, surveillance and intelligence now dominate the movements of contemporary life, he has argued. Spatiality has been consumed by temporality. We have been propelled by war into the service of the internal combustion engine, the camera, the microchip, robotics and biotechnologies. The human body is perpetually in transit. Our view – through television screens, monitor screens and windscreens – has become surveillance, conceptualized by the lens and the logic of the cinematic image:

> These 'images of time' in a desertified urban landscape amounted to a perfect illustration of SPEED [*VITE*] as the new VOID [*VIDE*], the presence-absence of the fleeting immured in vehicular dissipation, isolated by the violence of the driving energy, the resident closed within the distance of an accelerated trajectory, less 'inhabitant' now than a survivor, less 'a member of society' than a temporary resident. (Virilio 2005)

Virilio has famously named the dissolution of fixed geographical locations into the science of speed as 'dromology': '*the means of communication of dimension*, vectors or vehicles (surveyors, lenses, microscopes, telescopes, automobiles, satellites . . .) being simultaneously the *means of extermination of dimensions*' (Virilio 2005). Speed, image and violence conspire to repress and dominate: 'the vector becomes the last dimension of a world that is now reduced to the *desert of the moment*' (Virilio 2005: 144). Architecture in the Virilian speedscape is dromographic, its physical fixity lost to the violence of acceleration. Its inhabitants have become passengers, dromologues carried along by the militarizing logistics of technology. And the representations of architecture have become images for consumption.

Whatever their sympathies for Virilio's densely elaborated prose, most architects will recognize the daily implications of such accelerations. Our managerial age demands quantifiable delivery.

Architectural quality is no longer a function of built space (Dutoit, Odgers and Sharr 2010). No longer is it to be found in rooms which can astonish, console or contain, or in the elegant resolution of a functional diagram into form; instead, it pertains to predictable processes. Quality now describes the delivery of information to the construction team on time, in regularised formats, towards the efficient production of space.[4] Any qualities which are largely felt rather than measured, which are primarily subjective rather than objective, are subsumed into the speed of predictable, monitorable progress. Likewise, where architects once led construction, on large projects often they are now but one contributor to a Building Information Model, a live interactive 'drawing' on a closed intranet containing and controlling every aspect of the project which all consultants – engineers, project managers, quantity surveyors, health and safety experts – can access and manipulate, their changes transmitted simultaneously to all participants (Smith and Tardif 2009; Garber 2009). Live, in 'real time', cost and specification data can be instantly managed and supervized. Where buildings were once constructed for lifetimes, many professionals – including professional clients – now find it difficult to focus much beyond opening day. 'Long term' in construction regularly describes the finance period for a project; often a few months, rarely longer than five or ten years (Isaac 2003). Warranties issued by the manufacturers of building products – from roofing systems to basement tanking systems – exert much control over the design (Lupton 2000). Although they too rarely cover more than five or ten years, achieving the warranty can become more important than any quality of the space. The ruthless dromography of military logistics – the unstoppable computer-controlled distribution of stock, material or information to the campaign – has grown to dominate life beyond the military-industrial complex. The influence of logistics on supermarkets and agriculture is now widely acknowledged but it remains less acknowledged in construction and design. Nevertheless, its accelerating power seems all-pervasive.

Numerous architects have found design ideas in these trajectories. Since the 1970s, many famous architectural conjectures have been kinetic: mobile, adaptable, 'plug-in' structures, following those imagined by Cedric Price, Archigram and the Situationists (Matthews 2007: Sadler 1998, 2005). Since the 1990s, others – like NOX and Greg Lynn – have conjured parametric shape fantasies, generating complex forms instantly in three- and four-dimensional computer models, their constraints determined by rules programmed in computer script (Rappolt 2008; Spuybroek 2004). As architectural imagination arguably becomes more kinetic, so its anticipations become more cinematic. The static plane of the drawing has been supplanted for all by the CAD monitor, and for many by the fly-through of the visualization and the pulling-and-pushing of form in software such as Rhino (Piedmont-Palladino 2006). Seen through Virilio's gunsight, architecture, like society, has become caught up in an enterprise of perpetual acceleration.

The Bruder Klaus chapel, while it might not be the timeless edifice that Zumthor imagines it to be, does seem somehow out of time. Although it was designed, much of its design was not about predictability but instead about providing opportunities for chance. Who could anticipate with certainty what a three-week-long fire would do? Predictably unpredictable, its process seems to have been calculated backwards from the qualities of built architecture, rather than conceived as a management process in fulfilment of itself. The *Feldkapelle* contains no warrantied building products. It leaks – deliberately. Its geometries required no computer script. Its time-span appeals at once to the myths and mysteries of a fifteenth-century saint and to the anticipation of a long future. The building has an ambiguous relationship with the accelerating trajectories of architecture identified by Virilio.

3.

Those who seek a Virilian architectural aesthetic could easily claim the *Feldkapelle* for their canon. Superficially, it bears a resemblance to Virilio's own primary architectural production: the 'bunker church', *L'Eglise de Sainte-Bernadette-du-Banlay* in Nevers, designed with Claude Parent and completed in 1966 (Armitage and

Roberts 2007; Bouron 2000). Virilio has likened this boardmarked concrete carapace to an atomic shelter[5] and it was clearly indebted to the German fortifications of the French Atlantic coast that he presented in *Bunker Archeology* (Virilio 2004). Virilio writes how, in peacetime, 'the bunker appears as a survival machine':

> 'There is an affiliation between armor and the diving suit; the field of warfare extends to the totality of space, and natural landscape is replaced by a more original one in which everything is volatile, indeed, flammable . . . If the bunker can be compared to a milestone, to a stela, it is not so much for its system of inscriptions as it is for its position, its configuration of materials and its accessories: periscopes, screens, filters etc. The monolith does not aim to survive down through the centuries; the thickness of its walls translates only the probable power of impact in the instant of assault. (Virilio 2004: 39)

These are undoubtedly the iconographies of the 'bunker church': protection, shelter, the absorption of impact:

> The poetry of the bunker is in its still being a shield for its users, in the end as outdated as an infant's rebuilt armor, an empty shell, an emotionally moving phantom of an old-fashioned duel where the adversaries could still look each other in the eye through the narrow slits of their helmets. The bunker is the protohistory of an age in which the power of a single weapon is so great that no distance can protect you from it any longer. (Virilio 2004: 39)

The bunker church is no literal shelter but instead expresses the idea of shelter. As John Armitage and Joanne Roberts have argued, it manifests the flowing, slanting architecture that Virilio and Parent advocated in *The Function of the Oblique* (Parent and Virilio 1996), hoping to address and encapsulate Cold War emotions of anger, anxiety and futility (Armitage and Roberts 2007).

It is straightforward to liken the Bruder Klaus chapel, as an architectural artefact, to the church in Nevers and to the black-and-white photographic inventories of *Bunker Archeology*. Its materials are similarly martial: concrete, lead and steel. It stands on its hilltop as a concrete blockhouse, its monolith commanding the

Image 3.4: The chapel commands its landscape like the shelters catalogued in Virilio's Bunker Archeology *(Adam Sharr).*

roads and railway of its valley landscape (Image 3.4). The dumb inscrutability of the chapel's exterior has the eerie mystery which Virilio locates in the revetments and casemates of the Atlantic beaches. While it may appear more sharply cut on the skyline, the *Feldkapelle* has its metal blast door and it gives the impression that – like the bunkers – it is a structural whole whose foundations are integral with the walls, permitting it to sink and tilt similarly if the land were to shift and erode around it. The jagged-edged opening to the roof, once chimney to the chapel's founding fire, is a periscope whose reveal echoes the stepped embrasures of the Todt programme bunkers (Image 3.5). But it is trained resolutely upwards rather than outwards – like a guerrilla James Turrell

Image 3.5: The jagged-edged oculus *open to the sky (Adam Sharr).*

artwork (Turrell 2001; Etherington–Smith 2006) – and only the door permits contact with the ground or the horizon.

These parallels belong, however, in space rather than time. They are matters of location and construction rather than of trajectory. They belong more with the fixed categories of art-historical archi-tectural history than the Virilian notions of *vite* and *vide*. There is more that separates the chapel from Virilio's work than they have in common. If Virilio's work charts the shifts of acceleration, if the *Feldkapelle* should be studied as part of an all-embracing global acceleration rather than as a static object, then it is appropriate to ask the question: what is the course of its vector?

4.

The consumers of architectural media mostly know the Bruder Klaus chapel, like many contemporary buildings, through photographs in professional magazines and on the Internet. Through its images, the building has acquired cultural capital, finding a small place, framed by the digital lens, in the canon of contemporary expert architecture (Bourdieu 1989). Here, its speed is that of the global media world where incessant journalistic deadlines consume text and images which travel the globe digitally in seconds, demanding their instant manipulation – using ever-faster software from Microsoft and Adobe corporations – to fit a predetermined page grid. However the chapel is also consumed by a different constituency: by visitors, whose speed is less predictable and in whose motions the building acquires another status.

The chapel is accessible only on foot. Visitors will walk either two kilometres from the train, half a kilometre from the bus or a quarter of a kilometre from the car park. Paths shift from tarmac to gravel, slowing your walking speed, aided by the gradient to the door. The steel doorleaf is heavy to pull and you must pause while dragging it open (Image 3.6). The narrow entranceway, its inclined walls shaped by the ghosts of the timber props, causes you to hunch (Image 3.7). And, as you step in gingerly, your eyes take a few disorienting seconds to adjust to the gloom. The space inside is disarmingly small and its emphasis tilts from the horizontal to the vertical as you take a few paces forward, reorienting you from the plane of the lead floor to the jagged oculus open to the sky. Your pace slows once more as your gaze is drawn upward and the jewel-like glass baubles glow around you in their strange half-light. The mysterious bronze cogwheel figure – it takes time to calculate its iconography – glints with highlights from above. Readjusting to the horizontal, you take in the flickering votive candles, curious to watch their flame playing on the burnt-black concrete surface behind. Then what? It seems too soon to turn around and walk the few paces back outside. In my observations, people seem strangely drawn to linger for a few minutes, perhaps without quite knowing why. They pace around awkwardly, watching the scudding clouds

Image 3.6: The heavy triangular steel door (Adam Sharr).

overhead, drawn to touch the oddly juxtaposed rough and smooth surfaces, or taking the single seat to adjust for a while to the accommodating awkwardness of this hard echoey void. A sign outside sternly forbids photography and, despite the lack of supervision, people seem to self-police this instruction. Besides, the void is so small and strangely shaped that it remains delightfully impossible to capture in photographs, except in the most abstract way, without specialist lenses. It is hard to view this interior through a screen; neither windscreen nor camera viewfinder. While the military-industrial complex may be compelling the world into ever-increasing acceleration, the Bruder Klaus chapel seems able

Image 3.7: The entrance leads mysteriously into the gloom (Adam Sharr).

to slow its visitors and, in itself, also displays a decreasing rate of change.

The building is in negative acceleration. It has slowed in its short life. Its interior void began in an instant, with the lighting of a match. Its temperature increased rapidly to around a thousand degrees as the flames began to consume the logs. As the fuel was used, its temperature subsided more slowly, over days and then a fortnight, until only ash remained in the concrete shell. The lead floor was cast over a period of more weeks. Washed by the motions of rain and snow, the acrid stench of burning has faded almost totally over two years, leaving only the visual rather than the olfactory traces of fire. Changes to the building are now most likely to be those of weathering and decay. The soot impregnation of the concrete will fade, as it has already begun to around the chimney opening. Perhaps it will take a century to weather back fully to the interior colour of the concrete. The lead floor may take another century to wear away in places, ground down by the incessant footfall of visitors. The concrete, while it will chip and wear, contains no steel reinforcement so its life may approach the thousands of years over which Roman concrete has retained its structural capacity. As weathering takes hold, the chapel's rate of change decreases (Leatherbarrow and Mostavi 1993).

If the chapel's negative acceleration – its rate of change – were to be plotted on a graph, then its curve may resemble that of radio-active half-life. Just as the authors of the Bunker Church hoped to find an architecture for the nuclear age, so the chapel also contains echoes of atomic culture. Here, frenzied destructive activity is fading quickly to a long but steady declining trace.

The chapel itself, and the experience of visiting it, seem to describe a decelerative motion. The *Feldkapelle* demands immediacy of its visitors. In its approach, its materials, its atmosphere, it seems to emphasize body and senses; to call for time; to require scrutiny; to slow experience. The visitor may feel that they find some transient fixity in the 'desert of the moment'. If *vite* becomes void, might there also be, here, some fleeting void in the *vite*?

5.

The prospective longevity of the chapel and its materials seem to highlight acceleration. In an age when development finance and the warranty periods of mass-produced building products determine long term to be ten years, the Bruder Klaus chapel may last a thousand. Virilio argues that '[s]peed is identified with premature aging, the more and more the movement accelerates, the more quickly time passes and the more surroundings are stripped of their significance; displacement becomes a kind of cruel joke' (Virilio 2005). The chapel seems to offer-up a counter motion. Its interior hints at a momentary slowing of bodily experience in the face of a disembodying and ever-increasing accelerative displacement. Or at least it permits a fleeting image of negative acceleration. It is, in the most radical sense of the word, an emplacement.

The Atlantic bunkers are perhaps more analogous to the Bruder Klaus chapel in relation to the vectors of time than in relation to the aesthetic qualities of object. Their mass was capable of absorbing energy on the impact of assault. The force of incoming ordnance would be dissipated into the concrete. The bulk and longevity of the material, while no match for sustained assault, permitted some resistance in the moment. There is a parallel here with certain non-combat martial arts practices whose power lies not in fighting back, but in absorbing violent energy and reflecting it slowly, channelling it and dissipating it. The redoubt of the *Feldkapelle* might appear to act similarly. In its aesthetic evocation of the bunker, in the longevity of its tough materials, the chapel becomes a simulacrum of the military-industrial complex itself. Its image is indistinguishable from the accelerative enterprise while its constructional and experiential time-lag permits the idea of resistance to it. In experience, the *Feldkapelle* seems to channel forces of acceleration, answering them with some dromocidal counter motion. It does so in the moment of contact, in the instant of experience, in atmospheric immersion in the physical building rather than its reproduced images. By no means does this constitute an equal and opposite reaction. Instead, it is one which feels as though it might afford some temporary respite, however fleeting.

How, then, does the chapel effect its channelling of speed? Virilio writes: 'Thanks to the double projector, at once producer of speed and images (cinematic and cinematographic), everything is animated; the disintegration of vision begins, preceding somewhat the disintegration of the matter of the physical bodies that appears with the first studies of the forms of least resistance (aerodynamics)' (Virilio 2005: 125). It is helpful to extend this aerodynamic metaphor. The chapel achieves its drag force not in some impossibly romantic rejection of the present, in some doomed idea of retrieving a lost fixity, but in the momentary slipstreaming of acceleration. The potential of the *Feldkapelle* – assisted by its bunker iconography – is as an architecture of least resistance. Its potential consists in its fluid dynamics. Wind tunnel models – employed to simulate the effects of cars, locomotives and aeroplanes as well as buildings – use streams of silica in the flow of air to reveal moments of highest and least resistance. No matter how efficient the form being tested, there are always pockets of slower movement, eddies in the swirling vortex of speed. The chapel, imagined as a structural whole, is a vessel, propelled by the onslaught of acceleration. In its temporal, material and experiential density, the vessel exerts a temporary drag. It has capacity to find pockets of back-flow, to deflect temporarily some of the pressures of acceleration brought to bear upon it.

Zumthor's rhetoric locates the chapel as some kind of timeless expression of architectural essentials. But it is no architecture of statics. Virilio's illustration of the power of acceleration demonstrates clearly that any such essentials, that the idea of timelessness, are no longer possible, even if they were desirable. The chapel cannot be a place of stillness because acceleration is too all-pervasive for that to be within reach. Nor is the building capable of decelerative force. The best that such architecture can achieve is a condition of slipstream, seeking out momentarily the pockets of least acceleration. Its experiences offer the image – or evoke the atmosphere – of slowness. The Bruder Klaus chapel remains part of a perpetually accelerating world, but it is a fragment which offers the simulacrum of a slower speed; a whole world, a structural whole, in miniature; the evocation of a decelerative vector.

From the statically cycling pockets it finds in the slipstream, the *Feldkapelle*, arguably, acquires the capacity to act as an instrument for the measurement of flow. Virilio is clear about the politics of speed and acceleration:

'. . . speed extends the advantage of violence, a society where the affluent class conceals the class of speed . . . The progress of speed is nothing other than the unleashing of violence; we saw that breeding and training were economic forms of violence, or, if you like, the means to sustain violence, indeed render it unlimited. The conservation of metabolic energy was not therefore an end but an orientation of violence; *the means to prolonging it in time*; the technological motor resulted in the long standing pursuit of the *perpetuum mobile*, and with it the release of this violence. (Virilio 2005: 45)

Violence is the trajectory of speed, he argues. A dromocracy takes advantage of speed to promote its agendas and perpetually accelerate them. Arguably there are parallels here between Virilio's analysis and Naomi Klein's popular exposé *The Shock Doctrine* in which she outlines attempts by Friedmanite free-market economists, and their political conspirators, to seize a profitable privatizing initiative in the immediate wake of war or disaster – to the extent where they provoke, or fail to mitigate, violence in order to generate wealth for themselves (Klein 2007). Acceleration becomes, for Virilio, an opportunity for a certain elite to achieve domination and profit. His analyses by no means indicate any easy opportunities to resist this dromology. But the first step towards a decelerative politics, perhaps, is to find refuge from the most extreme vectors of acceleration, however momentary; a fleeting void from out of which their power and influence might be appraised. In a dromological culture whose daily accounting is contrived to occupy its citizens, professionals and intellectuals to the point of extreme time-poverty, to the point where they have little pause to contemplate actions which might conceivably disrupt the *status quo*, such eddies in the flow are hard to come by (McGinnity and Calvert 2009; Gershuny 2005). Architecture can contribute here, in the evocative potentials of its atmospheres – or its dromospheres – offering vectors which project the image of a vortex for reflective measurement of acceleration. The architecture of slipstream allows, perhaps, the beginnings of an architecture of resistance. This is not to say that only religious buildings like chapels, temples, mosques and synagogues – or for that matter other contemplative spaces like galleries or libraries – can offer such potential. The issue is not one of architectural type but of architectural acceleration.

Architecture is increasingly discussed according to the rhetoric of sustainability; but this is often sustainability as defined by the construction industry and viewed through the lenses of speed (Kibert 2005; Addis 2001). The industry makes and distributes energy-consuming devices to reduce the energy consumption of other devices. Manufacturers, professionals and governments formulate new regulatory codes to promote material and product development (Burchell and Rydin 2006). Expensive consultants become adept at arguing the sustainable credentials of glass and concrete high-rises from London to Shanghai and Abu Dhabi. Much of this sustainability industry shares a vector with the military–industrial complex, focused on architecture as the production of dromological space. Buildings – sustainable or otherwise – are understood here primarily as the objects of dynamic management processes, as devices of functional performance, as consumers of energy and allocations of logistical resource (Burchell and Rydin 2006). The Bruder Klaus chapel is hardly sustainable according to any conventional measures: its concrete and lead are neither local nor ecological materials, and the processes of burning and smelting hardly constitute environmentally-friendly construction. But its inflammatory capacity to find pockets of least acceleration might be sustainable in another way. Niklaus von Flüe was dedicated to a life of slow reflection now consumed by an accelerative project that he would likely find unimaginable. A little of his spirit remains, though, in the image of architectural atmospheres which have the resistant capacity for slipstreaming. If sustainable architecture is possible, then it is hardly compatible with the priorities of the military–industrial complex. Nor can it be achieved through any simplistic rejection of (late) modern culture or fantasy of dropping-out. Instead, first and foremost, it belongs with opportunities to slipstream, measure, and challenge, the military–industrial vectors of acceleration.

Notes

1. This approach to architectural research will be outlined in my forthcoming book: Adam Sharr (ed.) (2011), *Architecture and Culture*. London: Routledge.
2. www.klb-deutschland.de/ (accessed 20 January 2010).
3. Reinhold Martin has explored relationships between architecture and the military-industrial complex in the post-war West: Reinhold Martin (2005), *The Organisational Complex*. Cambridge, MA: MIT Press.

4. See Hall (1994), Nashed (2005), Bowyer (1981) and Lloyd Thomas (2004).

5. '. . . of course the emblematic building *par excellence* was the atomic shelter. My church is meant to be an architectural equivalent of all that. At the time, I said that, in the present-day, a church could only refer to the eventuality of total destruction. Hence, the bunker church is not modelled after its German namesake. Instead it is modelled after – and is a pointer to – the atomic shelter.' Paul Virilio and John Armitage (2001), 'The Kosovo W@r Did Take Place', in John Armitage (ed) (2001) *Virilio Live: Selected Interviews*. London: Sage.

References

Addis, William (2001) *Sustainable Construction Procurement: A Guide to Delivering Environmentally Responsible Projects*. London: CIRIA.

Armitage, John (ed.) (2001) *Virilio Live: Selected Interviews*. London: Sage.

Armitage, John and Roberts, Joanne (2007) 'On the Eventuality of Total Destruction', *City*, 11, 3: 428–32.

Bevan, Robert (2006) *The Destruction of Memory: Architecture at War*. London: Reaktion.

Bourdieu, Pierre (1989) *Distinction: A Social Critique of the Judgement of Taste*. London: Routledge.

Bouron, Sylvie (2000) 'Concrete Beliefs', *World of Interiors*, 20,11: 112–17.

Bowyer, Jack (1981) *Practical Specification Writing: A Guide for Architects and Surveyors*. London: Hutchinson & Co. (Publishers) Ltd.

Burchell, Kevin and Rydin, Yvonne (2006) *Sustainable Construction: Policy, Planning and Implementation*. London: London School of Economics.

Dutoit, Allison, Odgers, Juliet and Sharr, Adam (eds.) (2010) *Quality Out of Control: Standards for Measuring Architecture*. London: Routledge.

Etherington-Smith, Meredith (ed.) (2006) *James Turrell: A Life in Light*. Paris: Somogy.

Garber, Richard (ed.) (2009) *Closing the Gap: Information Models in Contemporary Design Practice*. London: Wiley.

Gershuny, J. (2005) 'Busyness as the Badge of Honor for the New Superordinate Working Class', *Social Research*, 72, 2: 287–314.

Glazier, Michael and Hellwig, Monika K. (eds.) (2004) *The Modern Catholic Encyclopedia*. Dublin: Columba Press.

Hall, Francis (1994) 'Specifying for Quality', *AJ: Architects, Journal*, 8 June.

Harries, Karsten (1997) *The Ethical Function of Architecture*. Cambridge, MA: MIT Press.

Isaac, David (2003) *Property Finance (Building and Surveying)*. London: Palgrave Macmillan.

Kibert, Charles J. (2005) *Sustainable Construction: Green Building Design and Delivery*. London: Wiley.

Klein, Naomi (2007) *The Shock Doctrine: Rise of Disaster Capitalism*. London: Allen Lane.

Leatherbarrow, David and Mostavi, Mohsen (1993) *On Weathering: The Life of Buildings in Time*. Cambridge, MA: MIT Press.

Lloyd Thomas, Katie (2004) 'Specifications: Writing Materials in Architecture and Philosophy', *arq: Architectural Research Quarterly*, 8, 3–4.

Lupton, Sarah (2000) *The Architect's Job Book*. London: RIBA Publications.

Lynch, Patrick (2009) 'Peter Zumthor Speaks to the Architects' Journal', *AJ: Architects' Journal*, 14 April.

Martin, Reinhold (2005) *The Organisational Complex*. Cambridge, MA: MIT Press.

McGinnity, F. and Calvert, E. (2009) 'Work-Life Conflict and Social Inequality in Western Europe', *Social Indicators Research*, 93, 3: 489–508.

Matthews, Stanley (2007) *From Agit-Prop to Free Space: The Architecture of Cedric Price*. London: Black Dog.

Nashed, Fred (ed.) (2005) *Architectural Quality Control: An Illustrated Guide*. New York: McGraw Hill Professional.

Parent, Claude and Virilio, Paul (1996) *The Function of the Oblique*. London: AA.

Piedmont-Palladino, Susan (2006) *Tools of the Imagination: Drawing Tools and Technologies from the Eighteenth Century to the Present*. Princeton, NJ: Princeton Architectural Press.

Rappolt, Mark (ed.) (2008) *Greg Lynn: FORM*. New York: Rizzoli.

Sadler, Simon (1998) *The Situationist City*. London: MIT Press.

— (2005) *Archigram: Architecture without Architecture*. Cambridge, MA: MIT Press.

Sharr, Adam (ed.) (2011) *Architecture and Culture*. London: Routledge.

Smith, Dana K. and Tardif, Michael (2009) *Building Information Modelling: A Strategic Implementation Guide for Architects, Engineers, Constructors, and Real Estate Asset Managers.* London: Wiley.

Spuybroek, Lars (2004) *NOX: Machining Architecture.* London: Thames and Hudson.

Turrell, James (2001) *The Other Horizon.* Ostfildern-Ruit: Hatje Cantz.

Virilio, Paul (2004) *Bunker Archeology.* New York: Princeton Architectural Press.

— (2005) *Negative Horizon: An Essay in Dromoscopy.* London: Continuum.

4

Vector Politics and the Aesthetics of Disappearance

Sean Cubitt

He (or she) smarted off until she (or he) encountered a bullet of *flawless vector*

(Dorn 1978: 64)

people make films on the internet to show that they exist, not in order to look at things

(Jean-Luc Godard, cited in Lovink 2008: 9)

The aesthetics of disappearance

In March 2010, the *San Jose Mercury News*, local paper of Silicon Valley, ran a brief item on YouTube, Google's colossally loss-making and increasingly controversial streaming video server (Swift 2010). Google had announced automatic captioning of videos, using voice-recognition software, initially in English with plans to expand to other languages. The announcement was attended by staff and students of the California School for the Deaf, and welcomed by speakers from Stanford and the University of California system's webcast services. Quietly unobserved was the possibility of extending Google's search capacity from the printed word to speech, and from speech to gain an entry to the holy grail of search: video. Video searching will allow Google to respond to two major complaints about the service: the posting of violent and bullying videos, and the fraught question of copyright infringement. It will also do just what Google says it will: open video to more users, especially the hearing-impaired, with more access and greater facility. It will not solve the problem of severe financial losses which, in a flurry of news stories in April 2009, were estimated at US$470 million for the year by Credit Suisse (Wang and Sena 2009), with other commentators claiming larger or smaller figures, among them bloggers announcing the end of streaming video. Google's deals with Hollywood studios, the booming uploads, the transmission and storage costs, and the failure to marketize the advertising revenue which is Google's stock in trade on the video platform, all combined for a long-term forecast of what, for a smaller company, would be catastrophic losses. Google, which reported US$26 billion profits for the year in 2009, can afford a loss, even a big one, if the payback is sufficient. The paybacks here may be old-style corporate goals: improved service at marginal cost per extra user, increased brand loyalty, or excluding newcomers from the market. Or they may be, as the corporation's mission statement has it, the fruit of a desire 'to organise the world's information and make it accessible': a goal which chimes more with the emergent peer-to-peer economics of the network.

It is not impossible to imagine Virilio's response to the YouTube phenomenon. 'It is thus our common destiny to *become film*' (Virilio 2001, cited in Colman 2009: 201). Today YouTube is one of the leading platforms through which we substitute the immaterial immediacy of filmic representations for the felt materialities of existence, of life. Or perhaps he might argue that 'the acceleration that is presently rushing towards us, is not that of Sassen's global city but that of the "*city-world*"!' (Armitage 2009: 103). Perhaps the global commons of the Internet is exactly this city-world, or rather its cinematic apotheosis, the substitute lives we wish we were living instead of the catastrophic intensification of urban living, itself drenched in the unrealities of urban screens and automobile windscreens. What is missing from this vision is the detail. YouTube is not alone: other services offer less draconian copyright provisions, more open software, deeper socializations and affiliation to political movements.

But if Virilio is correct, and we are on the brink of a city-world, isn't the word he's looking for *cosmopolis*? This was the goal of the Enlightenment, at least as expressed by Kant: the species destiny of humanity to come to a global union. The Fifth and Ninth theses of the *Plan for a Universal History with a Cosmopolitan Intent* read:

> The greatest problem for the human species, whose solution nature compels it to seek, is to achieve a universal *civil society* administered in accord with the right.

> A philosophical attempt to work out a universal history of the world in accord with a plan of nature that aims at a perfect civic union of the human species must be regarded as possible and even as helpful to this objective of nature's. (Kant 1983: 33, 38; original emphasis)

Kant's premise is that every creature is born with capacities which, over the course of its life, it will realize; and that the same is true of species, most of all the human species, whose destiny it is to combine into ever larger, peaceful and righteous unions. Admittedly, he puts a brake on the trajectory: the nation is the largest political unit. As a result, there can be no planetary government. But there can be an inter-governmental peace based on the principles of the Treaty of Westphalia (1648) which first established the body of laws which still govern international relations. It is the duty of the philosopher to provide support for this peace. This thesis is taken up warmly in Habermas' recent writings on international politics, in the form of an argument for legal (rather than political) instruments to resolve the problem that there is no global polity to address war between nations (Habermas 2006). Such cosmopolitanism in the realm of international relations chimes too with the late papers on Europe and cosmopolitanism by Jacques Derrida (2001), where the figure of the stranger and the law of hospitality ring with a parallel generosity to the Kantian idea.

That such cosmopolitanism is not integral to Virilio's platform, despite his devotion to the cause of the homeless, may well derive from a founding phenomenological critique. It is not necessarily that Virilio is against world governments or global legal and moral regimes ensuring peace otherwise than through the armed stand-off and threat of total annihilation of which he was such a powerful critic in the last years of the Cold War (Virilio 1986). Rather he takes his stance against, not the principle, but the practice of cosmopolis: a cosmopolis in which the material city of touch and contact is lost in the ephemeral, disappearing city of images and connections mediated by images.

Some of the clearest expressions of this theme appear in the pages of *The Aesthetics of Disappearance*, where he cites the radical psychoanalyst Reich: 'You don't have bodies, you are bodies!' was the cry once of Wilhelm Reich; to this, power and its techniques now respond: 'You have no speed, you are speed!' (Virilio 1991: 43). The speed of automobiles and planes, the way their wind-screens pass into the role of film screens, how the unmoving seats of cinemas, cars and planes cocoon passengers and viewers alike and absent them from experience: these are precursors of or parallel expressions to the optical nature of modern warfare. In aerial photography, in targeting, and in the reaction against both that led to the adoption of camouflage, the terrain of war is a visual terrain, its weaponry also visual. The prosthetic seeing of weapons is a tool for the annihilation of what they see. Military, transport and optical technologies share a concern for speed, and the paradoxical destruction of perception by the barrage of sensations they offer in its place. 'The development of high technical speeds would thus result in the disappearance of consciousness as the direct perception of phenomena that inform us of our own existence' (Virilio 1991: 104). What is at stake is not just power, then, as we might have expected in a direct critique of cosmopolis as solution. Power is itself a pursuit of mastery over space and, even more fundamentally, over time, as Virilio argues from the case of Howard Hughes, whose withdrawal from the world was, he suggests, in fact an attempt to take total control over it. Rather, the loss of perception and its replacement with sensation throws into doubt the very capacity for being which humans derive from their experience of the world. Deprived of or abstracted from that experience, we no longer *are*. If, as for Bishop Berkeley, *esse est percipi,* to be is to be perceived, then it is also the case that in our rush to sensation, not only do we no longer perceive the world, but it no longer perceives us. When, in a historical process that may extend as far back as the baroque, 'the intense visualization succeeded touch, contact with matter' (59), the anchorage in direct haptic experience was lost, and with it the grounds of human being, truly expressed.

What then do we become, when we cease to be? Playing with metaphors from the physics of the speed of light, Virilio's argument in *The Aesthetics of Disappearance* is that human *being* as such is no longer possible. In a reversal of Heidegger, he argues that the world persists, but we are no longer in or of it. At a critical stage of the argument, Virilio writes that 'the lack of variation of landscapes scoured by speed favours the driver's attempts to identify with the vector' (Virilio 1991: 68). As acceleration pushes the surrounding landscapes away into the distance beyond the imperial space of the car's interior, at the same time smearing them out into motion blur like a poorly adjusted camera pan, there remains nothing to the world of its Kantian transcendental dimensions of space and time. All that remains is the direction of movement through it, a pure geometry which, moreover, has historically uprooted the making of cities and buildings: 'architecture is no longer in architecture but in geometry, the space-time of vectors' (Virilio 1991: 64).

Vector politics

The term 'vector' occurs in at least three discourses: biology, mathematics and contemporary media theory, where its meanings depend on which of the first two categories provide the etymological or metaphorical substrate. In biology, a vector is any moving entity capable of carrying another organism from place to place, especially those organisms like viruses and parasites which require hosts in order to survive and reproduce. This is the sense used for example by McKenzie Wark (2004: ¶314–45) to describe the 'vectoral class' to whom he attributes the control of network regimes and the extraction of value from data flows. The viral model of control over the distribution of data suggests that such control includes ruling over the sustainability, indeed the very existence, of data traffic. In an argument redolent of Virilio's own, Wark suggests that 'The abstraction of information from the world becomes, in turn, the means of abstracting the world from itself' (¶319). Wark's vectoral class, which presides over the virtualization of the world as both nature and second nature, becomes itself a function of the vectoral principle, which constitutes an inhuman or a-human locus of power. Yet the vector in this sense is not determined by the class structure Wark describes: it retains a capacity for openness which leads towards a less biological and more mathematical model.

It is clear that Virilio too is speaking of the mathematical vector. Here again are two usages. In Newtonian mechanics, a vector is the sum of forces acting on an object to provide its motion with a specific direction and force. More generally however, the continuing action of changing forces on objects which are potentially malleable gives a wider definition of 'vector'. In these more general and therefore abstract regions, a vector is an algorithm expressing motion. A crucial characteristic, then, of vectors as opposed to mere lines, is that they have direction: the line segment A–B is not identical to the line segment B–A because there is direction involved, and therefore time. Geometrical vectors are directions, tendencies, future-oriented in that their algebraic expressions can lead to unforeseeable, chaotic, catastrophic or repetitive structures, or towards random and unforeseeable futures. It's for this reason that the vector holds such an important place in the politics of an age which is increasingly mathematized.

Vectors are used extensively in computer graphics, although for a time they were excluded in favour of arithmetic mappings known as bitmaps or raster, where each point (actually a square pixel) is given a numerical address and a number instructing it what colour to display. Vectors operate quite differently, not using numbers but algebra, algebra which instructs the computer to create a geometrical figure. So digital vectors operate not only over time but in complex spaces as well. They are used in computer-aided design and manufacture (CADCAM) and in architectural software to design complex curves: one early expression of vector geometry was a description of a plane surface from which various weights are suspended causing it to deform in complex curves. Typically used in 3D graphics systems for cinema and games, vectors provide not only the shapes of objects but instructions on the behaviours of light reflecting from their surfaces, so giving a visual impression of texture for objects created entirely as code. Virilio however derives his particular interpretation from a much earlier instance of vector mathematics: the complex curves explored using vectors by John von Neumann during the pioneering days of computing, when he was charged with providing gunnery tables for artillery working under a variety of weather conditions (Heims 1980). The connection between gunnery, optics and geometry as fatal intersection is quite clear in Virilio's account of the vector as an alternative to architecture, and as the mode of annihilation characteristic of automobile transport.

Geometry, however, despite its reappearance in contemporary computer design and manufacture, is far from the dominant form of order in contemporary media, an observation which troubles the conduct of Virilio's argument, especially his periodization, while opening up important vistas on the ontology of disappearance. It can be argued that arithmetic enumeration, not vectors, is dominant in contemporary media, and, indeed, in the conduct of contemporary life. This is why the meanings of vectors are the object of struggle, as we will see. What is more, far from enemies of *being*, vectors might potentially restore being from the arithmetic wilderness in which it has been lost.

Western media, and by implication the political economy of the West and more recently of globalization under Western terms, have been conducted under three regimes since the Renaissance, and are, perhaps, ready to change again. As late as the fifteenth-century Northern Renaissance, emblem and colour ordered the visual world in semantic hierarchies; as Edgerton (2009) notes, Brunelleschi's perspective was the last gasp of the spiritual Middle Ages – linear projection revealed God's order – as much as it was the beginning of the scientific world-view. As a tool, however, linear perspective outlived its allegorical origin. The Enlightenment reordered the world geometrically, notably in the perspectival projections of Alberti and in Mercator's map projections, universalizing them in the design and use of Galileo's telescope and Hooke's microscope. The central dispute of the ensuing era concerned the origin of projection: the eye or the vanishing point, the self or the world. The dialectic, perhaps best expressed as the argument between Newtonian and Goethean optics, embodies all the contradictions of the Enlightenment: rationalism versus Romanticism, realism versus republicanism, the terms of democratic individualism versus scientific discipline. We might think of it as the era of the dissemination and introjection of the panopticon, an era uneasily equilibrating exchange and use. These older semantic and realist, hierarchic and geometric formations still operate as deep layers in the manipulation and construction of media, and as paths not yet exhaustively explored for the future.

During the last century or so, a new mode of organization has been in formation. It is primarily arithmetic and probabilistic. As technique, it emerges from early nineteenth-century printing technologies, through the cathode ray tube, to the near-universal raster grid of data screens. As organization, it learned from emergent statistical social sciences to average the idiosyncrasies of perception, and from quantum mechanics to average the probability of photon-scale events. Screens, scanners, camera chips, motherboards and now the operating systems and transmission standards that connect them serve to separate the elements of the grid arithmetically, as rigidly as the keys of the keyboard separate letters from words (Kittler 1990). These structures are not restricted to the kinds of perceptual apparatuses that Virilio deals with, but extend to the dominant media of the twenty-first century: databases, spreadsheets and geographic information systems which form the basis of contemporary biopolitical rule as well as of practical economics. The processes of averaging, which align the flux of the world with the capacities of binary computing, necessarily round up or down to whole numbers, producing an automated process of enumeration which in turn governs the presentation of outputs on printers, screens and, to take just two more examples, the shadow-masks incorporated into TVs and data projectors, and the design of fields and hierarchies in such ubiquitous tools as PowerPoint (Tufte 2006). What all these techniques share is a radical spatialization: from the time-based ledger filled day by day to the synoptic spreadsheet; from the traveller's account of journeys undertaken to the layered data of geographic information systems and their managerial perspective on the control of populations through statistical aggregation. While it would be wrong to suggest a technologically determined structure of causation, nonetheless the enumerative architecture founded on statistical averaging is as precise a fit with the contemporary database economy as the Newton-Goethe dialectic and its projective geometry was with disciplinarity and with the factory system.

If this highly compressed account accurately describes the current case, then the vector is not the enemy that Virilio suggests. On the contrary. Used in the first digital graphics programme, Ivan Sutherland's Sketchpad (2003), and dominant in the early arcade games industry (Wolf 2007), the vector-based oscilloscope does not scan the screen but directs its beam only to the points requiring illumination. The economics of mass production made it too expensive to maintain in the games business; and standardization saw it ousted from all but specialist applications in scientific instruments, such as radar. Like many other experimental media – including the plasma screen – it dropped out of sight, but unlike the plasma screen it has yet to drop back in. Curious, because vector graphics, after being ousted from the centre of digital imaging in the later 1970s, have made a comeback as the centrepiece of digital animation and computer-aided manufacture and design since the late 1980s. The algorithmic vector has the virtue of efficiency: a relatively small algebraic expression replaces a comprehensive list of pixels to be illuminated. But it also has one characteristic which distinguishes it from both the raster grid, with its arithmetic separation and enumeration of action, and the projective geometry of the Renaissance and the Enlightenment: time. Like a gesture, the vector propagates across space but also through time. It is not increased realism or efficiency that makes vectors so important, nor even the tactile qualities of reflection and texture they make possible, but their quality of temporality. Quite distinct from the spatial projection of linear perspective or the arithmetic coding of bitmaps, the vector is lithe, transformative, relational and future-oriented.

Potentially, these qualities can exist on the kinds of oscilloscope screens Sutherland used in the 1960s. But since all current screens are bitmaps, allocating each pixel a numerical address and ascribing to it a numerical description of colour, vectors have to be translated into bitmaps for display. In typical blockbuster or advertising effects sequences, vectors have to be expressed in composites, that is as layers which first move from the four dimensions (three space and one time) of the vector to the two of bitmap, and secondly combine layers created in vector formats with other layers created in two dimensional bitmaps, such as photographic images, now almost universally either digitally generated or converted to digital intermediaries for post-production and editing. This process might be read as flattening the composite landscape of the two modes of digital image generation into a single format; but the traces of their compression into a single plane is often still discernible in the resulting sequences. From the eye-straining 3D planes of *Avatar* to the hand-rendered shadow colour of *Cars*, the restrictions of the grid are constantly argued with by the adversarial vector world. In experimental works like *Ryan,* (Chris Landreth, 2004, National Film Board, Canada, 13 mins 54 sec, http://nfb.ca/film/ryan/), such contradictions blossom into preemptive visions of another aesthetic.

Ryan was a critical and popular success, despite its fourteen-minute runtime. An animation portrait of animator Ryan Larkin, Landreth's film uses advanced 3D graphics to animate interviews with Larkin, at the time an alcoholic living on the streets of Montreal, and his friends, lovers and associates, as well as the director, who appears on camera as a 3D avatar, like Ryan mutilated and deformed in ways expressive of emotional and artistic trauma. One of the curiosities of the film is its inclusion of two short animations by Larkin from his heyday at the national Film Board of Canada, both of them meticulously observed line drawings of bodies in motion. One of the pieces excerpted is Larkin's *Street Musique* of 1972, which likewise moves between realms, cinematography, line animation, colourful organic abstraction. Near the beginning of *Street Musique*, a photographed image of a musician is displaced by a line drawing, as if in advance of the rotoscoping that is now so integral to digital animation technique (for example in Richard Linklater's 2001 animated feature *Waking Life*). At the second transition, motion studies of a man's body transform into a pattern which becomes the basis for colour abstractions migrating across the screen, at first in the form of line shading, but then in washes of colour. These migrations – from location film to line, from line to colour field – seem to be spurred on by an early photographic image of an older man in a hat, smoking, dancing drunkenly with a female member of the group. The world evoked is entirely improvisational: lines become figures or landscapes, a hat becomes a bathtub becomes a pair of trousers becomes a nude figure. This constant mutation, with no apparent goal, nor clear rationality, as if unplanned, made up on the spur, is a characteristic of the vector, whether hand-made or digitally animated. It has the freedom and openness of doodling.

Migration between formats is one of the capacities which artists' animation preserves, where feature animation tends to prefer the coherence of a single technique – such as CGI – and a single style – for example the realism of *Cars* or the reference to old Hanna-Barbera cartoons like *The Flintstones* and *The Jetsons* in *The Incredibles* – governing the whole film. Landreth's brief animated biography of Larkin moves between a number of styles and techniques, including Larkin's own hand-drawn vectors, rotoscoping and fully-rendered 3D environments and characters, to the extent that in certain passages, especially the interviews with friends and colleagues, we are unsure whether we are watching generated or treated images. Though the soundtrack – using a technique going back to Aardman Animation's *Creature Comforts* (1989) – is from dialogue recorded with the subjects, the visual universe is a constant commentary on the truths, half-truths and illusions of those subjects (again including the director himself). Despite this motivation of the images by the sound, the mode of images, and the content of specific realizations, has that same improvisatory quality as Larkin's work thirty years earlier. This is the improvisatory, unexpected and unforeseeable quality of the vector, here breaking through the coherence of the picture plane, opening up the depth and time of the flat fields of bitmaps – and of spreadsheets, databases and geographic information systems – to reveal their ambitions for totality, and their actual circumscriptions of infinities they cannot contain, and which point to the radical differences of futurity.

Yet even if the vector is a saving grace, we cannot pretend that it is intrinsically 'good'. As the film critic André Bazin, stemming from the same school of Catholic phenomenology as Virilio, already knew, no technique escapes its co-option into habit. Film's mission to redeem reality from our failures of perception, he argued, fell victim to the very techniques it used in order to renew perception, allowing reality to become

> identified in the mind of the spectator with its cinematographic representation. As for the filmmaker, the moment he has secured this unwitting complicity of the public, he is increasingly tempted to ignore reality . . . He is no longer in control of his art. He is its dupe. (Bazin 1971: 26-7)

Rather than provide a certain technique for cancelling or escaping the regime of the grid, the vector reveals the internal contradiction of the database economy: its lack of temporal dimension. The vector is always directional: it points towards the future, to what is not the case, and in doing so demonstrates that the vector itself is not identical to itself: the vector is what becomes other. But just as cinematic realism promised, for Bazin, release from the banalities of an ideological life, even at the risk of canonizing specific techniques to the point that they were no longer able to slice through the veils of habit, so, too, the vector is a technique which, at risk of becoming normative, still has the power to rip open the veils of digital efficiency and normativity.

Unsurprisingly, and perhaps proving the case for their significance, vectors are indeed the site of struggle between a variety of forces on a variety of terrains. Vectors are algorithms, mathematical expressions which anyone is free to use. The case of vector prediction techniques in image compression and decompression tools (codecs) is a case in point. It is clear to most users that the compression-decompression algorithms employed in transmitting media are not all of a kind. The H.261 codec which undergirds Adobe's Flash standard and is the primary codec in use on YouTube uses three major compression techniques, GoBs (groups of blocks), automated key-framing and vector prediction to analyse what it deems redundant differences between frames.

GoBs compile areas of similar colour over a period of time and ascribe a single colour or colour gradient to them. Key-framing selects frames where major changes occur, establishes the intervening frames as far simpler transitions, and reduces the amount of information inside the sequence. These techniques combined produce the blocky colour fields and smeared gradients we have come to tolerate on YouTube. Vector prediction is deployed in both techniques to assess the direction and rate of movement on the frame, regularize it mathematically, and reduce the detailed data in the image to a series of instructions to change this or that GoB over the duration marked by key-frames. Almost all the major codecs, including the dominant MPEG-4, use similar techniques to reduce file size in audio and video components. When combined with the poor colour gamuts of digital screens, which render only about 40 per cent of the visible spectrum (with the exception only of some professional devices), the colour management, textural detail and overall veracity of the transmitted image to its source data is seriously and in many instances terminally compromised.

As Adrian Mackenzie (2008: 49) has it, 'Codecs affect at a deep level contemporary sensations of movement, colour, light and time.' What is significant is not just the political economy, even the possible emergence of a network economy significantly different from contemporary capital, but also our phenomenological 'sensations of movement, colour, light and time' or, as David Garcia has it concluding a major collection of essays on YouTube, 'when the temporality of television (the paradigmatic "live" medium) collides with the "timeless time" of the database' (Garcia 2008: 213). Vector prediction is a case in point. The predictive aspect is based on an a-temporal machine reading of the sequence of frames: it is not, as the term 'prediction' would imply, a future-oriented practice. It is instead a translation of time into space, and an extension of the properties of one moment across many. Vector prediction is in effect a delay, a mechanism for extending the present into a foreseeable and plannable future. The vector-based principles of the artisan animation tradition inaugurated by Emile Cohl (briefly referenced in Virilio's book) indicate the capability of distributed light to contribute towards the emergence of new modes of order

(Cubitt 2004: 70–98). Vector prediction takes this future-oriented principle and turns it to the uses of managerial control, naturalizing it as the modes of representation and perception through which we learn to organize space, time and experience.

Such codecs are the stuff of global governance procedures. The key instrument for the most widespread is the Motion Picture Experts Group (which lends its initials to MPEG and mp3 codecs), a sub-group of the Internet Engineering Task Force reporting also to the International Telecommunications Union. The former is a part of ISOC, the Internet Society, which has an open membership and a fundamentally Habermasian mode of action: 'We don't believe in presidents, kings or voting. We believe in rough consensus and cutting code' (Froomkin 2003). The latter is part of the United Nations system, an inter-governmental body which has in recent years begun to open its decision-making committees increasingly to corporate players (MacLean 2003). The open membership model is under attack from both corporates and from nation states, especially China, India, Brazil and Indonesia, who contest the 'Americanization' of the web and the lack of a role in internet governance for nations. Codecs and algorithms are among the fundamental protocols whose future rule is being hotly debated on a global scale. Here, too, the vector demonstrates its foundational role in the emergence of any future internet, and to that extent any future possibility of global democracy, in a century where political access will be mediated or it will not be.

There is a further challenge to the unexpected autonomy of the vector. Currently it is a founding tenet of patent law that algorithms and other mathematical expressions do not constitute 'patentable materials'. This tenet has been the basis for legal battles over the legality of taking out patents on software. In almost all jurisdictions, it is impossible to take out a patent (copyright may be feasible, but there the algorithm is not in question, only its realization: the visual features of a game for example, not its code). Lawyers have found ways to protect their clients' software through sleights of hand, such as patenting devices for the expression of software (for example in driver software, which connects a computer to a printer or other peripheral). One result of this is that the only patents applying to vectors which I have found are associated with Adobe's TrueType fonts, where it is not the line but the mechanism for translating the vector into printable bitmap format that has been consolidated. However, there are moves in the European Union, and disputed cases in the US Supreme Court, which indicate that a new attempt is afoot to bring software, and thus algorithms and necessarily vectors, into the regime of private or corporate property.

As Wark observes, hackers seek to liberate the vector from the rule of the commodity: curiously however, vectors are unexpectedly exempt from that rule. Unlike colour – which has been enumerated and commodified through firms like Pantone – line, the vector, has not. It is true that major software companies have significant control over major sectors of the market for vector graphics. Adobe and Autodesk between them dominate the two- and three-dimensional markets, aided by workflow management systems of extreme sophistication, which currently far outstrip the capacities of free/libre open source software (but see FLOSS Manuals, http://en.flossmanuals.net/, for current work on producing them). Virilio's complaint against the vector is then misplaced: the vector is not the trance-inducing passage into abstraction but a hotly contested capability for change. This displacement reveals a key limitation in his thought, while also opening up Virilio's analysis for reuse in a less apocalyptic, more hopeful scenario.

Vector ontology

At the heart of Virilio's fears for the future lies the resumption of a human being in jeopardy from the loss of tactile, immediate experience. It is a tenet of media analysis, however, that the *im-mediate* is a contradiction in terms: our every experience is mediated through the senses, in a process which takes a measurable amount of time, at thresholds which vary from species to species, and which govern the exact duration of the lapses of consciousness which Virilio observes in the opening pages of *The Aesthetics of Disappearance*. Such moments of lapse are of course the very same that plunge us into darkness twenty-four times a second in

the movie theatre. This is the model of disappearance, a plum-
meting into the abyss which is, for Virilio as it was for Aristotle,
an abhorrence. Acceleration will result, Virilio says, 'in the disappearance of consciousness as the direct perception of phenomena
that informs us of our own existence' (Virilio 1991: 104). Howard
Hughes' abandonment of the pursuit of high-speed flight in favour
of an anonymous room equipped only with a cine projector is the
forerunner of this newly de-realized humanity:

> the abandonment of the vehicular speed of bodies for the strangely
> impressive one of light vectors, the internment of bodies is no longer
> in the cinematic cell of travel but in a cell outside of time, which
> would be an electronic terminal where we'd leave it up to the instru-
> ments to organize our most intimate vital rhythms, without ever
> changing position ourselves, the authority of electronic automatism
> reducing our will to zero. (Virilio 1991: 104)

Even down to the bed-sores, Hughes predicts the abnegation of
being, which for Virilio is expressible in the word 'zero'. The non-
existent is the opposite of being, the very antithesis of the human
which Virilio upholds. The lost fullness of being, its repleteness
with itself, its state of unity posed as self identity, stands at the
opposite end of a philosophical spectrum to some key thinkers of
the twentieth and twenty-first centuries.

The opening sentence of Wittgenstein's *Tractatus* (1961) – 'The
world is all that is the case' – results in the kind of unmediated
presence which Virilio upholds, yet from critical perspectives it
appears as a single undifferentiated environment, a unity held in
the present tense by its wholeness and integrity, a world without
change. Thus Adorno stands

> against scientism, for example Wittgenstein's position that fundamen-
> tally consciousness has to do only with that which is the case. That
> might call forth another definition: metaphysics is the form of con-
> sciousness in which it attempts to know what is more than the case, or
> is not merely the case, and yet must be thought, because that which, as
> one says, is the case compels us to do so. (note on the *Tractatus* cited in
> footnotes to Adorno 2000: 196)

clarifying the proposition in one of the late lectures:

> only what can be refuted, what can be disappointed, what can be
> wrong, has the openness I have spoken of. It is in the concept of open-
> ness, as that which is not already subsumed under the identity of the
> concept, that the possibility of disappointment lies. (Adorno 2000:
> 141)

Adorno's metaphysics of determinate negation clearly stands poles
apart from Virilio's concept of a lost immediate unity between
experience and world. Such immediacy is, for Adorno, the stifling
closure of the identity of the concept: the idea that my thought of
a thing is identical with the thing itself. Kant, of course, had merely
bracketed the thing-in-itself: for Adorno its contingency remains
the worm in the bud of rationalism. Far from overcoming the
contingency of the physical world, (the laws of physics), humanity
has made itself slave to the laws of physics by ascribing to the *idea*
of scientific concepts the definitive and complete description of
the world.

The thought of the vector, however, does suggest a possible
rapprochement between Virilio's phenomenological and Adorno's
metaphysical approaches. Implicit in these passages from Adorno
(but explicit elsewhere in his late works) is the idea of the non-
identical, of a world which he conceives of as fundamentally
dialectical, that is a world in motion. Motion, and change, imply
a lack of identity between the present, the past and the future.
Linked though they are, and evidenced by the temporal process of
change, the present cannot be set up as the apotheosis of all that has
gone before and its culmination. Change, if indeed it is to merit
the name, involves becoming other than what exists at present.
The future, Adorno and his long-time sparring partner Ernst Bloch
agree in a late lecture, is defined by its difference from the present,
to the extent that imagining a content for the future is a betrayal of
its capacity for radical otherness (Bloch 1988).

At the heart of the vector as an expression of this contentless
utopianism lies its own fundamental non-identity: the vector is the
line of change as it extends unpredictably into the future. This is
why it has been and remains so important to drag it back to the

arithmetic grid of the contemporary database economy, to propose to patent its forms, and to turn it into an instrument of spatialization, that is of the eternal present. Ontologically, this means that, strictly speaking, the vector does not exist. For the mathematicians, 'Since nothing falls under the concept "not identical with itself", I define nought as follows: 0 is the number which belongs to the concept "not identical with itself"' (Frege 1974: 87). The vector – and this is the core of Virilio's hatred of it – fails to exist as self-identical and therefore complete being. It belongs to the 0, the point of origin from which, eternally mysteriously, it derives, and the unknown trajectory it takes through space and time. Here, too, Virilio slips up: the vector does not have a destination: that is the characteristic of Euclidean geometry, where a line is a distance between two points. A vector has origin and trajectory but no predetermined end point; and moreover it is endlessly and infinitely, indeed infinitesimally malleable.

Alain Badiou (2006) has erected his ontology on a similar basis, arguing from the non-existence of the empty set for a metaphysics of foundational multiplicities. In the counting which characterizes the digital, there is either a count of one or there is no count (the 0 of binary electronics is a duration without a signal). The nothing, the void as Badiou terms it, the 0 is a marker of an event that doesn't occur. Such counting depends then on union, the one. But in the set theory of the late nineteenth century which fires Badiou's concept, the one hides a secret. To derive one, we begin with the empty set, the minimal point prior to being. This set without contents or elements is, however, a set, and as such it has logically to have the capability to be a member of other sets. To do so, it must be counted: the number of the empty set is one, and one, which pretends to lordship over the measurable world, hides within it the void of non-existence on which it is founded. (An alternate exposition: how many numbers are there on a blank page? None. We write the number zero on the page as a result. How many numbers now? One. So all counting numbers can be derived from zero.)

In his haste to decry the vector, Virilio has unconsciously set his tent in the camp of the count, the account, the diagrammatic presence of unity, of 'all that is the case'. Far from observing the culprit in the disappearance of reality, he has isolated the one great hope we have for overcoming the actually existing reality of the database economy: the biopolitical government and commodification of information and creativity which characterize the current state of the human universe and which have failed so signally to respond to the challenges of poverty, disease, war and environmental catastrophe.

It is a long cry from the mathematics of the vector to the solution of global challenges. Virilio's great contributions are first to identify the nature of those challenges, especially the integration of the military ethos throughout our political, aesthetic and ethical relationships, and secondly to insist that these degradations cannot be distinguished from the aesthetic, that is the sensual experience which constitutes the way we live in the world. If, as argued above, the vector is gestural, common to the drawn line (or the thrown ball) and its digital expressions, it stands apart from the overwhelmingly dominant geometry of the grid which enlaces our core engines of rule and trade as well as aesthetic experience. The relation of these experiences to bodily experience is complex. The physiological experience of gaming, for example, is not the same as the emotional one, involving rhythms of tension and relaxation, and sensations of touch, of impact, of flying or violence. The reverse is also the case: vector graphics represent bodies in novel ways. As Anna Munster (2006: 179) points out, they allow 'an entirely different kind of portrait: an image of the self or body no longer based upon appearance but instead expressed through motion and across time'. From Virilio's perspective, this could perhaps appear as another example of 'bad' vectorization. Yet, as Scott Lash (2002: 63) writes, in his work (as in that of Bruno Latour) 'it is the objects that become structure, that possess agency'. Virilio is concerned for the ill effects of this mutation of the subject-object relation, but his astute observation that it is occurring opens the way to another evaluation: that the new condition allows us to meet objects as agents equal to ourselves. This is the experience of gaming, of participation in online projects like Wikipedia and Linux, and, as several researchers have noted, of players in the global financial services network (Sassen 2006, Knorr Cetina and Bruegger 2002). There is indeed, as Virilio argues, a new phenomenology, one in which humans give up an element of their sovereignty over the world, but they do so in exchange for an expanded polity, and an expanded sensorium, in which we humans are articulated with networks in which we have, for the first time, the opportunty not to enslave machines but to greet them as our fellows in the creation of the future.

To build a new future is the greatest of challenges. When Virilio forces us to look into the abyss of final catastrophe, he makes us consider not only what is at stake, but how we might address it. In his pioneering work on ecological politics he demonstrates how much depends on how we see ourselves in relation to the world. Today, as the terrains of 'immaterial labour' and the physical infrastructure of the network coincide, Virilio, in common with feminist phenomenologists of digital media like N. Katherine Hayles (1999), Margaret Morse (1998) and Michele White (2006), argues against the mind-body split that informs the cyber-visionary desire to leave behind the crumpled, painful 'meat' of the body. Instead, Virilio argues, we have to understand that the general accident is not just a technological flaw, as in his insight that the inventions of the train, the airplane, nuclear power, internet and bio-engineering are always simultaneously the invention of the train crash, the plane wreck, meltdown, information crash and the genetic time-bomb. The condition is, however, more general and formative than that: Virilio notes that 'the production of any "substance" is simultaneously the production of a *typical accident*' (Virilio 1993: 212). As Jussi Parikka observes of this passage, 'An accident . . . is not in this context intended to mean the opposite of absolute and neccessary, as Aristotelian metaphysics has maintained. Instead, accidents are an inherent part of an entity' (Parikka 2007: 4). This might recall Adorno's praise of disappointment, and perhaps also signal the danger attendant on construing the future not as risk management but as unknowable other. In other words, Virilio points us towards an aesthetics of failure: of the inherent risk that any object – and phenomenologically therefore any subject – runs of failing to continue to *be*. It comes down then to a duty of care, for the planet, and consequently therefore also for the people who inhabit it. It seems then that Virilio is correct: a putative vectoral network, one that is not self-identical, that evolves without notice, that plunges into accident and disappointment, and in which machines have as much say as humans is a terrifying risk. But it may also be the only way to escape the stifling grid of destruction which is the military, economic, political and cultural stand-off of a present which denies hope to the mass of humanity and the planet itself.

Google's launch of speech-recognition searches for YouTube videos not only opens its content to search. One reason Google appears to keep the loss-making YouTube venture afloat is because the site contains a second form of invaluable data. Along with the videos, YouTube is a zoo for the observation of mass online behaviours: meta-tagging, folksonomies, word-searches, serendipity. Human behaviour is in itself information, and in line with the company's mission statement, this information too needs to be organized. What is characteristic of human behaviour, even in so corralled a space as the YouTube portal, is that it is, again, non-identical. It shows little order, little rationality, only tendencies. Instead it is a perpetual flocking and scattering, a hive of direction-less activities. Google's network entreprise is to understand that zero-degree of indistinct, irresolvable activity, to turn it into data. Characteristically in this era, the result will be a grid, a matrix of projections and simulations, an artificial future which is instead a continuation of the present, indeed, just such a virtualization as Virilio fears. What the vector teaches as ontology and as politics is that there are behaviours that are significant, even if they do not appear so from the biopolitical vantage where they are merely statistical anomalies. Portals like YouTube will come and go (who still uses MySpace and Friends Reunited?) but vector politics will continue in protocol wars (DeNardis 2009) and in the wide field of information governance, as we struggle over the soul of change. If it is not to be permanently managed as a statistical grid of probabilities, we will need to continue the intellectual, creative and political fight for openness. Those struggles always start in very specific, material terrains. YouTube contains in its unchanging page structure billions of repetitions – of TV clips and home movies – but also many ravishing strange works that, like *Ryan*, point to the internal contradictions of the present and reveal the void at its centre; or gesture towards the exit door beyond which lie untold changes and radical alterity.

References

Adorno, Theodor W. (2000) *Metaphysics: Concept and Problems*. Polity: Cambridge.

Armitage, John (2009) 'In the Cities of the Beyond: An Interview with Paul Virilio', in the Dutch Cahier on Art and the Public Domain *OPEN 18. 2030: War Zone Amsterdam*, ed. Brigitte van der Sande. Amsterdam: NAi Publishers, SKOR, pp. 100–11.

Badiou, Alain (2006). *Being and Event*, trans. Oliver Feltham. Continuum: New York.

Bloch, Ernst (1988). 'Something's Missing: A Discussion between Ernst Bloch and Theodor Adorno on the Contradictions of Utopian Longing (1964)', in *The Utopian Function of Art and Literature: Selected Essays*, trans. Jack Zipes and Frank Mecklenburg. Cambridge, MA: MIT Press, pp. 1–17.

Colman, Felicity (2009) 'Paul Virilio', in Felicity Colman (ed.) (2009) *Film Theory and Philosophy: The Key Thinkers* Durham: Acumen, pp. 201–11.

Cubitt, Sean (2004) *The Cinema Effect*. Cambridge, MA: MIT Press.

DeNardis, Laura (2009) *Protocol Politics: The Globalization of Internet Governance*. Cambridge, MA: MIT Press.

Derrida, Jacques (2001) *On Cosmopolitanism and Forgiveness*, trans. Mark Dooley and Michael Hughes, preface Simon Critchley and Richard Kearney. London: Routledge.

Dorn, Ed (1978) 'Correct Usages of some Words Widely Misused or Abused in Modern Conversation and Poetry', in *Hello, La Jolla*. Berkeley: Wingbow Press.

Edgerton, Samuel Y. (2009) *The Mirror, The Window and the Telescope: How Renaissance Linear Perspective Changed Our Vision of the Universe*. Ithaca: Cornell University Press.

Frege, Gottlob (1974) *The Foundations of Arithmetic*. trans. J.L. Austin. Oxford: Blackwell.

Froomkin, A. Michael (2003) 'Habermas@Discourse.net: Toward a Critical Theory of Cyberspace', *Harvard Law Review*, 116, January: 751–873.

Garcia, David (2008) '(Un)real-time Media – Got Live If You Want It', in Geert Lovink and Sabine Niederer (eds.) *Video Vortex: Responses to YouTube*. Amsterdam: Institute of Network Cultures, pp. 293–6.

Habermas, Jürgen (2006) *The Divided West*, ed. and trans. Ciaran Cronin. Cambridge: Polity Press.

Hayles, N. Katherine (1999) *How We Became Posthuman: Virtual Bodies in Cybernetics, Literature and Informatics*. Chicago: University of Chicago Press..

Heims, Steve (1980) *John von Neumann and Norbert Wiener*. Cambridge, MA: MIT Press.

Kant, Imanuel (1983) *Perpetual Peace and Other Essays on Politics, History and Morals*, trans. Ted Humphrey. Indianapolis, IN: Hackett Publishing.

Kittler, Friedrich A. (1990) *Discourse Networks 1800/1900*, trans. Michael Metteer with Chris Cullens. Stanford, CA: Stanford University Press.

Knorr Cetina, Karin and Urs Bruegger (2002) 'Traders' Engagement with Markets: A Postsocial Relationship', *Theory Culture and Society* 19, 5/6: 161–85.

Lash, Scott (2002) *Critique of Information*. London: Sage.

Lovink, Geert (2008) 'The Art of Watching Databases', in Geert Lovink and Sabine Niederer (eds.) *Video Vortex: Responses to YouTube*. Amsterdam: Institute of Network Cultures, pp. 9–12.

Mackenzie, Adrian (2008) 'Codecs', in Matthew Fuller (ed.) *Software Studies: A Lexicon*. Cambridge, MA: MIT Press, pp. 48–55.

MacLean, Don (2003) 'The Quest for Inclusive Governance of Global ICTs: Lessons from the ITU in the Limits of National Sovereignty', in *Information Technologies and International Development*, 1, 1: 1–18.

Morse, Margaret (1998) *Virtualities: Television, Media Art, And Cyberculture*. Bloomington: Indiana University Press.

Munster, Anna (2006) *Materializing New Media: Embodiment in Information Aesthetics*. Hanover, NH: Dartmouth College Press/University Press of New England.

Parikka, Jussi (2007) *Digital Contagions: A Media Archaeology of Computer Viruses*. New York: Peter Lang.

Sassen, Saskia (2006) *Territory, Authority, Rights: From Medieval to Global Assemblages*. Princeton: Princeton University Press.

Sutherland, Ivan Edward (2003 [1963]) *Sketchpad: A Man-Machine Graphical Communication System*, with a new preface by Alan Blackwell and Kerry Rodden, dissertation submitted January 1963 by the author for the degree of Doctor of Philosophy to the Massachusetts Institute of Technology, University of Cambridge Computer Labs technical reports, Cambridge, www.cl.cam.ac.uk/TechReports/

Swift, Mike (2010) 'YouTube plans to caption most videos automatically', *San Jose Mercury News*, 3 March.

Tufte, Edward R. (2006) *The Cognitive Style of PowerPoint*, (2nd edn). Cheshire, CT: Graphics Press.

Virilio, Paul (1986) *Speed and Politics: An Essay in Dromology*, trans. Mark Polizotti. New York: Semotext(e).

Virilio, Paul (1991) *The Aesthetics of Disappearance*, trans. Philip Beitchman. New York: Semiotext(e).

Virilio, Paul (1993) 'The Primal Accident', trans. Brian Massumi in Brian Massumi (ed.) *The Politics of Everyday Fear*. Minneapolis: University of Minnesota Press, pp. 210–18.

Virilio, Paul (2001) 'The Last Vehicle', in Chris Kraus and Sylvère Lotringer (eds.) *Hatred of Capitalism: A Semiotext(e) Reader*. New York: Semiotext(e), pp. 151–60.

Wang, Spencer and Kenneth Sena (2009), 'Deep Dive Into YouTube; 1Q09 Preview', Credit Suisse Equity Research 3 April. Geneva: Credit Suisse.

Wark, McKenzie (2004) *A Hacker Manifesto*. Cambridge, MA: Harvard University Press.

White, Michele (2006) *The Body and the Screen: Theories of Internet Spectatorship*. Cambridge, MA: MIT Press.

Wolf, Mark J.P. (ed.) (2007) *The Video Game Explosion: A History from PONG to PlayStation and Beyond*. New York: Greenwood Press.

5

Virilio's Media as Philosophy

Scott McQuire

The theme of media is hard to isolate in the overall context of Virilio's work: while traces can be found in many places, 'the media' is rarely the central focus in itself. Although Virilio almost entirely ignores the themes which have historically dominated the academic discipline of media studies – namely, institutional ownership and control, textual analysis, and studies of production and reception – media nevertheless constitute a privileged site in his understanding of a broad range of phenomena including perception, power, the transformation of urban space, and, of course, the practice of war. If, for Virilio, media are not an end but a middle, this middle passage does not conform to the idealized cybernetic model of a neutral conduit transmitting a discrete message from sender to receiver. By treating media as complex transformers, Virilio manages to avoid what Morley (2009) refers to as the media-centric analysis of much media studies, which limits its consideration to an overly narrow object and set of effects. The fact that he does so by positioning media as integral to the fundamental transformation of human modes of being in the modern world, carries its own risks – namely technological determinism – but also creates a thought-provoking analysis rarely matched in the present.

Despite his disinterest in dominant approaches, Virilio's work has gained purchase within media studies over time. This stems largely from his influential role in conceptualizing two trajectories that have become central to contemporary media studies: the globalization of media flows, and the impact of 'real time' transmission, especially in the context of war. I'd also add a third aspect: Virilio's long insistence on the importance of joining analysis of media space to our understanding of physical spaces such as cities and buildings. In this respect, Virilio's work can be aligned to an important paradigm shift in understanding media, exemplified by the contemporary explosion of interest in geo-spatial data and geographic information systems. This development confirms the extent to which the traditional analysis of media in terms of 'representation' – which ultimately depends on the vexed and often unarticulated assumption of a 'reality' that exists outside mediation – has given way to analysis of media as embedded within everyday life.

For Virilio, the trajectories of globalization and 'real time' are more properly conceived as a single horizon located under the master sign of 'speed'. By conceptualizing media as *motor*, and foregrounding speed as the determinant force in contemporary society, Virilio has opened up an original and highly productive problematic. The global milieu in which light-speed media become ubiquitous not only inaugurates the historically distinctive and urgent problem of what Virilio calls 'critical space', but fundamentally interrupts human capacity for understanding and judgement. If media speed represents the general extension of military logistics into the terrain of everyday life, Virilio's work implies that the formulation of an *ecology of speed* becomes an integral part of any meaningful political settlement in the present.

Medium theory and technological determinism

At first blush, Virilio's approach to media shares common ground with the tradition Joshua Meyrowitz (1994) has called 'medium theory'. Deriving from the work of Harold Innis and Marshall

McLuhan, medium theory foregrounds the transformative role of media technologies by ascribing specific powers or consequences to the introduction of new media platforms. Key historical thresholds, such as the introduction of paper-based communication (Innis), or mechanical printing and electronic media such as television (McLuhan), are posited as the central factor underlying a range of social, economic and political changes (for example, McLuhan's assertion that 'print' was the 'architect of nationalism'). In fact, the logic of medium theory can be found in many places: Debord's (1983) spectacle, Baudrillard's (1983) simulation, Anderson's (1983) print-capitalism, Castells' (1996) network society, all depend on the assertion of a formative connection between the introduction of new media platforms and a series of broader social, economic and political shifts. The key point of contention is, of course, the degree and directness of any causal relation that can be ascribed to 'media' as the origin of certain effects. In the mid-1970s Raymond Williams' (1990) well-known critique of McLuhan made a generation of media theorists wary of 'technological determinism'.

Insofar as this promoted critical reflexivity instead of treating specific media platforms as ahistorical and autonomous causes which simply dropped from the sky, this was well and good. However, as Lister et al. (2009: xiv) point out, critique sometimes flipped over into its polar opposite, denying technology any substantive role. Moreover, while Williams' Marxist-humanist frame provided the formative matrix for thinking the relation of culture and technology within media studies, the field has since undergone significant changes. Understanding human agency in societies with a growing dependence on complex technological systems, including distributed networks such as the Internet, raises new challenges. The rise of new theoretical accounts insisting on the relative autonomy of technology, such as actor-network theory's stress on addressing both human *and* technological agency as constitutive of complex, heterogeneous assemblages (see, for example, Latour 2005), is one marker of this difference. The resurgence of interest in a 'digital McLuhan' in the 1990s, from the academic approach of those such as Paul Levinson (1999) to the uncritical embrace of *Wired*, who seized McLuhan as their 'patron saint', is another.

Virilio's work cuts obliquely across these debates. While he is susceptible to charges of technological determinism, dismissing his work on this basis risks missing both its critical ambivalence *and* its generative possibilities. Although Virilio has little interest in the sort of situated, empirical studies called for by actor-network theory, his work shares the aim of re-evaluating the possibilities of human agency in relation to the agency of 'things', as the contemporary city becomes a highly mediated environment comprising automated sensors, surveillance cameras, data tags and pervasive screens. However, rather than the 'post-humanist' systems orientation adopted by someone like Friedrich Kittler (2009), Virilio's stance has remained resolutely *humanist*. Awareness of the extent to which contemporary technology threatens the space-time of embodied subjectivity is the ethico-political heartbeat reverberating through his thought.

If Virilio's take on technology is frequently pessimistic, he insists that this is a matter of saying what is too often left unsaid: 'Today we are faced with a kind of slack-jawed optimism with respect to new technologies, which for me is perhaps the latest conformism' (Virilio and Lotringer 2002: 156). Sylvère Lotringer offers a perceptive analysis, arguing that, rather than simple negativity, Virilio in fact displays a profound ambivalence towards technology which 'is impossible to shrug . . . away in any simple way'. Lotringer adds:

> [R]eaders will be shocked again and again to realize that this prodigious prophet of speed, undoubtedly the most important thinker of technology since Martin Heidegger, actually hates technology with a passion. And yet passion there is, possibly stronger even than hate, and so infectious that this absolute rejection of technology could also be experienced as a form of love or devotion. . . . Virilio's world is a crepuscular one, but so flamboyant and poetic that it could easily be mistaken for a new dawn. (Virilio and Lotringer 2002: 8)

Reading this poetic rejection of technology – a rejection that, in its passion, could be mistaken for a declaration of love – underlines the fact that, for Virilio, the question of media can never be reduced to a reform agenda, but necessitates a rethinking of fundamentals. In short, he calls for a new *philosophy* of media. More

than most of his contemporaries, it is this sustained reflection on
the unstable grounds of media that his work has consistently sought
to provide.

Media, space and time

What Virilio particularly shares with Innis and McLuhan is their
emphasis on the role of media technologies in the production of
new space-time frames which not only affect social experience
– including the form of the social bond and the exercise of
political power – but which profoundly shape conceptual paradigms, including those dominant in science, art and religion. As
McLuhan (1974: 16) put it when distinguishing his approach
from then-dominant forms of content analysis: '[T]he "message"
of any medium or technology is the change of scale or pace or
pattern that it introduces into human affairs'. McLuhan's work was
strongly influenced by Harold Innis' thesis concerning the spatial
or temporal 'biases' of different media as fundamental to explaining changes in political and economic processes and organizational
forms. Innis' basic contention was that durable media, such as clay
and stone, have a temporal 'bias', while less durable media such
as papyrus and paper, which are 'light in character', have a spatial
bias. Where time-biased media are conservative and 'helped sustain
centralised religious forms of tradition', Innis (1951: 116) argued:
'Transportable media favoured the growth of administrative relations across space, thereby facilitating the decentralised growth of
secular and political authority.' In his account, the invention of
paper, and its spread from China to the Middle East and then to the
West, constituted a central factor in the decline of oral culture, and
the subsequent emergence of spatially extensive forms of political
authority such as the Roman empire.

McLuhan's particular audacity was to apply Innis' logic to the
new technological threshold of electronic media, most notably
television. His famous thesis about television ushering in the post-
rational era of the 'global village' is built around a *gestalt* model
of perception and information patterning which had first been

promoted in the US by avant-garde design figures such as Gyorgy Kepes. While Virilio is clearly aware of McLuhan's work, his analysis of electronic media runs completely counter to McLuhan's optimistic vision. For Virilio (Virilio and Wilson 1994):

> [T]elevision is a media of crisis, which means that television is a media of accidents. Television can only destroy. In this respect, and even though he was a friend of mine, I believe that McLuhan was completely wrong.

Virilio's difference with McLuhan is, above all, a difference in reading the social and political effects of television's impact on time. McLuhan argued that television had the potential to restore the unity of human consciousness, which had been fragmented by centuries of print culture, through the televised creation of the 'absolute present' of the 'global village'. Virilio certainly acknowledges the radical aspect of live television, positioning it as the apex of an historical trajectory in which the value of information has increasingly become a function of its speed. When the production of 'news' was industrialized in the nineteenth century, the news cycle was measured by the relative speed of technologies including the telegraph, telephone and rail networks. However, in the twentieth century, print media found itself overtaken by new platforms allowing the instantaneous global distribution of information to mass audiences. Recalling the first multiplex radio broadcast in 1938, when CBS correspondents were linked live from Rome, Berlin and Paris, Virilio notes:

> Subscribers were not so much buying daily news as they were buying instantaneity, ubiquity – in other words, their own participation in universal contemporaneity, in the movement of the future Planet City. (1995a: 49)

This incipient global arena was strengthened by the first satellite link-up of all five continents for a live television broadcast in 1964, and finally confirmed by the emergence of CNN as an explicitly global television network in June 1980. As Virilio (1991: 17) argued: 'In 1980, for example, when Ted Turner decided to launch Cable News Network as a round-the-clock live news station, he transformed his subscribers living space into a kind of global broadcast studio for world events.' However, in stark contrast to McLuhan's faith in television's redemptive capacities, Virilio (2000c: 52) argues that 'the global village Marshall McLuhan hoped for does not exist; there is only *a centre of inertia* that freezes the present world in each of its inhabitants'.

Tracing Virilio's recapitulation of this history demonstrates how his conception of television as a 'media of crisis' relates to both its predilection for *showing* violence, but also to its status as a *violent form of showing*. If the first strand of analysis prefigured the recent profusion of work on the relation between media and crises such as war and terrorism, the second shares common ground with Avital Ronell's (1994) perceptive analysis of the ontological effects of television.[1] However, rather than Ronell's psychoanalytical framework, Virilio argues that the violence of television is measured, above all, by speed. When Virilio describes contemporary television as *anti-democratic*, this is partly a reflection of its annexation for the transmission of propaganda, but more directly a function of its imposition of a velocity of communication that is inimical not only to democracy, but to properly *human* modes of being. As he put it in an essay first published in *Le Monde Diplomatique* (Virilio 1995b): 'To have reached the light barrier, to have reached the speed of light, is a historical event which throws history into disarray and jumbles up the relation of the living being towards the world.'

Media as metaphor

I began this chapter by noting the difficulty of pinning down Virilio's conception of media. This is partly because of its wide distribution throughout his work, but also arises from the fact that media serve a double function as both symptom and source. If his essays return time and again to criticism of the 'effects' of media technologies, they are also littered with examples, such as public statements or descriptions of recent events, gleaned from newspapers and television. This technique of montage feeds Virilio's highly distinctive style of writing. McLuhan was fond of launching what he called 'probes', presenting his work through evocative phrases and visual designs that traded rational argument for a patina of effects. Virilio is also renowned for his pungent aphorisms and unconventional argument, which Lotringer positions as a deliberate pedagogy:

> Like Hegel, you often try to condense the various contradictions and innovations of a period in a single hero, the way you often bounce an idea with a striking quote. But for you they are more than representatives of their times, they embody an idea poetically through their own excess. (Virilio and Lotringer 2002: 97)

Virilio's own take on his approach – 'I'm an old painter, you see. I don't just do theory, I make images when I write' (Virilio and Lotringer 2002: 141) – suggests an affinity with Benjamin's concept of 'dialectical images'. For Benjamin, dialectical images were figures capable of condensing contradictory historico-political currents, and then releasing their latent and potentially liberatory power when mobilised in critical contexts.[2] This underlines the importance of exploring the specific resonances of the images that Virilio develops and deploys. Take, for example, three of the most striking metaphors under which television appears in his work: the 'third window', the 'last vehicle' and 'the museum of accidents'. Each performs a double act by articulating television in relation to another milieu, respectively architecture, transport and technological systems. This technique supports Virilio's approach of positioning media as a transformer which is not itself the fixed centre of analysis. Inasmuch as media technologies shape fundamental social trajectories, media is nevertheless conceptualized as a partially unbounded *and radically unbinding* milieu, producing effects which always point elsewhere.

For example, by introducing the notion of the 'third window', Virilio succinctly places television in a new historical lineage, analysing it via its impact on architecture and urban space. He describes the advent of the 'third window' as an 'event of considerable importance', adding:

It reaches to the heart and soul, the principle and nature of architecture; it relegates the protocol of physical access – as well as the necessity
of an effective presence – to a secondary plane of actual experience.
(1991: 99)

By situating television in relation to two previous thresholds in
human dwelling space (with the first window constituting the
entrance to the primordial cave, and the second window constituting the advent of a dedicated opening for light and air),
Virilio focuses our attention on television as an epochal force. By
asking us to think of television as a 'cathode window' which no
longer opens onto its immediate surrounds but interrupts spatial
contiguity to shed an indirect light which increasingly de-localizes
all surrounds, Virilio positions television as symptomatic of the
profound realignment of dimensions and experience central to
the current phase of globalization. In the same move, he offers a
productive image for registering the integral link between macro
and micro scales, relating changes in the material boundaries
and existential dimensions of the private home to the destabilization of the geography and borders of the nation state. By
shifting attention from Enlightenment enthusiasm for light and
transparency to the contemporary potential for *overexposure*, he
undercuts McLuhan's image of an incipient global family with
Bauman's (2000: 7–8) sombre warning of a coming ethos of
'universal comparison':

> Thanks to this 'real-time' illumination, the space-time of everyone's
> apartment becomes potentially connected to all others, the fear of
> exposing one's private life gives way to the desire to over-expose it
> to everyone. . . . The much-vaunted globalization requires that we
> all observe each other and compare ourselves with one another on a
> continual basis. (Virilio 2000a: 60–1)

The metaphor of the 'last vehicle' traces a similar historical
trajectory, but this time in relation to the extensive forms of
movement entrained by modern vehicles. Where successive
waves of 'dynamic' vehicles, from the steam-powered ship to
the airplane, were implicated in the circuits of mobility essential

to the growth of industrial capitalism and the expansion of colonial power across the globe, the light-speed of television instantiates a new type of vehicle: 'the static *audiovisual vehicle*, a substitute for bodily movement, and an extension of domestic inertia, which will mark the definitive triumph of sedentariness'. (2000b: 18) In place of extensive movement through the world, Virilio argues that television (and later the Internet) address us quite differently:

> The whole panoply of the latest technologies invites us suddenly to be stuck at home, under the house arrest of telematics and the electronic workplace, which turn erstwhile televiewers into teleactors in an instantaneous interactivity that exiles us from real space, from contact with our fellow man. (2000c: 63)

This is not simply a lament directed at the laziness of 'couch potatoes'. Rather, it points to a social condition in which media, which generally appear under the democratic sign of individual freedom, are in fact implicated in the production of a new *carceral* society. Virilio (2000b: 33) suggests: 'Here Bentham's panopticon is no longer in the detention centre but in the apartment or city, or even the country at large.' As with his optic of overexposure, the implications of this thesis extend beyond the televisual to contemporary digital networks, exemplified by current debates over privacy concerns in relation to social networking sites such as Facebook and Google Buzz.

Finally, consider the metaphor of the accident museum. One of Virilio's most striking dictums is his assertion that each technical threshold involves the appearance of a new accident (see 2000c: 54; 2007). This can perhaps be most readily understood in relation to the railway, which inaugurates the train accident as an integral part of its expansion of modern mobility. However the assertion becomes more complicated in relation to media technologies. Virilio argues that the formation of global media networks has introduced a new type of accident, of which computer viruses are exemplary. In contrast to the train wreck, a localized accident which occurs in the determinate time and place underpinning classical physics, the *informational* accident exists in quantum space-time where distribution cannot be precisely localized, but is a statistical function of probability.

It is in this context that Virilio proposes his provocative notion of an 'accident museum', a museum which could undertake the paradoxical task of exhibiting the accident as the *contingent and yet inevitable* horizon of technological society. In some respects, Virilio's argument here parallels Ulrich Beck's (1992) description of 'risk society', in which the unintended consequences of industrial modernity mean that traditional debates concerning the distribution of social 'goods' have morphed into arguments about the distribution of social 'bads'. However, where Beck's exemplars are environmental issues such as nuclear waste and pollution, Virilio's focus is increasing societal reliance on information technologies. For Virilio, the accident museum is not a matter of exposing a new range of objects, but creating a new kind of scenography in which '*only what explodes and decomposes is exposed*' (2000c: 56). Finally, it is television's preoccupation with disaster scenarios that leads Virilio to proclaim that 'the *accident museum* exists': 'I've come across it: it is a TV screen' (2000c: 60).

From here it is only a short step to Virilio's primary metaphor for the computer: the 'information bomb'. This refers not only to the widely observed phenomenon of 'information overload' but to the way that rapid information processing underpins two other key trajectories of technological modernity: the development of atomic weapons and the advent of genetic engineering. Positioning information at the centre of this unholy trinity confirms Virilio's longstanding analysis of the implication of media technologies in modern warfare.

Media as war machine

Virilio has often situated his own formation in relation to the experience of war. Not surprising, then, that the role of war in modern technological development has been a pervasive theme in his work. In his landmark book *War and Cinema*, Virilio traced the extent to which visual technologies had become an integral part of contemporary weapons systems, establishing a 'deadly harmony' between the functioning of eye and weapon (1989: 69). This reconceptualization of the traditional 'theatre of war', according to the new forms of indirect vision deriving from photography and opto-electronics situates the manner in which the customary role of war-time media – to disseminate propaganda directed at civilians – is now complemented by tactical and strategic representations directed at the combatants themselves. In a second phase of this process, some of the same images become increasingly available to the broader public via civilian media circuits.

Virilio's perspicuity in tracing the historical genesis of this interdependence ensured that the 'missile cam' images that amazed viewers and commentators alike in the 1990–1 Gulf War were less new developments than confirmations of a trajectory he had already sketched. In retrospect, the key development in *War and Cinema* was less his analysis of the growing role of photography and film in military observation, but his connection of this process to the general *informationalization* of warfare. Arguing that increases in firepower introduced by industrialized warfare not only enabled long-range destruction, but necessitated new forms of reconnaissance, Virilio notes that the First World War is marked by a growth in military photography, especially from the air, and a growing reliance on *serial* forms of imagery (both still and moving) to cope with the heightened mutability of the front line subjected to massive bombardment. By the Second World War the old logistics of 'positional warfare' has given way to a new war of movement, creating a strategic demand for new information flows capable of keeping up with mobile mechanized armies. Information not only had to be gathered from new perspectives, but transmitted in new ways so as to minimize the gap between sending and receiving, and finally assembled according to new protocols. Developments such as short-wave radio and onboard radar systems for airplanes were coordinated by new command posts, as warfare increasingly came to depend on the 'special effects' of audio-visual reconnaissance. By harnessing new possibilities for radio communication-at-a-distance, command posts could be situated well behind the lines, eventually falling back to capital cities themselves:

> No longer having any real extension in space, these centres of interaction received an endless mass of information and messages from the most scattered points and radiated it back into their own, defined universe. (1989: 50)

Here the military command post has become the prototype for the post-war era of broadcast media, in which a central 'studio' disseminates controlled data (programmes) to a dispersed but defined audience. Virilio couples this insight to his insistence on the historical role of wartime photography and cinematography as precursors for modern information flows. In this regard, he delineates two trajectories, each of which will extend well beyond war. The first concerns the emergence of the *sight machine* (what he will later call the vision machine), describing a technological mode of observation that, in its desire to transcend all natural obstacles, increasingly loses any dependence on a human viewer. The second concerns the gradual conversion of warfare to a problem of *data management*. If the advent of the sight-machine steers military strategy towards a radical dependence on a 'general system of illumination that will allow everything to be seen and known, at every moment and in every place' (Virilio 1989: 4), the need to interpret the resultant data changes the practice of warfare in a fundamental way.

> The problem, then, is no longer so much one of masks and screens, of camouflage designed to hinder long-range targeting; rather, it is a problem of ubiquitousness, of handling simultaneous data in a global but unstable environment where the image (photographic, or cinematic) is the most concentrated, but also the most stable form of information. (1989: 71)

Once the problem of military observation becomes an informational problem of managing data flows, the threshold of computerized warfare is also inevitable. Many of the trajectories first identified in *War and Cinema* reappear in Virilio's subsequent writings on military campaigns. However, by the 1990s this is not simply a matter of the military's growing use of sophisticated weapons systems incorporating real time surveillance, but the growing strategic need to manage the data flows of civilian media. For Virilio, the 1990–1 Gulf War signalled the terms of a new 'imbalance', in which real-time miliary intelligence found its correlate in real-time information flows to the home front. Rapid information flows once demanded military systems, such as the strategic formation of rapid media networks as part of the *blitzkreig* that enabled film shot at the front to be screened in German cinemas within a day. By the time of the Gulf War, satellite broadcasters such as CNN were routinely able to match the speed of military data flows, effectively placing global society on a permanent war footing. This, in turn, forced the military to find new means of influencing media coverage. Tactics have included the institutionalized daily briefings and lavish provision of military footage including 'missile cam' in the 1990–1 Gulf War, and the 'embedding' of journalists in the 2003 Iraq campaign.[3] In his analysis of media strategy in the Kosovo war, Virilio (2001: 24, 27) also highlighted the increase of direct interventions into civilian media through tactics such as jamming and bombardment, comparing the decision to cut off Yugoslav television by removing its satellite feeds to the strategic destruction of electricity supply using graphite bombs.[4] What seems most significant to me in Virilio's analysis of the turn to 'info war' is less its insight into the relation between broadcast television and the Pentagon's 'revolution in military affairs', but the profound shift it registers in the relation between media and politics.

Mediating politics

In conventional theory, the media's capacity to contribute to democracy is dependent on the construction of a functioning public sphere that enables the circulation of relevant information and rational discussion of alternative policies. Building on this ideal image, Joshua Meyrowitz (1985: 323) has contended that television has 'the potential of the closest thing the earth has witnessed to participatory democracy on an enormous scale'. In contrast, Virilio perceives contemporary media as profoundly *anti-democratic*,

instituting radical forms of *non-communication* (2002b 39–40).
Observing media coverage of the Kosovo 'info war', Virilio argued
that older forms of political control based on repression had been
displaced by deliberate over-supply:

> [W]hereas in the past it was lack of information and censorship which
> characterized the denial of democracy by the totalitarian state, the
> opposite is now the case. Disinformation is achieved by flooding
> viewers with information, with apparently contradictory data. The
> truth of the facts is censured by **over-information**, as we have seen
> from the press and the television discussing the Balkans. (2001: 48)

Over-information is correlated with information acceleration.
Where Virilio (1989: 53) argues that the failure of the public
sphere in the first decades of the twentieth century was a function
of the rise of a new form of spectacular politics, exemplified by fas-
cism's fusion of the roles of director and dictator, the fundamental
problem in the present is *speed*. The media circuits of the 'live'
Gulf War signalled the ascendancy of a new paradigm of rapid
decision-making:

> Indeed the Gulf War has marked the beginning of serious doubts
> about the reign of instant information: Can one democratise ubiquity,
> instantaneity, immediacy, which are precisely the prerogatives of the
> divine – in other words, of autocracy? (2000c: 30)

Speed intensifies the pressure on public opinion, not so much
according to traditional demands for 'the people' to accept a singular 'truth', but through a form of synchronization that, for Virilio,
threatens to eviscerate the *time* of democracy:

> After the era of the standardization of products and manners of the
> industrial consumer society comes the era of the synchronization of
> opinion – the age of an information revolution in which parliamentary
> geopolitics suddenly gives way to a *chronopolitics* of instantaneity, that
> 'live' coverage of which television possesses the knack, with the rise
> of a genuine virtual democracy – that is to say, a *ludic* democracy for
> infantilized tele-citizens – still to come. (2002b: 31)

If Virilio attributes the infantilization of the citizenry in part to populist politics, in which 'telecracy' produces 'the triumph of audience ratings over universal suffrage' (2002b: 30), it is also a function of the reduction of the temporal horizon of 'deliberative democracy' to atomized instants. From this perspective, far from constituting the life blood of democracy, light-speed media rings its death-knell.

> From ancient Athens up to the transport revolutions of the 19th century, the *democratisation of relative speed* was a major historical constant in the development of Western civilisation. But can we seriously envisage a *similar democratisation of absolute speed* in the age of the instantaneous transmission revolution? . . . Personally, I doubt it . . . (2000c: 31)

While the older mode of politics clearly had its own problems, its replacement is equally unpalatable. Symptomatic is the symbiotic relation between live television and terrorism that Virilio was one of the first to perceive. In response to the 1993 bombing of Manhattan's World Trade Center, he argued that the event signalled the emergence of a mutant form of militant politics:

> With the New York bomb, we thus find ourselves faced with the latest escalation in the kind of military-political interaction that is based simultaneously on a limited number of actors and *guaranteed media coverage.* (2000c: 19, emphasis added)

When the spectacle of orchestrated violence has become a recognized form of political strategy, the repeat screening that constituted 9/11 eight years later was, tragically, all too predictable.

Rethinking the politics of media philosophy

For Virilio, the displacement of the theatrical space of traditional political power is no longer simply a problem of the over-concentration of power in the hands of twentieth-century media moguls, of whom Berlusconi and Murdoch are perhaps the last remnants. The new political terrain is defined by expansive dreams of 'global information dominance', itself an outgrowth of demands for omniscient vision in the military field of operations.[5] It is the capacity of media technologies to seemingly 'transcend' previous spatio-temporal limits that Virilio sees fuelling the contemporary displacement of religion and philosophy as bodies of knowledge capable of *situating* human life. From this perspective, Virilio (2001: 22) asks us to consider the *ethico-religious* aspects of this and similar projects, 'the attributes of which are indeed those of the divine'.

One outcome of this displacement of the gods is the creation of new *fundamentalist* investments in technology itself. Or, as Avital Ronell (1994: 308) wryly puts it: 'The death of God has left us with a lot of appliances.' The expansion of contemporary media into a mode of omniscience previously reserved for the gods underpins Virilio's demand that we understand media not only in relation to the political-strategic problem of 'critical space', but also as the unstable ethico-philosophical ground of contemporary human existence. This sets a difficult, if essential, task: as Friedrich Kittler (2009: 23) has noted, media philosophy – or rather a philosophy of media – has been an historical blind spot.

Long ago Marx famously rejected philosophy in favour of the priority of political action. If his point about changing the world still remains to be achieved, it has always been far too simple to assert that conceptual frameworks have no role to play in social and political transformation. While Virilio's political activity has always shown solidarity with marginal communities such as the homeless and refugees, I would argue that his writing on media has made its most significant contribution in advancing thinking about media *as philosophy*. More than any of his contemporaries, he has continually posed the problematic of media technologies in terms of key philosophical questions of time, space and being. The transformed conditions in which embodied human beings are required to make judgements, exercise agency, and form relations to others – to past and future, to the natural world and to particular living environments – underpins all Virilio's writing about media. The limit to this emergent philosophy of media is its unremitting negativity.

Before I address this issue in more detail, I think it is important to understand the internal logic of Virilio's stance. Insisting that 'negativity is a positive task', Virilio argues:

> Only critique is possible right now, precisely because we no longer have the power to stem these tendencies. Why not? Because we can no longer fall back on a philosophical power or a religious power in the broad sense of wisdom. . . . Today, the power of absolute speed, of live transmission, of cybernetic information technology is such that traditional power which used to rely on force, on armies, on police, etc., and even on wealth, can no longer hold it back. (Virilio and Lotringer 2002: 161–2)

In other words, it is the acceleration in all areas of social life engineered by media and information technologies that creates a tipping point, defined by the loss of historical measures for judgement and action, so that the social milieu is fundamentally transformed and the political space of subjectivity is subsumed. In this context, Virilio suggests that media technology is no longer susceptible to dialectical understanding, but can only be thought from the standpoint of its *excess*. It is from this position that we can understand, if not necessarily subscribe to, Virilio's powerful dramatization of the *depletion* of life in a mediated society, one which has long forsaken the Enlightenment demand for rational illumination for the brave new world of mediatized overexposure and the surveillance capitalism of Google search. Virilio is sharpest when he dissects the imbrication of media in contemporary military campaigns and the militarization of society as a whole, or when he riffs on the role of pervasive media in inculcating a 'surveillance society' that eviscerates social relationships. These are part of the big picture through which he connects media to ideas of the 'good life' – or rather, of its negation. But negativity has its limits. The general thrust of his pronouncements leaves no space for recognizing the many important counter-initiatives using digital media technologies, particularly those associated with peer-to-peer collaborative networks. This is a real shame, because the fundamental political question asked by Virilio's philosophy of media – *how might we build a more varied ecology of speed?* – is intimately connected to the question of what new transversal forms of political action, what new spaces and rhythms, are possible and appropriate in global networked societies.

Since the 1960s, many cities have learnt – painfully and still only partially – that what Le Corbusier famously dubbed 'cities built for speed' are not the recipe for 'success' that he imagined in the 1930s. In the face of the incessant demands of traffic engineers, it has been recognized that cities need spaces for lingering and socializing, spaces for inhabitation as much as rapid transit. In other words, a successful city is defined by its capacity to engender and sustain a variety of speeds; the more complex the urban ecology of speed, the more likely the city will not only prove inhabitable to a variety of people, but will incubate a rich mix of social inter-actions and cultural innovations. It is increasingly apparent that a similar lesson needs to be learnt in relation to the always on, always available, media networks that are now recalibrating social life.

Virilio's work is useful in providing a pungent critique of the kind of thinking manifest in tracts such as Bill Gates' (1999) *Business @ the Speed of Thought*. The extent to which this logic remains dominant is evidenced in the common use of 'league tables' comparing the broadband capacity of different nations as an index of their social and economic contemporaneity.[6] Virilio's insistence on speed as an *existential* issue is not an abstract issue but provides an important corrective to disturbingly one-dimensional policy frameworks. It also opens a critical perspective on the way in which social networking sites such as Facebook and Twitter are currently normalizing the continual reporting and scrutiny of users' everyday actions, thus underlining the growing implication of digital networks in the micro-colonization of 'real time'. Finally, Virilio's focus on speed offers a vantage point to question the tactics and strategies of some who ostensibly advocate alternatives to multinational-led globalization. Despite manifest differences in the political and social outcomes sought, the default assumption in both camps is too often the belief that problems can be overcome by increased speed – greater bandwidth, more processing power, universal access, ubiquity, pervasiveness. Virilio, on the contrary, asks us to consider that such 'improvements' may well be part of the problem, not only because they impact on our capacity to sustain deliberative debate and make political judgements, but also because they threaten to undermine the fundaments of our social relations.

Recently, the mobile phone overtook the wristwatch as the single, most carried, personal device. From its origins in the medieval monastery, the adoption of clock time orchestrated immense changes in economic, social and cultural life, as it gained ascendancy over other ways of measuring and coordinating time. If the city clock tower symbolized the victory of secular clock time over the religious order of the day, the wristwatch exemplified the suffusion of clock time into the interstices of daily life. While it is possible, and indeed likely, that the mobile phone signifies changes of a similar scope and magnitude, we need not imagine that the outcomes are already written. The partial breakdown and displacement of traditional forms of social bonding based on spatial proximity and the relative durability of social actors levies a clear and urgent task on the present. Suggesting that '[t]he bonds will have to be reinvented', Virilio (1993: 80) asks: 'Will we rediscover the religious bond, and so re-establish sociability? Are there new, as yet unimaginable bonds?' As a media philosopher, Virilio has put serious questions on the table – or rather the screen – at a moment when relatively few others have been prepared to ask them. As yet, this philosophy remains an outline, long on critique and short on strategy. Finding 'as yet unimaginable' forms of solidarity and empathy for the paradox of life lived in a time defined by light-speed transmission; this, then, is the task Virilio announces for media theory to come.

Notes

1. Ronell examines the politico-ethical framework of television through the lens of the Rodney King incident and the Gulf War.
2. On Benjamin's concept of the 'dialectical image', see Buck-Morss 1991: 218.
3. One could add the strategic design of the short, sharp military campaigns themselves. This lesson, rehearsed by the US in

Granada in 1981 and tellingly exploited by the UK in the Falklands in 1982, peaked with the triumphalism of the '100 hour' Desert Storm campaign in 1991. However, it had seemingly been forgotten in the post-2001 'regime change' ambition for Afghanistan and Iraq.

4. An even more brazen example was the destruction of the al-Jazeera offices by US tank fire in Baghdad in 2003.
5. The logic of information dominance is evident in the ambitious scope of projects such as the Total Information Awareness programme announced in the US following the 2001 attacks (since partially discontinued).
6. This logic underpins the Australian Government's decision in 2009 to construct a national high-speed optical fibre-to-the-premises network costing up to Aus$43 billion of public funds.

References

Anderson, B. (1983) *Imagined Communities: Reflections on the Origins and Spread of Nationalism*. London: Verso.

Baudrillard, J. (1983) *Simulations*, trans. P. Foss et al. New York: Semiotext(e).

Bauman, Z. (2000) *Liquid Modernity*. Cambridge: Polity Press.

Beck, U. (1992) *Risk Society: Towards a New Modernity*. London: Sage.

Buck-Morss, S. (1991) *The Dialectics of Seeing Walter Benjamin and the Arcades Project*. Cambridge, MA and London: MIT Press.

Castells, M. (1996) *The Rise of the Network Society*. Cambridge, MA: Blackwell.

Debord, G. (1983) *Society of the Spectacle*. Detroit: Black & Red.

Gates, B. (1999) *Business @ the Speed of Thought: Using a Digital Nervous System*. Ringwood: Viking.

Innis, H. (1951) *The Bias of Communication*. Toronto: University of Toronto Press.

Kittler, F. (2009) 'Towards an Ontology of Media', *Theory, Culture and Society*, 26, 2–3: 23–31.

Latour, B. (2005) *Reassembling the Social*. Oxford: Oxford University Press.

Levinson, P. (1999) *Digital McLuhan: A Guide to the Information Millennium.* London and New York: Routledge.

Lister, M. et al. (2009) *New Media: A Critical Introduction* (2nd edn). London and New York: Routledge.

McLuhan, M. (1974) *Understanding Media: The Extensions of Man.* London: Abacus.

Meyrowitz, J. (1985) *No Sense of Place: The Impact of Electronic Media on Social Behaviour.* New York and Oxford: Oxford University Press.

——(1994). 'Medium theory', in D. Crowley and D. Mitchell (eds.), *Communication Theory Today.* Stanford, CA: Stanford University Press.

Morley, D. (2009) 'For a Materialist Non-media-centric Media Studies', *Television & New Media*, 10, 1: 114–16.

Ronell, A. (1994) 'Trauma TV: Twelve Steps beyond the Pleasure Principle', in *Finitude's Score: Essays for the End of the Millennium.* Lincoln: University of Nebraska Press.

Virilio, P. (1989) *War and Cinema: The Logistics of Perception*, trans. P. Camiller. London and New York: Verso.

——(1991) *The Lost Dimension*, trans. D. Moshenberg. New York: Semiotext(e).

——(1993) 'Marginal Groups', *Daidalos.* 50: 72-81.

——(1995a) *The Art of the Motor,* trans. J. Rose. Minneapolis: University of Minnesota Press.

——(1995b) 'Speed and Information: Cyberspace Alarm!' *Ctheory* [www.ctheory.net/articles.aspx?id=72].

——(1997) *Open Sky*, trans. J. Rose. London and New York: Verso.

——(2000a) *The Information Bomb*, trans. C. Turner. London and New York: Verso.

——(2000b) *Polar Inertia*, trans. P. Camiller. Thousand Oaks and London: Sage.

——(2000c) *A Landscape of Events*, trans. J. Rose. Cambridge, MA: MIT Press.

——(2001) *Strategy of Deception*, trans. C. Turner. London and New York: Verso.

——(2002a) *Desert Screen: War at the Speed of Light*, trans. M. Degener. London: Continuum.

——(2002b) *Ground Zero*, trans. C. Turner. London and New York: Verso.

——(2007) *The Original Accident*, trans. J. Rose. Cambridge and Malden, MA: Polity.

Virilio, P. and S. Lotringer (2002) *Crepuscular Dawn*, trans. M. Taormina. New York: Semiotext(e).

Virilio, P. and L. Wilson (1994) 'Cyberwar, God And Television: Interview with Paul Virilio', *CTheory*. [www.ctheory.net/articles. aspx?id=62].

Williams, R. (1990) *Television: Technology and Cultural Form*. London: Routledge.

6

Empathetic Vision: Aesthetics of Power and Loss

Elin O'Hara Slavick

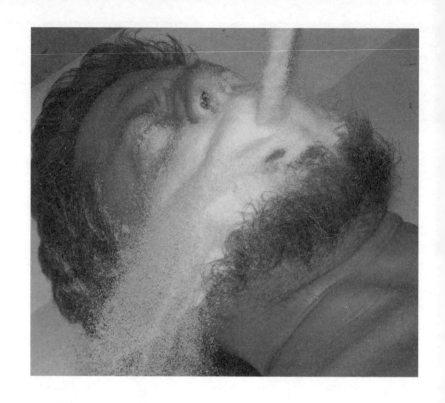

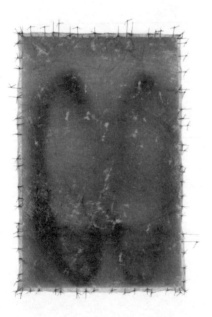 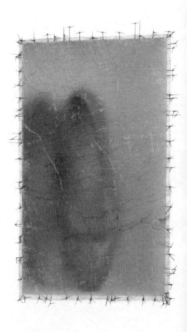

s Response
Iraq Killings

Iraq. A senior Pentagon official said it could be several days before Defense Secretary Donald H. Rumsfeld receives a complete briefing on the matter, and before a redacted version of General Chiarelli's findings are made public.

In addition to General Chiarelli's review, a separate inquiry by the Naval Criminal Investigative Service is examining whether crimes were committed when a squad of marines killed the 24 Iraqi civilians after a roadside bomb killed a member of the Third Platoon of Company K, Third Battalion, First Marine Regiment, in the early morning of Nov. 19.

In April, when the Third Battalion returned to Camp Pendleton, Calif., from Iraq, the battalion and company commanders were relieved of their commands for what their commander said was "a lack of confidence in their leadership."

According to one of the defense officials, General Chiarelli embraced all of General Bargewell's findings and expanded upon some of them. In one instance of a missed opportunity to investigate further, the official said, General Bargewell noted that the comptroller of the Second Marine

War Plan Requests More U.S. Troops and a Job

ranks. But they emphasized that the American influx, which would be focused in Baghdad and Anbar Province but could also include a contingency force in Kuwait, could be re-evaluated at any point.

The American officials who described the plan included some who said they were increasingly concerned about Mr. Maliki's intentions and his ability to deliver. They said senior Bush administration officials had been deeply disturbed by accounts from witnesses to last Saturday's hanging of Saddam Hussein, who said they believed that guards involved in carrying out the execution were linked to the Mahdi Army, the Shiite militia that is headed by Moktada al-Sadr, whose name some of the executioners shouted while Mr. Hussein stood on the gallows.

"If that's an indication of how Maliki is operating these days, we've got a deeper problem with the bigger effort," said one official, who insisted on anonymity because he was discussing internal administration deliberations over a strategy that Mr. Bush has not yet publicly announced.

The White House has refused to talk publicly about any of the decisions that Mr. Bush has made about his plan, which is tentatively titled "A New Way Forward." Even though speechwriters are already drafting Mr. Bush's comments, several of the crucial elements are not final, officials warned. That apparently includes the exact amounts of money Mr. Bush will ask of Congress to fi-

Iraqis inspected the wreckage after a car bomb exploded in Baghdad yesterday. The bomb ently intended to strike an Iraqi police patrol, killed a civilian and wounded three police of

ent Iraq," one in which the passion for fighting for sectarian control of neighborhoods may outweigh interests in obtaining employment.

The new effort, officials said, would cost between a half billion and a billion dollars, some of which would be spent on other efforts to achieve

Internal d
a project t

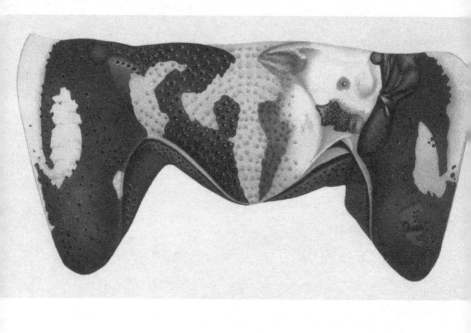

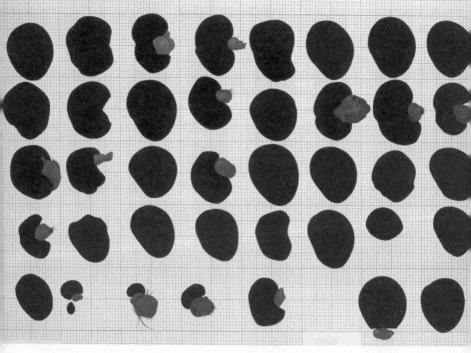

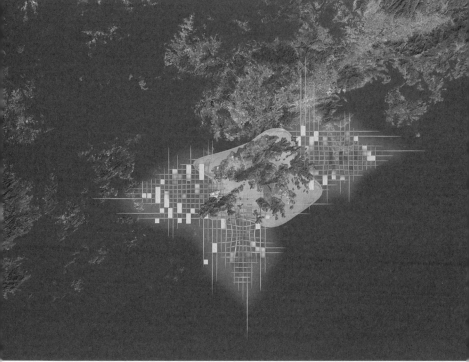

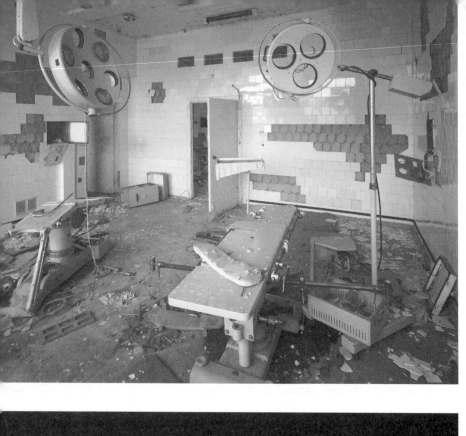

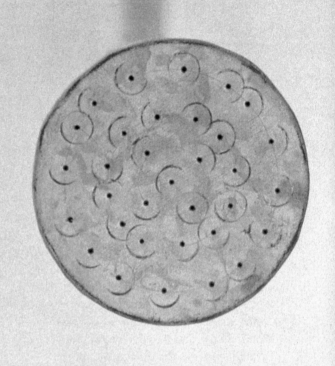

List of plates:

Leah Bailis, *Fence*, 2007, cardboard and paint. Courtesy of the artist.

Alfredo Jaar, *Infinite Cell, (Gramsci Trilogy)*, 2004, iron bars, concrete, mirrors. Courtesy of the artist and Galeria Lia Rumma.

Doris Salcedo, *Shibboleth*, 2007, concrete and metal, Turbine Hall, Tate Modern. Courtesy of Alexander and Bonin, New York.

Nestor Armando Gil, *Azucar*, 2008, still from the performance *Boca: Your Memories Are My Myths*. Courtesy of the artist.

Doris Salcedo, *Atrabiliarios*, 1995, drywall, four shoes, cow bladder and surgical thread, two niches. Photo: Bill Orcutt. Courtesy of Alexander and Bonin, New York.

Miyako Ishiuchi, *Hiroshima: A-Bombed False Teeth*, 2008. Courtesy of the artist and Third Gallery Aya, Osaka.

Andreas Tapia-Urzua, video still from *Loverdosis*, 2000, 15 minutes colour, stereo. Courtesy of the artist.

Alfredo Jaar, *Lament of the Images*, 2002, three illuminated texts, light screen. Courtesy of the artist and Galerie Lelong, New York.

elin o'Hara slavick, *Hiroshima Mask*, 2008, cyanotype of steel fragment from the A-Bomb Dome.

Huong Ngo, *Escape*, 2008, public performance with felt HAZMAT suit (direction: Huong Ngo; photography: Paul O'Reilly; performance: Daniel Martin). Courtesy of the artist.

Sophie Ristelhueber, *WB* (West Bank), 2005, chromogenic print. Courtesy Sophie Ristelhueber / ADAGP, Paris.

Robert Polidori, *Unit 4 Control Room, Chernobyl*, 2001, Fuji Crystal Archive print mounted on aluminum. Courtesy of the artist.

Becca Albee, *War Plan Requests* and *Response Killings*, 2008, archival inkjet prints. Courtesy of the artist.

Lance Winn, *Plane Collision II*, 2002, plastic, paint, light. Courtesy of the artist.

David Tinapple, *Time Slip Waves*, 2008, video still. Courtesy of the artist.

Cornelia Hesse-Honegger, *Pentatomidae, Carpocoris Purpureipennis*, 1999, watercolour and *Eyes of Drosophilia melanogaster, Mutante ey. Opt*, 1987, watercolour. Courtesy of the artist.

Arthur Ou, *Untitled (Test Screen 3)*, 2008, pigment print on silver rag paper. Courtesy of the artist.

Jane D. Marsching and Mitchell Joachim/Terreform 1, *Future North: Ecotarium,* 2008, video projection. Terreform architects: Makoto Okazaki; Maria Aiolova; Melanie Fessel. Courtesy of the artists.

William Kentridge, drawings for the film *Sobriety, Obesity and Growing Old*, 1991. Courtesy of the artist.

Robert Polidori, *Operating Room in Hospital #126, Pripyat*, 2001, Fuji Crystal Archive print mounted on aluminum. Courtesy of the artist.

elin o'Hara slavick, *Hiroshima Autoradiograph*, 2008, silver gelatin contact print of x-ray film exposed by lingering radiation in a fragment of an A-bombed tree.

Hiroshi Sunairi, *Tree Project: Chinaberry Seeds,* 2008 and *Chinaberry Seedling,* 2009, inkjet prints. Courtesy of the artist.

Lisa Ross, *Mauthausen,* 2003, silver gelatin prints. Courtesy of the artist.

The author would like to thank Reuben Ayres for his expert assistance with this project.

Elin O'Hara Slavick

... let's not become *negationists of art*.[1] – Paul Virilio

As Victor Hugo put it: *The rope doesn't hang, the Earth pulls*. In this age of the sudden pollution of the atmosphere, it is about time we revised our perception of appearances. *To raise your eyes to the heavens* could become more than a sign of helplessness or exasperation. A secret perspective is, in fact, hidden *on high*. Reverse vertigo may well force us to change the way we think about the landscape and about the human environment. Our sky is vanishing. Soon we will have to learn to fly, to swim in the ether.[2] – Paul Virilio

There is urgency in Virilio's manifestos, but I am not sure what he is asking of us. He makes me want to put up a fight. Virilio implies that artists, willingly or not, utilize the same corrupt codes and violent means as those who operate oppressive systems of power. I would argue that there are exceptional artists deliberately working against this idea. Virilio writes about many artists, from Beuys and Warhol to ORLAN and Cattelan, and it is hard to tell if he *approves of* them. Susan Sontag asks us: 'What does it mean to protest suffering, as distinct from acknowledging it?' (2003: 40) and one could formulate a similar question regarding Virilio. If an artist illustrates Virilio's dark theories, is she complicit in that darkness? Can we disengage ourselves from the vice grip of power(lessness) that technology, speed, warfare, circuits of wealth and the maze of the market have on our imagination, vision and action? Howard Zinn writes: 'Here in the US, the public, as was true of me [while a Second World War bombardier], does not understand – I mean really understand – what bombs do to people. That failure of imagination, I believe, is critical to explaining why we still have wars, why we accept bombing as a common accompaniment to our foreign policies, without horror or disgust' (Zinn 2007: 9). This failure of the imagination should not be surprising if we study Virilio. Virilio's books are full of fear, cold panic, turbo-capitalism, terrorism, accidents and disasters. He does not celebrate these things, but his language seems to revel in this cyborgian predicament of our furious world.

Perhaps we are responding to what Virilio has identified as the intensifying speed of warfare over the twentieth century.

If bombing, like other war technologies, is a primary engine of history and if 'history progresses at the speed of its weapons systems' (Virilio 1986: 68), how can art respond to this problem? While I feel defeated by this idea, I think it's true. However, I am more interested in Virilio's idea that our real enemy is more internal than external. We are racing against ourselves, bombing ourselves. I am more afraid of my own government than I am of 'terrorists'. (How does one tell the difference between a terrorist and a soldier?) John Armitage writes in the introduction to Virilio's *Art and Fear*: 'When Virilio considers the aesthetics of disappearance, he assumes that the responsibility of artists is to recover rather than discard the material that is absent and bring to light those secret codes that hide from view inside the silent circuits of digital and genetic technologies' (Armitage 2003: 9). Indeed, Virilio's *Art and Fear* is a chilling book for an artist to read. Like W.G. Sebald in *On the Natural History of Destruction (2003),* Virilio makes me feel as if there is no manner in which to properly, effectively or truthfully represent or respond to the horrors of war, genocide and the holocaust. Yet, they both attempt to do just that and they do it very well.

While some artists – mostly those working with electronic media – attempt to keep up with the intensifying speed of everything around us – warfare, information and communication systems – many artists are responding by trying to slow down, not only themselves but also viewers. I too want to slow people down and offer a different approach to seeing and thinking about war.

In Alfredo Jaar's *Infinite Cell (Gramsci Trilogy)*, the empty, waiting-to-be-filled prison cell goes on forever, endlessly reflected in a mirror. Leah Bailis painstakingly constructs a chain link rectangular cell out of cardboard and paint. Anyone, even a dog, could break free. These are clinical illusions symbolizing Guantanamo Bay, Abu Ghraib, our overcrowded prisons and the corrupt and unjust penal system, our relationship to other human beings.

Colombian Doris Salcedo is another artist who works slowly and who slows us down as viewers. She sews hair into heavy wooden tables and buries shoes belonging to 'the Disappeared' in walls. It is as if she is making work from the grave. In Salcedo's *Shibboleth*, a crack is cut into and across the gigantic floor of the Turbine Hall at the Tate Modern in London. Deep within the crevice, a chain link fence is embedded in the cement. Touching upon the impossible danger of illegally crossing borders and the discrimination and violence that occurs even with a legal migration, Salcedo sets us on edge. Nestor Gil has processed white sugar poured into his aching Cuban-American mouth until it overflows. Both artists render silence as tortured orifices. As Virilio says, 'No one is waiting any more for the REVOLUTION, only for the ACCIDENT, the breakdown, that will reduce this unbearable chatter to silence' (2003: 75). While Salcedo disorients us, Gil gags us.

Ishiuchi Miyako photographs A-Bombed artefacts that were once in direct contact with the victim's bodies – clothing, slippers and false teeth – from the Hiroshima Peace Memorial Museum. Miyako writes in her statement *For Things That Remain Forever,* 'It is difficult for human beings to survive for even one hundred years, but these objects have been bestowed with a longer existence. As parts of the longest scar the world has known, they will outlive us all, and never grow old' (2008: 76).

Andres Tapia-Urzua places a blindfolded man behind a steering wheel in *Loverdosis*, a video about love and mind/body relationships in the context of technology and telecommunications; about alienated existences within a techno-scientific world. This blind driver is *the man* in all of Virilio's books – the pilot and inventor, the soldier and artist, the scientist and computer analyst. Jaar's *Lament of the Images* illuminates the impotence and power of images. This project came out of his experiences in Rwanda in 1994, where he went to record the testimonies of the survivors of a genocide that claimed the lives of one million. Jaar chooses to erase the image in response to the constant overload of images that often does not represent these one million victims. We are left standing there *in the light,* frustrated and disillusioned, not blindfolded but blind. To lament is to mourn.

My *Hiroshima Mask* stares at you with a deadly emptiness. I placed a fragment of a steel beam from the A-Bomb Dome in Hiroshima on cyanotype paper and exposed it to the sun for ten minutes. I had Virilio in mind as I worked on this project, *Hiroshima: After Aftermath3* and I continue to struggle with the question: *ethics or aesthetics?* Armitage writes: 'Virilio places his hope in the 'accident of the visible' and the annihilation of the audio-visual by a politics of silence. . . .Virilio thus looks to reclaim a poignant or pitiful art and the politics of silence from an art world enchanted by its own extinction because to refuse pity is to accept the continuation of war' (Armitage 2003: 16, 24). I was shocked as I watched this mask appear in the bathtub of water as I rinsed the cyanotype into being. This is an accident of the visible rendered from a previously exposed object that survived the A–Bomb as 70,000 human beings were instantaneously annihilated (and another 70,000 would die by the end of the year as a result of the A–Bomb).

Huong Ngo places her lover in a handmade felt HAZMAT suit and *performs* this man across busy New York City intersections, in front of industrial sites, standing on a crowded commuter train. Passersby must be confused. 'Is there a contaminant that I am being exposed to?' (There are always contaminants that we are being exposed to.) 'Who is this man?' (He is all of us.) She is ready for the accident, for the future, for now. 'In the beginning, the term "empathy" had the primary sense of "touching" and referred to physical contact with tangible objects. With Edmund Husserl, it would come to denote the effort to perceive and seize the reality that surrounds us in all its phenomena, in all the forms in which that reality manifests itself. . . . A survivor of the 1943 bombing of Hamburg acknowledges its effects: "It was my initiation into the knowledge that looking means suffering; so after that, I could no more stand looking than being looked at"' (Virilio 2002).

Sophie Ristelhueber photographs ruined roads in Palestine. Her book *WB* contains over fifty colour images of these bulldozed, blockaded, dug up, blasted, or otherwise rendered dysfunctional roads in the West Bank. She says, 'I crisscrossed the West Bank – 300 kilometers from north to south, 50 kilometers from east to west. I thought about the historical marking of the region. It would have been easy to photograph the wall that separates the two camps, but I find the subject simplistic. These interventions in the landscape are much stronger and suffocating than the wall itself. I saw the land wounded like a body. And at the same time, this rubble was created three or four years ago, the grass is growing back, archaeology is being formed. These rock barriers imply that the landscape is turning against itself.'[4]

Robert Polidori's photograph of the *Unit 4 Control Room,*

Chernobyl, reveals the brutal cement and plywood facade at the core of such a dangerous facility. Polidori writes: 'As time passes, our memory of the Chernobyl catastrophe begins to fade. Our initial shock and fear are pushed aside by new world events and private dreams that populate the attention of each of our lives. The radioactive half-lives of elements, however, are not subject to this form of accelerated, subjective amnesia' (Polidori 2002: 111). The catalogue for the show that Virilio curated at the Fondation Cartier pour l'art contemporain, *Unknown Quantity*, is a book full of images of accidents, disasters, crashes, aftermath, wrecks, fire and artists' representations of such things. It is as if Virilio cannot help himself from imaging the things he despises and resents. It is also a book filled with brilliant writing, including an interview between Svetlana Aleksievich and Paul Virilio for Andrei Ujica's film *Unknown Quantity*. In it, Aleksievich talks about Chernobyl: 'The first sensation there, in the disaster zone, is that our biological machinery is not adapted to this. Human dimensions in general aren't adapted to it, because up to that point time was measured with our human dimensions. Perhaps this had already changed with the atomic bomb, and yet it was after Chernobyl that time took on a radically new dimension. Time transformed itself into eternity. The end and the beginning were joined. It seems to me that if we had understood Chernobyl, we would have written more about it. We are paralyzed by the knowledge of our ignorance' (Virilio 2002: 200, 202). What I most remember from this book of images, *Unknown Quantity*, are these *words* from his introduction, 'to invent the sailing vessel or the steam ship is to *invent the shipwreck*' (2002: 24, original emphasis). Becca Albee replaces war imagery from the *New York Times* with pretty pictures of flowers that were taken by her grandfather and community newspaper journalist, Ellis Albert Resch (1903–74), in the late 1960s and early 1970s. Below the headline *War Plan Requests More US Troops,* several white blooms float open-mouthed instead of the captioned image of 'Iraqis inspected the wreckage after a car bomb exploded in Baghdad yesterday'. Our expectations are thwarted and relieved. Albee's response to the fragmented headline *Response Iraq Killings* is to insert a snapshot of a cluster of blossoms, rather than bombs. Lance Winn responds to the incessant headlines of terrorism and war more literally with his *Plane Collision II*. Utilizing plastic, paint and light, Winn turns a toy plane into an explosive device, albeit one that most little boys would love to have as a nightlight.

David Tinapple's otherworldly landscape was made 'using a video camera and processing the footage to find time patterns. The result of processing the video is another video. What happens when you transpose dimensions in an image – dimensions being up, down, left, right, and back and forth. I've taken another dimension, time, and transposed it with the left-right dimension. Time and speed become inherently visible elements of the image. The techniques used to analyze this image are similar to those used for surveillance, the software the same as is used for simulations. We all have developed new logistics of perception in order to make sense of the logic of speed.'[5]

Cornelia Hesse-Honegger was trained as a scientific illustrator. Since 1969 she has collected and painted leaf bugs, Heteroptera. Since the catastrophe of Chernobyl in 1986, she has collected, studied and painted morphologically disturbed insects, which she finds in the fallout areas of Chernobyl, as well as near nuclear installations all over the world. She demonstrates – by way of a microscope and tiny paint brushes – that where the radioactive fallout from Chernobyl, or from normally working nuclear power plants, hits the ground, vegetation is contaminated and some insects become morphologically deformed. In *Pentatomidae, Carpocoris Purpureipennis*, a tree bug near La Hague reprocessing plant in France one may notice thorax deformation and in *Eyes of the Drosophila Mutant ey.opt.* parts of wings can be seen sprouting from some of the black orbs.

Arthur Ou's *Untitled (Test Screen 3)* is an indescribable explosion, a chemical disturbance, a stilled rupture, a frozen contamination. Jane Marsching and Mitchell Joachim's human-less futuristic animation is 'a simultaneously and unsettlingly dystopian and utopian view of a future in which our technological advances can preserve and forget at the same time. The *Future North Ecotarium* project imagines our future after irreversible climate change. Massive migrations of urban populations will move north to escape severe flooding and increasing temperatures. In this animation, entire cities float away from their flooded moorings and meet in a new North, reimagining the entire surface of our planet.'[6] In both Marsching and Tinapple's work, I see Virilio's *horizon of expectation*, 'What we are seeing here is the recent emergence of the *sense of the End of the world* – in no sense an apocalyptic or millenarian End, synonymous with an End of History, but, more simple, *an end of Geography*, as though the all-too-famous consumer society has ended up consuming planetary space-time, a role in which it has been duly replaced by the recently developed communication-based society' (Virilio 2002: 109, original emphasis).

William Kentridge's drawings for his film *Sobriety, Obesity and Growing Old* show a modernist building collapsing, dropping under its own weight, unable to sustain itself. Andrew Hennlich writes about this imagery: 'What is significant about this imagery is that it comes to represent inside *and* outside. Soho is destroying the building because he is consumed with sorrow over his wife taking a lover. Subsequently, he destroys the markers of his empire, the large rising buildings, one by one. As these buildings mark his power and tower over the views of Johannesburg we see in Kentridge's films, the crumbling of them symbolizes internal loss suffered. Soho's relationships at the time of political transition, though overwhelmed with grief, are not concerned with political transition. They are internal images. These hyper visible images mark a long series of inward turning shifts for Soho through the narrative of the entire project, and are at the end destroyed because of his sorrow.'[7]

Robert Polidori's *Operating room in Hospital #126, Pripyat* is another image of destruction: the end of things as we know (knew) them; disabled equipment and apocalyptic spaces as a result of Chernobyl. My *Hiroshima Autoradiograph* is a contact print of a sheet of x-ray film that captured, in 2008, lingering radiation in a fragment of a tree exposed to the A-Bomb in 1945, forty years before Chernobyl. In terms of radiation, there is little difference; both 'accidents' are permanent. Hiroshi Sunairi's generous art, *Leur Existence (Tree Project)*, recognizes this permanence. The trees that still live from the time of the atomic bombing in Hiroshima are called Hibaku trees. Sunairi collects seeds from these trees – seeds from Round Leaf Holly, Persimmon, Chinaberry, Firmiana simplex, Japanese Hackberry and Jujube trees that are the second or third generation of Hibaku Trees. He gives these seeds to people all over the world to plant.

Lisa Ross' photographs of showerheads at the Mauthausen concentration camp in Austria are bone dry. They arrest us. Ross writes: 'Each showerhead was different. In one, the holes are so small it is clear that water was never intended to come out. An anthropologist may see the showerheads as evidence of the prisoners' individuality. Prisoners built the camp. They may have made the showerheads. The gas Cyclon-B never came out of the showerheads. Water came out only after the corpses were removed to wet down the floor for mopping. Cyclon-B came in through a small hole in the wall, stored in a long metal tube that released the gas upon heating it. It took at least twenty minutes for prisoners to die from the gas and an hour before the doors were opened and the room considered gas free. It was called *disinfection*.'[8] One is struck by the simple force and beauty of Ross' artifacts. She overcomes the dilemma.

I do not intend for the art in this chapter to illustrate or argue against Virilio. I offer these images by artists as examples of empathy in a wrecked world of deliberate cruelty. How do we imagine that and how do we image it? I have chosen artists who address the past (history, memory, loss), the present (war, power, speed) and the future (possibility). Without knowledge of history, the memory of lives before us, or an acknowledgement of the past, we are doomed. Speed erases the pause, the chance to remember, to consider and reconsider, to think and be, to continue and to survive. Empathy, a prolonged gaze, a slow critical approach, an emotional archive, an attempt to see and represent ethically, a sincere gesture towards historical truth, an effort to do no harm – all of these exercises are movements of infinite possibility.

Notes

1. Virilio 2003: 39, original emphasis.
2. Virilio 1997: 2–3, original emphasis.

3. For more on this see elin o'Hara slavick in *The Asia-Pacific Journal: Japan Focus* [www.japanfocus.org/~elin_o_Hara-slavick/3196].
4. Sophie Ristelhueber (2009) in an email to the author.
5. David Tinapple (2009) in an email to the author.
6. Jane Marsching (2009) in an email to the author.
7. Andrew Hennlich (2009) in an email to the author. Original emphasis.
8. Lisa Ross (2003), *Mauthausen* artist statement. Original emphasis.

References

Armitage, John (2003) 'Art and Fear: An Introduction', pp. 1–24, in Paul Virilio, *Art and Fear*, London and New York: Continuum.

Polidori, Robert (2003) *Zones of Exclusion: Pripyat and Chernobyl*. Gottingen: Steidl.

Sebald, W.G. (2003) *On the Natural History of Destruction*. New York: Random House.

Sontag, Susan (2003) *Regarding the Pain of Others*. New York: Picador.

Virilio, Paul (1986) *Speed and Politics*. New York: Semiotext(e).

— (1997) *Open Sky*. London and New York: Verso.

— (2002) *Unknown Quantity*. London: Thames and Hudson.

— (2003) *Art and Fear*. London and New York: Continuum.

Zinn, Howard (2007) foreword in Elin O'Hara Slavick, *Bomb After Bomb: A Violent Cartography*. Milan: Charta.

7

Panicsville: Paul Virilio and the Aesthetic of Disaster

Nigel Thrift

We're here to go. That's what we're here for. We're here to go . . .
(Burroughs 1990)

Remorse, predictably, was the form taken by her distress, the merciless
whipping that is self-condemnation, as if in times as bizarre as these
there were a right way and a wrong way that would have been clear
to somebody else, as if in confronting such predicaments the hand of
stupidity is ever far from guiding anyone. (Roth 2004: 340)

'Just talk, talk, talk with you in'it. Yeah, you got the home, the education, the fucking past what weren't full of abuse . . . and now you want
me all tied up in explanations. That's what people like you wan't in'it
. . . But you can't. I haven't had it that simple. Why should you get to
put reasons on it when I've fucking lived it, and still can't.' (Masters
2005: 38)

Introduction

I have what I think is a pretty good test of whether a person is a
social scientist or not: do they eavesdrop on a fairly regular basis on

other people's conversations on trains and planes, on buses, in the street and so on? If they don't, I suspect that they really want to be a philosopher or an architect – or both. The difference is crucial for me. One kind of work (mainly) involves trying to figure out what other people are thinking as they are doing. The other (mainly) involves thinking. They are not the same.

Paul Virilio is probably best described as a philosopher architect who has some things to say about city and society. If he eavesdropped on conversations, I think it unlikely that he would write the way he does. Make no mistake, this is not to say that Virilio doesn't come up with interesting thoughts but for evidence he mainly seems to use other books and newspaper articles. In his writings at least, he is not up against people but against the idea of people. This wouldn't matter so much – he is hardly the first philosopher to offer synoptic readings of Western society on the basis of not too much in the way of evidence, after all – but Virilio keeps wanting to speak in the name of a putative humanity, and he seems pretty sure that he knows what that humanity is. I, on the other hand, am not so sure. As Burroughs put it, I think 'we're here to go' in the sense that I am not sure what the nature of human or thinking is or might be meant to be: our technologically enhanced ways of life are already barely tethered to an ancestral realm but I am not at all sure that that is necessarily a concern. After all,

> human thought and reason emerges from a nest in which biological brains and bodies, acting in concert with nonbiological props and tools, build, benefit from and then rebuild an endless succession of designer environments. In each such setting, our brains and bodies couple to new tools, yielding new extended thinking systems. (Clark 2003: 197)

Now there are some awful, awful things going on in the world as a result of the evolution of some of these technologically enhanced environments, to be sure. Only a lunatic would want to deny that. And it may be that whatever humanity is will eventually do itself in through one means or another. The list of candidates is a long one: precipitate global warming, a generalized ecological crisis, a gene-spliced pandemic, a runaway particle experiment, self-assembling nano-machines running amok and so on. And that's before we get on to warfare – or asteroids. In other words, Virilio's jeremiads about the future in the present, of which *City of Panic* is just the latest in a long line, have found their time. They have become part of a prevailing post-September 11th social mood of doom-saying (Geertz 2005). Indeed, on some counts, they are not extreme enough (Diamond 2004; Posner 2004; Rees 2004). Virilio is being outflanked.

But Virilio's relentless negativism about the future in the present does not seem to me to constitute an answer. Indeed, one might argue that it is likely to lead to despair, surely the ultimate political sin. Certainly, his brand of doom-saying seems to me to be profoundly out of kilter with prevalent tendencies on the left that are moving toward putting far more emphasis on constructing a politics of hope than before, both as the emotional ingredient that the left should be offering above all, and as a way of occupying a future that is too often reserved for the retrograde forces that have brought us to this pass.

Panic urbanism

I am sure that it is already clear that I find Virilio's work frustrating. Nowhere is this more the case than when it comes to his work on the city, for Virilio describes himself as an urbanist and he has the credentials to prove it: he has been a professor of architecture, after all. But, in his work on cities, we find both the best and worst of Virilio, as *City of Panic* shows all too well. True, there are some genuine insights but they are wrapped up in a hyperbolic apparatus that sometimes makes it very difficult to locate them and is unlikely to win many over who do not already subscribe to Virilio's vision of an all-but-terminal modernity.

So what is Virilio's vision of the city? The first thing that comes to mind is its resolute modernism. Virilio's city is a city of the swoosh of speed through a landscape of verticals and horizontals, of towers writing on (or indeed taking off into) the sky and of the featureless planes of endless suburbs, stirred by cataclysm and catastrophe, a landscape of perpetual accident. Sometimes it seems to me a bit like the view from *The Daily Planet* of a Metropolis-like comic-strip city: all it needs is some superheroes to finish the picture off. Then, Virilio's city is a phenomenology of despair: inhabited by populations that are drugged by emotion, can no longer see reality, are led astray by speed and information, have become mere pawns in the logistics of perception. They sit and watch the world go by. But, finally, Virilio's city has nowhere left to go. It's reached the edge of urban evolution. The city is now collapsing in on itself; its population is becoming incarcerated in an infosphere from which there is no escape.

Well, it's certainly a way of looking at things, and one with a long and honourable pedigree: let's face it, it's not often that you read social theorists who want to present garlands to the world. But I don't think it even vaguely holds up to serious scrutiny as an account of how the modern world is. If Virilio ever read much in the way of serious social science research, which is, after all, flooding in from all quarters of the globe, he would surely have to backtrack. Almost everything he says about the modern city would have to be seriously qualified or reconstructed or just plain retracted. Take information technology to begin with. Here detailed studies show that Virilio's idea that we are moving into a machinic age needs qualification, to put it but mildly. Thus, prompted by the growth of sociology of science, actor-network theory, material culture studies, and so on, there has been a systematic rethinking of what human might mean as a tool-using entity. The general conclusion is well summarized by Clark (2003: 198):

> Some fear . . . a loathsome 'post-human' future. They predict a kind of technologically incubated mind-rot, leading to loss of identity, loss of control, overload, dependence, invasion of privacy, isolation, and the ultimate rejection of the body. And we *do* need to be cautious, for to recognise the deeply transformative nature of our biotechnological unions is at once to see that not all such unions will be for the better. But if I am right – if it is our basic *human* nature to annex, exploit, and incorporate nonbiological stuff deep into our mental profiles – then the question is not whether we go that route, but in what ways we actively sculpt and shape it. By seeing ourselves as we truly are, we

increase the chances that our future biotechnological unions will be good ones.

Thus, there is a veritable legion of careful empirical studies of information technology that very often show the polar opposite of what Virilio would have us believe. Instead of taking on the cyberbole of firms and marketing agencies, researchers have gone out and looked at what people do with information technology and what information technology does with them and, surprise, surprise, there is a divergence. Just as one example, a common rule in this literature is 'the more virtual the more real' (Woolgar 2002), that is, the introduction of new 'virtual' technologies can actually stimulate more of the corresponding 'real' activity. Then, take speed. I have shown in numerous papers, as have many commentators now, that any serious historical analysis of the impact of increasing speed on society demonstrates that its impact is much more variegated than Virilio credits, and does not add up to any particular tendency (such as that sad old chestnut, the 'time-space compression' story). I, like many other commentators, have demonstrated this over and over again, pretty well to distraction – and largely to no avail, it has to be said. The idea that increasing speed somehow has causality is an urban myth so deeply engrained in Western individuals' idea of themselves and how they are that it is probably not dislodgeable – but that doesn't mean that philosophers have to power it up.

Then, last of all, take the impact of emotion on democratic politics. No one can deny that there are serious problems with the emotional content and thrust of current politics, which have been nurtured by concerted media campaigns, and most especially the construction of a state of fear (Altheide 2002; Bourke 2005; Robin 2005). But it is important to be careful. Emotion has always figured in politics and it is a crucial part of political thinking: it cannot be caricatured as likely to diminish a full consideration of an intended action or as likely to provoke action without thought (Marcus 2002). So there is nothing necessarily wrong in its appearance in the media: indeed, from the earliest days of print political media, emotion has been a routine means by which the press has plied its trade. More to the point it could and in fact has been argued that emotion is a vital part of political citizenship and communication, not some awful canker. Indeed, it is possible to argue that an able citizen is likely to be an emotional citizen. Though it is, in fact, a problematic distinction, we can argue with both Hume and Smith that whilst reason can give birth to understanding, passion gives rise to action. 'Democratic politics cannot be solely a space of calm deliberation. It must also be a sensational space, one that attracts and engages spectators. Only by doing so can it create the conditions for new possibilities' (ibid.: 148).

Most frustratingly, each one of these three areas is currently the object of attention of the liveliest of left politics. Thus, real thought is going into taking modern materialities seriously, thought that has led to a burgeoning literature that questions what we might mean by terms like 'material', 'life' and 'thought' (cf. Fraser, Kember and Lury 2005; Miller 2005), and which is already influencing the politics of a whole series of domains, from environmental activism to animal rights. Then, considerable thought is also being given to the fragmentary nature of globalization and how it consists of a whole series of speeds that in turn lead to quite different notions of political networks (cf. Ong and Collier 2004; Thrift 2005b; Tsing 2005). And, finally, as I have already mentioned, the politics of affect have become an important element of forward-thinking left politics: it is not acceptable to cede the realm of emotion, itself a powerful form of thinking, to the right (Thrift 2004; Wilson 2004; Probyn 2005).

So, why if so much of Virilio often seems misguided does he have such a following? I think there is an ironic reason for this: Virilio's books are themselves a part of the set up of the media age he so often decries, for they increasingly read to me as nothing so much as newspaper columns, philosophically inclined newspaper columns to be sure, but newspaper columns all the same. We increasingly live in the age of the column and the op-ed piece, and Virilio's books often read as extended versions of that particular genre. Indeed, I think *City of Panic* functions better and is much more understandable if thought of as a collected series of columns, rather than as a book.

Columnists have great advantages for editors: they cost less than running long investigations or a string of overseas correspondents

(Marr 2004); they fill all the space around the advertising; they save the editor from having to think what else might be there. They have similar advantages for columnists: 'many columnists do not have to go out and interview people, or check facts, or do anything much beyond spinning out an idle thought or a pet prejudice, and pressing the "send" key, followed by a monthly invoice' (Marr 2004: 367). Unfair? Of course. But remember two things: first, there are some great columns and columnists. Second, columns often act best when they function as momentary warnings that make us stop and think through the emotive power of their language and their consequent ability to convey the kernel of an argument. In other words, seen as a set of columns, *City of Panic* has a life that it is otherwise missing.

Cities

The really frustrating thing, of course, is that Virilio *has* had some interesting things to say about cities. His work on a phenomenology of movement is important and might be thought to be among the precursors of all the work in this vein now taking place on cities (cf. Amin and Thrift 2002). His work on the city as, in part at least, a product of war, similarly can be considered a worthy ancestor of all the important work on cities and war that is now arising (Graham 2004). His work on modern forms of perception again seems to me to have been one of the key precursors of a good deal of telling work, especially on forms of technological perception, and his notion of a logistics of images is surely a fertile one. But each time he goes round the park, he exaggerates and this exaggeration is not just of the 'well, this is an illustration of a general trend and should not be expected to play out equally everywhere', or of the 'well, take this as a warning of how things could become', or of the 'well, it won't come to pass exactly like this but near to it' variety. It is systematic. And such systematic exaggeration is of more than mild concern. First, it shows a fundamental misunderstanding of how cities and societies work, which is as generators of difference as much as of similarity. Modern cities throw all kinds of lives into contrast in variegated ways and demand a cultural literacy that is a source of hope as well as friction, a means of learning how to live plurality and conviviality (Gilroy 2004). Second, it consigns the political to 'resistance' against machines or whatever other looming presence is to be held responsible for the woes of the world when there always is a lot that can be done. The forces lined up against the left are certainly not inconsequential but nor are they insuperable (Amin and Thrift 2005). One of the things that is needed to fill the left's political arsenal is a sense of hope. One of my worries about Virilio is that his work can be read as if no hope exists. Third, it ignores specificity except as an illustration of something more general. But specificity is now regarded as crucial by many theorists, not just as an ethnographic undertow to urban life but as something that has value in its own right, a point to which I will return.

Worst of all, Virilio's work on cities, at least on the evidence of this book, has stopped progressing. Yet his work could still be a veritable inspiration if more was made out of some of the issues that it raises. Let me take just two examples.

The first is Virilio's modernist sense of urban space. Modernism has been around for so long that it has now become a folk model of how cities are, one which continually bubbles up in new ways in the culture. It therefore needs working with and developing, rather than dismissing (cf. Barley 2001). As just one example, Virilio's work on the city from the air could have been developed much more fully in ways that would have been wonderful in showing some of the paradoxes of the logistics of aerial images, to whose power we have in large part become inured. For example, Vanderbilt (2005) shows just what a wonderful boost to imagination being able to see cities from the air was and just how banal that imagination now is as aerial images have become routinely available in books (see, for example, Getmapping 2004) and on the Internet. These images need recuperating: their wonder needs bringing out again (see Dicum 2004). So do their emancipatory as well as carceral possibilities. Thus, in the middle of a security-obsessed United States, Vanderbilt is able to show the degree to which aerial remote sensing is a double-edged sword; he and a colleague pinpoint a probable new government bunker in Washington, DC, just by using images from the Internet: 'things the Soviets would have paid dearly for are a mouse click away' (Vanderbilt 2005: 35).

The second example is catastrophe itself. It has become increasingly clear that cities are actually extraordinarily resilient: they routinely bounce back from accident and disaster (Thrift 2005a). They are not the playthings of forces beyond their control but can have active agency through the institutional performances that they are able to mobilize, the mundane loops of maintenance and repair, and the reactions of networks of citizens, though these all have interesting and instructive cultural variations (Vale and Campanella 2005). Even the new information technology – which might be thought of as in a distributed state of siege from viruses and the like – turns out to be surprisingly robust. The lesson can be generalized to most urban networks, which might be thought to be more vulnerable because so many of them rely on each other: after September 11th, for example, most critical networks in New York had enough redundancy built into them to be able to recover quickly and with a minimum of fuss (Mitchell and Townsend 2005).

The overall point I want to make is that modern cities may not be in a twilight zone at all. They may be rather more efficacious than Virilio seems to consider, including under the most stressful conditions imaginable. They foster new imaginations and powers that cannot all be counted as bad. I want to take up this point again in conclusion.

Conclusions

By coincidence, at about the same time that I was reading *City of Panic*, I was also reading Philip Roth's *The Plot Against America*, a novel that is the equal of Virilio: equally speculative, equally urban, equally concerned with war and terror, equally vexed by the impact of emotion on democracy. But here is an author who eavesdrops, who listens to what people are saying – their gait and gesture as well as their speech – and who never sees cities as formless agglomerations. This is, in part, to be sure, because the fact of

Jewishness so obviously dictates geography in the book, from the fastness of Newark, to the Jewish families cast out into the desert of rural middle America, to the sense of danger that comes from straying outside a particular familiar urban space. But it is Roth who also understands that lights that go out can come on again because of simple decency, which though it may be washed by a certain nostalgia, also understands damaged lives and why they are sometimes redeemed – through sheer cussedness, through nego-tiating misunderstandings, through raw emotion – in ways which are irreducibly complex and cannot be read off from some grand analysis. So, for example, the Italian family that comes to stay in the apartment below (forced on the protagonist's family as a part of a 'racial integration' policy) includes an old grandmother who hates Jews – and a father who defends them, with a gun if needs be. And the cast of Jews includes the resister turned layabout, the sincere collaborator, the seeker after celebrity, the enthusiast, the tougher-than-tough businessman, the flawed but ultimately big-hearted demagogue, the gangster, the timorous and the scared, and the downright stubborn, all of them claiming the right to be American.

In other words, it is just not possible to read specificity off from theoretical positions: specificity speaks for itself and it speaks in many and varied ways that do not add back up to those positions but have their own power. I am reminded of the famous piece of badinage between Mark Tapley and Martin Chuzzlewit about how to paint an American Eagle (peculiarly relevant in these times, it has to be said): 'I should want to draw it like a Bat for its short-sightedness; like a Bantam, for its bragging; like a Magpie, for its honesty; like a Peacock, for its vanity; like a Ostrich, for its putting its head in the mud, and thinking nobody sees it . . . And like a Phoenix for its power of springing up from the ashes of its faults and vices and soaring up anew into the sky!' (Dickens 1951: 638).

Roth's book seems to me to signal a more general task too; that is, to bring writers like Virilio back to everyday life in all its every-dayness. I am always struck by how little Virilio ultimately has to say about that – a few reminiscences aside – and yet it seems to me to point to a pressing task: how to connect social theory, with its often imperious gaze, back to the lives of people in all their messi-ness. The other book I have been reading in parallel with *City of*

Panic and *The Plot Against America* has been Alexander Masters' *Stuart*, the story of one homeless man whose chaotic life and personality is almost impossible to capture in print – though Masters has a pretty good try. Stuart was a particular challenge to write about, precisely because his life lacked any conventional structure, seemed to fall down the cracks.

Now, I do not think that philosophy or synoptic social theory has to transform suddenly into a vast social tract or some kind of ethnography – as if it could. But the gap is currently so wide between the cogitations of most philosophers and everyday life, especially the everyday life of societies which, in Wacquant's (1996) telling phrase, suffer from 'advanced marginality' and which routinely trigger all kinds of much more directly carceral mechanisms than the flow of images – from ghettos to welfare retrenchment to prisons (Wacquant 2000) – that I do end up wondering if it is possible to find some means of proceeding that might be able to capture the presence of all the people who fall out of theoretical diagnostics (as Bourdieu (1999) might be thought to have attempted in *The Weight of the World*). I say this in part because it is well known that Virilio works with homeless people and yet I am struck by how little theirs and many marginal others' imprint seems to be felt in a book that is, after all, on the modern city. This is not, I should hasten to add, a plea for philosophical thinkers to get socially relevant or to theorize everyday life – there's plenty of that going on already. Rather, it is for them to bring people like Stuart into their thoughts as more than examples. One might argue that, in part at least, the future relies on being able to forge a new rapprochement between theory and practice, one that will not only produce all kinds of chaotic pleasures but might also be productive of genuine political advance, even if the times are as dark as Virilio paints them.

References

Altheide, D.L. (2002) *Creating Fear: News and the Construction of Crisis.* Chicago: Aldine.

Amin, A. and Thrift, N.J. (2002) *Cities: Rethinking Urban Theory*. Cambridge: Polity Press.

Amin, A. and Thrift, N.J. (2005) 'What's Left? The Future', *Antipode* (forthcoming).

Barley, N. (ed.) (2001) *City Levels*. London: August/Birkhauser Verlag.

Bourdieu, P. (1999) *The Weight of the World: Social Suffering in Contemporary Society*. Cambridge: Polity Press.

Bourke, J. (2005) *Fear: A Cultural History*. London: Virago.

Burroughs, W. (1990) *Dead City Radio*. Compact disc, Island Records.

Cavell, R. (2002) *McLuhan in Space: A Cultural Geography*. Toronto: University of Toronto Press.

Clark, A. (2003) *Natural-Born Cyborgs: Mind, Technologies, and the Future of Human Intelligence*. Oxford: Oxford University Press.

Diamond, J. (2004) *Collapse: How Societies Choose to Fall or Succeed*. New York: Viking.

Dickens, C. (1951) *Life and Adventures of Martin Chuzzlewit*. Oxford: Oxford University Press.

Dicum, G. (2004) *Window Seat: Reading the Landscape from the Air*. New York: Chronicle.

Fraser, M., S. Kember, and C. Lury (eds.) (2005) 'Special Issue on Inventive Life: Approaches to the New Vitalism', *Theory, Culture and Society* 22, 1.

Geertz, C. (2005) 'Very bad news', *New York Review of Books*, 24 March: 4–6.

Getmapping (2004) *New York: The Photo Atlas*. New York: Harper Collins.

Gilroy, P. 2004) *After Empire: Melancholia or Convivial Culture?* London: Routledge.

Graham, S. (ed.) (2004) *Cities, War and Terrorism: Towards an Urban Geopolitics*. Oxford: Blackwell.

Huyssen, A. (2003) *Present Pasts: Urban Palimpsests and the Politics of Memory*. Stanford: Stanford University Press.

Marcus, G. (2002) *The Sentimental Citizen: Emotion in Democratic Politics*. University Park: Pennsylvania State University Press.

Marr, A. (2004) *My Trade: A Short History of British Journalism*. London: Macmillan.

Masters, A. (2005) *Stuart: A Life Backwards*. London: Fourth Estate.

Miller, D. (ed.) (2005) *Materiality*. Durham, NC: Duke University Press.

Mitchell, W.J. and A.Townsend (2005) 'Cyborg Agonistes: Disaster and Reconstruction in the Digital Electronic Era', in L.J. Vale and T.J. Campanella (eds.) *The Resilient City: How Modern Cities Recover from Disaster*. Oxford: Oxford University Press.

Morris, D. (2004) *The Sense of Space*. Albany: State University of New York Press.

Ong, A. and S.J. Collier (eds.) (2004) *Global Assemblages: Technology, Politics and Ethics as Anthropological Problems*. Malden, MA: Blackwell.

Posner, R. (2004) *Catastrophe: Risk or Response*. New York: Oxford University Press.

Probyn, E. (2005) *Blush: Faces of Shame*. Minneapolis: University of Minnesota Press.

Rees, M. (2004) *Our Final Century? Will Humanity Survive the 21st Century?* London: Arrow.

Robin, C. (2005) *Fear: The History of a Political Idea*. New York: Oxford University Press.

Roth, P. (2004) *The Plot Against America: A Novel*. London: Jonathan Cape.

Thrift, N.J. (2004) 'Intensities of Feeling: Towards a Spatial Politics of Affect', *Geografiska Annaler*, series A, 86: 57–78.

—(2005a) 'But Malice Aforethought: Cities and the Natural History of Hatred', *Transactions of the Institute of British Geographers* (forthcoming).

—(2005b) *Knowing Capitalism*. London: Sage.

Tsing, A.L. (2005) *Friction: An Ethnography of Global Connection*. Princeton: Princeton University Press.

Vale, L.J. and T.J. Campanella (eds.) (2005) *The Resilient City: How Modern Cities Recover from Disaster*. Oxford: Oxford University Press.

Vanderbilt, T. (2005) 'Diary', *London Review of Books*, 31 March: 35.

Wacquant, L. (1996) 'The Rise of Advanced Marginality: Notes on its Nature and Implications', *Acta Sociologica* 20, 1: 34–46.

—(2000) 'The New Peculiar Institution: On the Prison as Surrogate Ghetto', *Theoretical Criminology* 4: 377–89.

Wilson, E.A. (2004) *Psychosomatic: Feminism and the Neurological Body*. Durham, NC: Duke University Press.

Woolgar, S. (ed.) (2002) *Virtual Society? Technology, Cyberbole, Reality*. Oxford: Oxford University Press.

8

Three Theses on Virilio Now

Arthur Kroker

Thesis 1: City of transformation – Paul Virilio in Obama's America[1]

It is surely the fate of every engaged political theory to be over-come by the history that it thought it was only describing. So too, Paul Virilio. His writings have captured brilliantly these twi-light times in which we live: *The Aesthetics of Disappearance*, *The Information Bomb*, *War and Cinema*, *City of Panic*, *Speed and Politics* – less writing in the traditional sense than an uncanny shamanistic summoning forth of the demonology of speed which inscribes society. A prophet of the wired future, Paul Virilio's thought always invokes the doubled meaning of apocalypse – cataclysm and remembrance. Cataclysm, because all his writings trace the history of the technological death-instinct moving at the speed of light. And remembrance, because Virilio is that rarity in contemporary culture, a thinker whose ethical dissent marks the first glimmerings of a fateful implosion of that festival of seduc-tion, fascination, terror, and boredom we have come to know as digital culture. A self-described 'atheist of technology', his motto is 'obey and resist'.

But for all that there is a raw materialism in Virilio's reflection, nowhere better expressed than in his grisly vision of information as suffocation. In his theatre of thought data banks have migrated inside human flesh, bodies are reduced to granulated flows of dead information, tattooed by data, embedded by codes, with complex histories of electronic transactions as our most private auto-biographies. Information mapping our lives – process, principles, concept, fact – we have all become measurable. In Virilio's writing, what Hannah Arendt once described as 'modern world alienation' rides the whirling tip of history as the spirit of pure negation that is everywhere today. Negative politics, negative subjectivity, nega-tive culture. It is impossible to escape the technological accident that has become us. But for all that history will not long be denied. Just as Nietzsche once prophesied in *The Gay Science* that with the birth of human subjectivity, twisted and scarred and deliriously unpredictable, the gods actually stopped their game of wagers and took notice because something new was moving on the earth – a going across, a tremulous wakening, a pathway over the abyss – so too with Virilio, the gods of history take notice once again. And not just take notice, but actively respond to the fatal challenge that is the thought of Paul Virilio.

Are we beyond *Speed and Politics*? What characterizes contem-porary politics is the unstable mixture of speed information and slow movements. Like the slow implosion of the manufacturing economy, the slow rise of evangelical visions of catastrophe, the slow ascent – the slow ubiquity – of the speed of technology, the slow descent of culture into the cold state of surveillance under the sign of bio-governance. You can see it everywhere. In the world economy, the speed of mortgage-backed securities, credit swap debt offerings, and complex derivatives always seeks to move at the speed of light. Iceland is the world's first country actually liquidated by hyperreality with debts amassed at light-speeds now constituting ten times its national wealth. Like Michel Serres' the perfect para-site, the Wall Street financial elite has worked a perfect number on the host of the world economies – implanting unknown levels of toxic debt everywhere in the circulatory system of finance capital, from China and Japan to the European Community. Waking up to the danger of hot debt moving at light-speed when it is definitely too late, Japanese bankers suddenly declaim that 'it is beyond panic'. Wall Street types say it is 'panic with a capital P'. Harvard economists, standing on the sidelines like a chorus of lament, wisely add that we are now between 'capitulation and panic' and 'debt is good'. That in a world of over-extended economies, sudden loss of financial credibility and a seizing up of credit mechanisms everywhere, the only thing to do, financially speaking, is wait for the **capitulation point** – that fatal moment when despair is so deep, pessimism so locked down tight in the investor's heart, that everything just stops for an instant. No investments, no hope, no circulation. And for the always hopeful financial analysts, this is precisely the point to begin anew, to reinvest, to seize financial redemption from despair. Definitely not a speed economy, then, but a politics and economy of complex recursive loops, trapped in cycles of feedback which no one seems to understand, but with very real, very slow consequences: like vanishing jobs, abandoned health care and trashed communities. In *City of Panic*, Virilio writes about the 'tyranny of real time', 'this accident in time belonging to an event that is the fruit of a technological progress out of political control'. For Virilio, we are now interpellated by a complex, three dimensional space-time involved in the acceleration of technological progress 'that reduces the extent, the fullness of the world to nothing' (Virilio 2007: 69).

Or something else? Not really a fatal oscillation between fast technology and slow society, but hyper-technologies of global financial manipulation that can move so quickly because, just as Jean Baudrillard long ago warned, the hyperreal, simulational world of derivatives, credit swaps and mortgage-backed securities long ago blasted off from material reality, reaching escape velocity, and then orbiting the world as star-like high finance satellites – purely virtual satellites which have no real meaning for the rest of us as long as they stay in space as part of the alienated, recursive loops of advanced capitalism. But when the meltdown suddenly happens, when that immense weight of over-indebtedness and toxic mortgages and credit derivates plunge back into the gravitational weight of real politics and real economy, we finally know what it is to live within trajectories of the catastrophic. Economists are quoted as saying the financial crisis affects 'everyone on earth'.

Is this Virilio's 'global accident?' Quite certainly it is panic finance: that moment when the credit mechanisms necessary for capitalist liquidity slam shut, a time made to measure for Virilio's brilliant theory of bunker archeology, with each bank its own toxic bunker of junk assets, each banker a born-again socialist. For example, always vigilant automatic circuit-breakers working in the darkness of night recently prevented a global plunge of the futures market. Alan Greenspan throws up his hands, exclaiming 'I'm in shocked disbelief.'

By one measure, the global economic meltdown is Virilio's accident, a searing demonstration of the truth of Virilio's proposition that every technology is born with a necessary accident in mind. This time it is not a trainwreck, a robo-trader or even 9/11, but a massive financial accident. Here, the brilliant software innovations and computerized trading programmes that run so much of the world's economy move so quickly but respond so slowly to the complex information feedbacks of recursive loops of bank failures and toxic debt and storms of warring political opinions that they do the only *logical* thing possible. They quickly, globally, and simultaneously abandon their own hyperreal world of virtuality, and go to ground in a panic search for authentic value. The machine-to-machine communication that makes the posthuman economy possible wants, in effect, the gold standard of real, measurable value. It demands the bottom line, the unleveraged mortgage, the real asset that its digital operations have worked so zealously to accident. And just when you think you have finally got the financial capitalists – those unfettered deregulators – they instantly reverse course saying 'Now that the capital is gone "something different" is needed – an emergency provider of equity.' That emergency provider, of course, is *us*.

But maybe it's not an accident at all. Perhaps Naomi Klein's theory of always predatory capitalism as a 'shock doctrine' is correct (Klein: 2008). Or perhaps Robert Reich's statement that, 'It's socialism for Wall Street and capitalism for the rest of us.' Perhaps we're experiencing a carefully planned accident, a trajectory of the catastrophic, that was allowed to run freely to its fatal destiny. A culture under the sign of the 'tyranny of the code', where we find ourselves biologically driven to unlock a code, where computer code literally reinscribes our genetic code and reconfigures our brains. Virilio suspects this. He most of all is an artist of the art of war, a theorist who understands that dromology has no real meaning outside of logics of capture and endocolonization and predation. When modern world alienation, Hannah Arendt's 'negative spirit', found its quintessential historical expression in the past eight dark years of Republicanism, it not only set out to accident the world, but it has succeeded, probably beyond its dreams, in doing so. Thinking the Middle East in terms of the *Book of Revelation* literally required world catastrophe for Armageddon, for a fatal clash of civilizations and ancient religions, which would usher in the seven years of the Anti-Christ, and thereupon the Revelation. Thinking American political economy first, and then world economy, in terms of a permanent paralysis of the progressive movement, has meant just what Thomas Frank's recent book described as the 'wrecking crew'. The party is finally over, the hosts are packing up to flee the premises, and everything is wreckage. Out of the coming crisis of massive state over-indebtedness and hyper-inflation can come only Democrats as night-watchman of the Tower: the imposition of a new austerity state for non-fungible labour – blue-collar workers, the weak and the dispossessed; the intensification of the disciplinary state to control the inevitable social unrest; and for the always unrepentant capitalist class, a massive replenishment of all the capitalist marketplaces of the world, with the state willingly held hostage, just as Virilio predicted, by demonologists wrapped in the masquerade of bankers and financiers and investment dealers. At this time, at this place, at this trajectory of the catastrophic, Kevin Phillips' admonition 'bad money always follows bad money', gets it just about right.

Or is it the reverse? In 1996 Virilio may have originally predicted a 'global accident' that would occur simultaneously to the world as a whole. Only twelve years later in the last autumn days of 2008 – exactly forty years after the tumultuous political events of 1968 – **was it possible that Virilio's 'global accident' has itself been accidented**? Slowly, inexorably, one resistor at a time, one mobilization, one march, one individual dissent, one collective 'no' at a time, with what Antonio Gramsci called the dynamism of the popular will, the global accident seemed to flip into a global political transformation. Signs of this at first political, and then technological, recircuiting of the popular will were everywhere. Entire empires had suddenly vanished, global social movements were everywhere on the rise, imperialisms had seemingly been checkmated, and the first tangible hints of a truly transformational politics were in the air. The political environment was charged with the electricity of the technological noosphere. It's the primal impulse, the desperate hope, of many progressive human hearts. It's why beyond all the rules of normal politics that the popular American Will – the world Will – now unified into a common current of information flows, of house-to-house organization, of state-to-state campaigning, of immense financial support by a microphysics of small donations, without illusions, without false hopes, it appeared that a truly transformational movement in American politics was underway. Marshall McLuhan once noted correctly that the United States *is* the world environment. Ironically then, just as the United States triggered Virilio's global accident, it just might be on the verge of **accidenting the accident**, revealing that the City of Panic might also be an American City of Transformation.

Thesis 2: Minor simulations and major disturbances[2]

Dreams of utopia are everywhere in Virilio's perspective. Definitely not as a metaphysics of presence, but as the necessary exclusion, the disavowal, the hauntology, the supplement, the margin which, as Derrida prophesied, is the structural condition always silently presupposed by Virilio's relentless exposure of exactly the opposite tendency in technoculture. In this sense, if Virilio can present us with such a searing vision of postmodern ruins as the animating impulse of technology, if he can write so apocalyptically about the radiating, and dangerous, positivity of data, that only indicates that the reappearance of precisely the opposite trajectory is already in motion, that from visions of technological apocalypse emerge the most inspiring intimations of utopian imagination. Consequently, to really understand the politics of Virilio Now it would be salutary to bring into presence the artistic practices of tactical media which have everything to do with the language of marginality, disavowals, hauntologies and supplements. In other words, seek out the actual political struggles informed by the specter of Virilio Now not in the fabled constructions of the great referential unities of power and language and sexuality and consciousness, but in those highly contested fields of undecidability and iterability where that which has been disappeared by the 'aesthetics of disappearance' makes its fatal reappearance. That's why, I would argue, one actual site for the politics of Virilio Now takes place on the southern borderlands of the United States, and involves artistic practices working on behalf of those who have been effectively marginalized by the global accident.

For example, consider what's happening in the (dromological) state of California. Here, the utopian imagination which animates the radical activism of tactical media has instantly created strange convergences in contemporary formations of power, namely between technocratic liberalism and atavistic conservatism. If California is the nervous breakthrough to the future anticipated in brilliantly bleak detail in all of Virilio's writings, perhaps that is because California literally wears the skin of Virilio. Everything that Virilio theorizes is present in California in excessive detail: accelerated flows of information, powerful media complexes, celebrity celebrations of 'hyper-active man', relentless evacuations of the biosphere in favour of 'pan planetary human physiology', and massive corporate efforts directed at the creation of 'biotechnological cybernetics'. It is as if California is a complex beta-tester of the applicability of Virilio's critique of the culture of speed, and of the impossibility of transforming the destiny of technology from within. In book after book, Virilio takes refuge in a deeply ethical Christian refusal of the technological imperative. Much like those dark visionaries of the technological future before him including Jacques Ellul, Teilhard de Chardin and Marshall McLuhan, Virilio can travel so deeply into the pathologies of 'biotechnological cybernetics', reprise so eloquently the viral logic of new media complexes and examine so carefully the logistics of dromological society because all his thought is based on a sincerely held Christian refusal of the will to absolute technicity. That the generative logic

of Christianity may itself be the metaphysical foundation of contemporary technology is itself a thought held at one remove from
Virilio's conceptualization of technological society. Indeed, while
Virilio's fidelity to Christian ethics permits him to think deeply
about the terminal culture of technology, it is combined in all his
writings with an equally resolute commitment to understanding
the paradoxical and contingent nature of technology. For political activists engaged in the resistance politics of tactical media, it
is precisely Virilio's brilliant conceptualization of the 'trajectory
of catastrophe' that is the digital future which has proven to be
so compelling about his writings. Confronted with the hard realities of the 'negative horizon', 'aesthetics of disappearance' and the
'information bomb', tactical media has had no other choice than to
theorize novel forms of political resistance capable of disrupting the
logic of technologically augmented societies. In this sense, Virilio's
persuasive image of the negative horizon of information culture
provides important clues for envisioning different technological,
economic and educational futures, all deeply inflected by social
justice and human creativity.

It is my sense that this is precisely what is taking place in the
present state of California, fittingly in the city of San Diego where
the attempted suppression of a university-funded art project,
the Transborder Immigrant Tool,[3] has exposed the vulnerable soft(ware) belly of dromological California. In the same way
that Virilio once argued in *The Art of the Motor* that distinctions
between centre and periphery have been eclipsed by the incredible
'shrinking effect' of digital media, I would argue with and, in some
ways, beyond Virilio that 'minor simulations' carried out by prac-
titioners of tactical media working on the southern borderlands of
American empire have an importance beyond their specific time
and place, namely that the deconstructive power of such tactical
media reveals very real weaknesses in the hegemonic aspirations of
the speed of culture. As Ricardo Dominguez and other activists at
B.A.N.G..Lab/Electronic Disturbance Theater at the University of
California San Diego declare: 'Just remember – Art is not a Crime.
Online protest is not a Crime. Online protest is Art.' So then,
beyond Virilio, a theorization of minor simulations and major
disturbances.

In an American empire culture marked by wild swings between technocratic liberalism and atavistic conservatism, any attempt to introduce a third political term (minor simulations, Transborder Immigrant Tool, Electronic Disturbances) into popular debate will definitely be met with powerful reaction-formations. In the case of atavistic conservatism, southern California is its homeland, from the bunkered suburbs of Orange County to the increasingly 'hardened' borderlands of San Diego. For technocratic liberalism confronted by a domestic crisis of economic over-indebtedness and a global crisis of cultural delegitimation, the 'markers' of political sovereignty must be reaffirmed. Since tactical media are necessarily all about transgressing borders, destabilizing the big 'markers' of power, economy, gender, sexuality and race and disturbing the hegemonic status of national borders, it is to be expected that the deployment of tactical media will do the politically impossible, namely unite the supposedly clashing politics of technocratic liberalism and atavistic conservatism in a common political project of saving the honour of the name (of the American homeland).

The always strong, always recidivist, reaction-formations directed against the Transborder Immigrant Tool by conservative activists, roaming border posses of white vigilantes, security state officials, and now University of California authorities, this new combination of technocratic liberalism and atavistic conservatism under the sunny skies of Southern California, is not really understandable without taking into account that there are actually two Transborder Immigrant Tool projects taking place. First, there is the Transborder project with its provision of innovative, repurposed cellphones to vulnerable, exposed, desperate immigrants from Mexico and many countries south. Here the question is: should the political sovereignty of borders trump basic human rights to water, safety and shelter? That the question of human rights is dangerous from the point of view of the state is clearly illustrated by the fact that American policing authorities have immediately resorted to a rhetoric of hysteria in critiquing the Transborder Immigrant Tool, suddenly speaking of the potential (mis)uses of this device by terrorists and drug-runners. However, there is another Transborder project running, namely the tactical deployment of 'minor simulations' against the authoritative borderlands of UCSD. While the University of California educational system might be shamed into supporting repurposed cell-phone networks on behalf of immigrants, it is equally quick to support its own logistics of academic sovereignty. As UC student and faculty critiques now circulating as part of *Communiqués from Occupied California* illustrate, the borders of power in the UC system are very much under general assault by a diverse activist coalition. By running minor simulations intended to re-imagine other alternative futures for education, tactical media literally disappears the (rhetorical) differences between technocratic liberalism (UCSD) and atavistic conservatism (posses of Tea Party activists). Here, the two sides of American empire, previously rhetorically separated but both necessary parts of the twisted strands of power, combine in a fateful rejection of that which they both commonly fear – minor simulations with very real potential for creating major political disturbances. Disrupt the binary logic of the borderlands, undermine the strict logic of inclusions/exclusions necessary to maintain state sovereignty, re-imagine other alternatives, insist that all borders be rethought in terms of contingency, paradox and complexity, and what results is literally a big bang in the logic of empire.

So then, the question: Now that the strategies of tactical media have successfully generated a big bang in the theory of American (empire) governance, now that atavistic conservatism and technocratic liberalism have found common cause in suppressing both the politics of minor simulations and the resistance art of the Transborder project, what are appropriate tactics to resist this newest iteration of empire power? After all, when atavistic conservatism and technocratic liberalism combine, something definitely new emerges, namely augmented empire. Augmented empire? That's technocratic liberalism with such rationalist excess in defending its academic boundaries from networked simulations that it flips into its opposite state – a dangerous form of liberal *realpolitik* animated by atavistic emotions running the psychological gambit from bureaucratic defensiveness to panic anger. Fully alert to the threat posed to previously impervious borders by minor simulations such as the Transborder Immigrant Tool, atavistic conservatism suddenly goes repressively liberal, justifying its attempt to shutdown the Transborder project in terms of 'responsible academic research'. Of course, when that does not work, atavistic conservatism always keeps in reserve other activist strategies ranging from congressional denunciations to very real death threats. As always, utopia is the bright angel of history.

Thesis 3: Which way the angel of history?

No one has understood technoculture with such theoretical finesse and unflinching commitment to truth-saying than Paul Virilio. Not simply a brilliant theorist of technology, the lasting legacy of Virilio's thought will be to have shown in detail and definition the full sweep of the negative spirit of technology, namely its evacuation of all that which is grounded, material and truly organic. While it was left to generations which preceded the twentieth century to have perhaps known something of a physical, material relationship to organic life, to have experienced at least something of the complexity of relationships among humans, animals, plant-life and inanimate objects, Virilio's thought is at the expressive height of a generation of postmodern theorists – most secular, some religious – who absorbed directly into their theorizations the full crisis dimensions of the present technological epoch. It is, I believe, no exaggeration to claim that Virilio's theoretical trajectory is that of a shock theorist, simultaneously traumatized by the negative spectre of cybernetics but, for all that, firm in his ethical dissent against the nihilism that is the will to technology. Refusing to bunker his thought in any of the great referents of intellectual refuge in a troubled world, Virilio does precisely the opposite. Whether the object of investigation be warfare, cybernetics, cinema, information bombs, biotechnological cybernetics or the art of the motor, Virilio always privileges the immersive, the tactile, the complex as necessary preconditions for any accurate understanding of the human impact of technology. In his writings is to be found nothing less than an epic history of the story of digital technology, from its emergence in the form of cinematic derealization as the much-feared yet fatally seductive destroyer of

Newtonian space and time, to its most mature representation as something which literally outgrows its bodily habitation on the way to the creation of extra-planetary quasi-human physiologies. Caught up in the speed of (theoretical) information generated by Virilio's pilgrimage across the space/time spectrum of techno-culture, the lasting impact is most definitely not suffocation but something very different, namely an urgent, fatal and increasingly desperate illumination of the uncanny nature of technology in society. While Virilio's theory of technology was formed in the spectral heat of twentieth-century technological anima-tions, his insights will, I believe, only be fully appreciated in the coming age of humans as both neurological appendages of min-istering (software) machines and utopian visionaries of the always all-too-human condition.

More than a theorist of information culture, Virilio is a cos-mologist of software culture, capturing in his analysis something truly ominous about the evolution of technicity, namely that in the operational language of data and codes there is present, first as a glimmer on the digital horizon, and later as the emblematic, animating feature of the digital future, the presence of the death instinct. Indeed, if there can be almost a Manichean divide in Virilio's thought between his deep immersion in the calculative logic of the 'information bomb' and his ethical refusal of the same, this may have its origins in something truly cosmological, specifi-cally that for Virilio the stakes of technology today are no longer, if they ever were, between domination and freedom but evoke the greater ethical fundamentals of good and evil. Consequently, it is only fitting to conclude this reflection on the politics of Virilio Now by calling into presence a radical experiment in 'augmenting' vision undertaken by a futurist tech lab on the Pacific coast of the United States. Here, the premonitory warnings issued by Virilio in his theses on the aesthetics of disappearance with its hijacking of human vision by the substitute vision of robotically controlled machine vision, suddenly goes one step further, in effect moving augmented vision from the outside of the body to the perspec-tival centre of the cornea itself. If what is implied in all Virilio's theory is correct, namely that the death instinct is embedded in the logic of technology, then perhaps in this futurist experiment with augmented vision we are present at the first historical appearance of the death of the eye.

The Virilio app: the death of the eye

Today, the death instinct is alive and well in all the software language surrounding ocular vision. That's what makes software for improved (technological) vision so vividly, and chillingly, dynamic. When the eye upgrades to digital eyesight, there's a simultaneous downgrading of human vision. If by human vision we mean not only what is rendered visible, but more importantly what remains invisible, not only what is perceived, but what remains obstinately outside the regime of perception, then software for improved digital vision effectively shuts down the invisible, the unperceived, all the forms of everyday blindness so necessary for the complex workings of human vision. With its deep nerve connection to the human nervous system, from the visual neurology of the brain to the orality of the mouth, the tactility of the limbs and the desires of (our) sexual organs, the eye is always a porous membrane negotiating the boundary of bodies and the world. When the eye first opened to the world of earth, air, fire, water and sky, it was as if the evolutionary story of human flesh finally had made an elemental, even indispensable, connection. With the opening of the eye, the human organism became a visual traveller: nomadic, curious, forewarned, always pulled out of the dark cavity of skull and skin and bones and blood to become something unmistakably human, namely that which Nietzsche first signalled − a going-across, a gamble, a thin spider's web over the abyss called life.

All that is about to change.

In the way of all truly momentous technological innovations, the death of the eye has been announced by way of a media report describing the latest adventure in technological futurism. It appears that a research team at the University of Washington, motivated by the desire to transform the contact lens into a digital platform like iPhones with its always growing menu of creative apps, has invented the world's first protoype of the fully augmented human eye. But why stop there?

According to the leader of the research team:

> The human eye is a perceptual powerhouse. It can see millions of colors, adjust easily to shifting light conditions, and transmit information to the brain at a speed exceeding that of a high-speed Internet connection.
>
> In the Terminator movies, Arnold Schwarzenegger's character sees the world with data superimposed on his visual field – virtual captions that enhance the cyborgs' scan of a scene. In stories by the science fiction author Vernon Vinge, characters rely on electronic contact lenses, rather than smartphones or brain implants, for seamless access to information that appears right before their eyes.
>
> These visions (if I may) might seem far-fetched, but a contact lens with simple built-in electronics is already within reach; in fact my students and I are already producing such devices in small numbers in my laboratory at the University of Washington, in Seattle. These lenses don't give us the vision of an eagle or the benefit of running subtitles on our surroundings yet. But we have built a lens with one LED, which we've powered wirelessly with RF. What we've done so far barely hints at what will be soon possible with this technology.[4]

In the usual way of all scientific experiments with the human body, the animal species selected for a digital eye implant is the rabbit. Definitely not mindful of Virilio's warnings concerning the exterminist ambitions of 'hyper-active man' nor, for that matter, Donna Haraway's understanding of animals as 'companion species', the body of the bunny is scientifically repurposed to become a platform for digital lenses. Did anyone think to ask: what's a bunny's vision of the world? Or did the bunny consent to seeing fields of edible grass in a newly augmented digital way?

That the bunny was never consulted about the advantages of augmented reality is itself perhaps very revelatory of the impoverished vision of a scientist. Isn't there an indispensable ethical reflex associated with human vision, a carefully nurtured sense that human vision is not simply about appropriation, but appreciation? Strip human vision of a complex sense of critical appreciation of the world around us, and aren't we suddenly left in a world of bunnies as objects of technological appropriation, objects of abuse-value?

But perhaps that's unfair. In the larger story of technology, of which this research innovation is a brilliant digital example, no permission is ever required to secure an animal's consent to a digital eye implant in order to become the world's first pilgrim of the digital eye. Consciousness of the bunny as a unique, complex species-being is always disavowed, and this disavowal is the first, most important avowal of scientific experimentation. On the path to the augmented human eye, animals occupy the diminished role of unwilling test-beds.

But not, of course, for humans. Appropriating human agency is never really required because, unlike bunnies, humans are seemingly always ready to become leading objects of digital augmentation. In response to the announcement in a story headlined 'A Twinkle in the Eye', one net correspondent immediately said: 'Wow. I would be more than willing to risk losing eyesight in one of my eyes to test this out as the technology matures.' Perhaps shutting down human vision and opening up an augmented reality of the enhanced digital eye requires, in the first instance, something not really technological, but metaphysical. When the digital eye blinks for the very first time, when the augmented iris is streamed, networked and vectored, an indispensable ethical preparation has already taken place, namely a prior human willingness to identify itself with its technological future with sufficient intensity to override any remaining (human) quibbles concerning animal rights, human dispositions, and what's lost with the coming-to-be of the fully realized universe of augmented reality.

In the amazing blast of technological creativity, such ethical reservations have no necessary cultural standing. How could they? Networking the eye, augmenting human vision, implies that the eye will now port information moving at the speed of light. The iPhone becomes an ocular implant, texting literally becomes a blink of the eye, the cornea opens onto an iris repurposed as a mobile device. Even for those standing on the sidelines with ethical reservations ready to hand, the accidenting of the eye by digital vision can only be understood ambivalently. If individual human autobiography can be linked so intimately to the unfolding adventures of technological biography, perhaps it is because that which is soon to be acquired in such experimentation easily outpaces the slow reservations of ethical remembrance.

Everything about the digital lens is amazing. Slip the digital lens onto the cornea and the world opens up as code-work. Shimmering columns of data slipstream across the expectant iris, reality suddenly goes bifocal with distance for ordinary human eyesight and nearness for data feeds, astigmatism is instantly corrected since the irregularly shaped cornea is forced to retool itself as a platform for always undistorted information, and human vision itself becomes multifocal, mediated and multitasked.

That the digital lens may reduce vision to monovision with compromised (ethical) depth perception is, in the end, a matter best left to those soon to be left behind by augmented reality in a contact lens.

In the future, could one accidented remnant of digital vision, this sacrifice of human eyesight before the altar of augmented reality, be a sudden increase in ethical myopia? For Paul Virilio such ethical myopia has occurred long ago, the ethical imperative now being to find a way of clarifying human vision in a culture of technological nihilism.

The sign of Virilio

In the way of all truly serious thought, honouring Paul Virilio means treating his theoretical insights in precisely the same way that he himself has theorized. At every point, Virilio has insisted that thought itself cease its purely representational function, becoming instead a critical probe of digital technology. Theory as critical probe? That's the aesthetic strategy common to all of Virilio's writings, from his searing visions of bunker archeology, pure war and speed politics to his eloquent theorizations of information bombs, cinematic derealization and aesthetics of disappearance. Before Virilio, technological futurism could sometimes vacillate between the utopian aspirations surrounding the technological mastery of human and non-human nature and the dystopian warnings of a form of theory which always held itself at one fatal remove from direct engagement with the operational logic of technicity. After Virilio, theory pays the price for losing its techno- logical innocence by drawing into public consciousness that which was previously obscured by the fast acceleration of a fully technical society, namely that the trace of technology is always accompanied by violent scenes of accidents, dromology, and disappearances. In other words, after Virilio, theory becomes a truth-sayer of that which is lost with the historical realization of the empire of tech- nology, from the eclipse of autonomous subjectivity to the shutting down of human vision, and deadened ethics. More than most, Virilio's thought, while always accurately portraying the particulars of the technological spirit of the age, from cinema and computa- tion to cyber-war and automatic vision machines, recuperates the more ancient voice of lament. Certainly not lament for things rendered obsolete with the appearance of networked culture, but a more indefinable, yet urgent, lament for ethical possibilities instantly foreclosed by the grammar of technology. Refusing to think outside of the real material history of information culture, Virilio's thought can identify so accurately, often decades in advance, the likely human and non-human impact of technology precisely because his comportment towards technology is so deeply inflected by the speed of lament, namely the relentless dissection of technological culture at a pace of thought which, in its accelerated effects and intensity of purpose, transforms the language of lament itself into something moving faster than the speed of (digital) light. Indeed, Virilio can write so insightfully about the bending of light- time and light-space under the pressure of the digital imperative because his own thought has already moved ahead of the unfolding digital universe of light-time and light-space to carefully consider the dawning age of the global accident.

The three theses developed here – City of Transformation, Minor Simulations and Major Disturbances, and Which Way the Angel of History? – are reports *after* the global accident. Skipping the polite pretence that technology continues to evolve towards an open, yet undetermined, future, these theses listen intently for the sign of Virilio in the accident of global culture, art and politics that surrounds us. While the City of Transformation might con- clude on a hopeful note alluding to a political epiphany, even that glimmer of utopia is held in check by the more realistic understanding that today atavistic conservatism and repressive liberalism are twin sides of the very same coin of technology. That this is the case in art as much as politics is illustrated by the second probe of Minor Simulations and Major Disturbances where the language of increasingly technological politics is reduced to a powerful form of semiotic manipulation. As for the question of technology itself, the report on the death of the (rabbit's) eye in a west coast tech laboratory with the consequent opening of the newly augmented digital eye draws the necessarily grim conclusions anticipated by Virilio's understanding of machine vision. That the three theses are suggestive only, neither foreclosing alternative interpretations nor excluding other sitings of the spreading debris field of the global accident, indicates that, more than the content of his analysis, Virilio's theoretical legacy may have its most lasting implication as a highly original and compelling methodology for understanding technology. Moving by a doubled logic of deep immersion in the field of technology and complex intimations of the digital future, Virilio's method privileges the question of that which is disavowed, excluded and proscribed in the otherwise seamless rhetoric of information culture. In one word, Virilio's method is that of hauntology, simultaneously rendering visible the critical codes of technology while drawing into presence that which is disappeared by the rush to augmentation and mobility.

Notes

1. 'City of Transformation', by Arthur and Marilouise Kroker, was originally published on CTheory, www.ctheory.net (10/30/2008).
2. An earlier, shorter draft of 'Minor Simulations and Major Disturbances' was published on Empyre, 14/10/2010 (empyre@lists. cofa.unsw.edu.au).
3. The border between the US and Mexico has moved between the virtual and the all-too-real since before the birth of the two nation-states. This has allowed a deep archive of suspect movement across this border to be traced and tagged – specifically anchored to immigrant

bodies moving north, while immigrant bodies south much less so. The danger of moving north across this border is not a question of politics, but vertiginous geography. Hundreds of people have died crossing the US/Mexico border due to not being able to tell where they are in relation to where they have been and which direction they need to go to reach their destination safely. Now, with the rise of multiple distributed geospatial information systems (such as the Google Earth Project, for example), GPS (Global Positioning System) and the developing Virtual Hiker Algorithm by the artist Brett Stalbaum, it is possible to develop a Transborder Tool for Immigrants to be implemented and distributed on cracked Nextell cellphones. This will allow a virtual geography to mark new trails and potentially safer routes across this desert of the real. A Mexico/US Border Disturbance Art Project, by Ricardo Dominguez and Brett Stalbaum (Principal Investigators) and Micha Cardenas and Jason Najarro (Lead Researchers), www.post. thing.net.

4. IEEE Spectrum: Augmented Reality in A Contact Lens, 2 September 2009 (http://spectrum.ieee.org/biomedical/bionics/augmented-real ity-in-a-contact-lens/0).

References

Klein, Naomi (2008) *The Shock Doctrine: The Rise of Disaster Capitalism.* Toronto: Vintage.

Virilio, Paul (2007) *City of Panic*, trans. Julie Rose. Oxford: Berg Publishers.

9

The Accident of Finance

Paul Crosthwaite

On Monday, 19 October 1987, stock markets around the world collapsed. In the United States – where the Dow Jones Industrial Average fell by 22.6 per cent, its largest ever one-day decline – losses were amplified by the widespread use of 'programme trading' software, which automatically issued transaction instructions as market conditions shifted. A particularly significant role was played by 'portfolio insurance', a common form of programme trading in which positions in index futures (derivative contracts traded in accordance with expectations about the future levels of stock indexes, such as the Standard & Poor's [S&P] 500) are adjusted in response to fluctuations in the value of a portfolio of stocks. From the opening of trading on 19 October, a devastating positive feedback effect arose, whereby portfolio insurance schemes responded to price falls on the New York Stock Exchange at the end of the previous week with such heavy sales of S&P 500 futures contracts at the Chicago Mercantile Exchange that futures prices fell to disproportionately low levels relative to their underlying index, leading arbitrageurs to attempt to exploit the discrepancy by selling more stock on Wall Street, which, in turn, succeeded only in triggering portfolio insurers to sell yet more index futures at the Merc.[1] In the weeks following 'Black

Monday', as it soon came to be known, Mark Rubinstein, a Berkeley professor and partner in the dominant portfolio insurer Leland O'Brien Rubinstein Associates, fell into what he would later recognize as a period of clinical depression, brought on by concern that the field of financial engineering he had pioneered might have contributed to one of the worst crashes in US history. In particular, he was wracked by an obscure yet insistent fear that the Soviet Union would exploit the weakness and disarray of the American markets to instigate a military confrontation akin to the Cuban missile crisis, leading to the possibility of full-scale nuclear war (interview cited in MacKenzie 2006: 206). Today, this eerie psychodrama, in which anxieties regarding the global economy, geopolitics and the very fate of the planet converge with personal concerns over reputation and self-image, appears at once wildly at odds with the reality of the situation and weirdly prophetic: at odds with reality because, whatever the weakness of the US and its allies in the wake of the '87 crash, it was as nothing compared to the decrepitude of a Soviet empire that, far from plotting an assault on the West, was even then struggling to postpone its own collapse; and yet prophetic because, as the work of Paul Virilio makes clear, over the last two decades, systemic financial crises have become to the age of globalization what thermonuclear holocaust was to the Cold War era, with the exception that, whereas nuclear warfare remained confined to the realms of strategy, game play, simulation, imagination, and nightmare (remained, in Jacques Derrida's famous words, 'fabulously textual' (1984: 23)) financial crises have been frequent occurrences (whilst, however, being in many ways themselves 'fabulously textual').

In August 1998, just over a decade after Rubinstein experienced his disturbing premonition, the world was plunged into turmoil by convulsions emanating from Russia. These were not missiles blasting forth from remote silos in the Siberian wastes, however, but bursts of debt and illiquidity triggered by devaluation and default in Moscow, which homed in at near light speed on the world's financial centres via a planetary grid of satellites, modems and fibre-optic cables. According to the financial journalist and historian Paul Blustein, the resulting crisis, which annihilated the massive American hedge fund Long Term Capital Management

(LTCM) and threatened to destabilize the entire western financial system, 'with no malice intended, created a threat more devastating to the West than anything the friends of communism had ever concocted during their decades in the Kremlin' (Blustein 2001: 238).

Black Monday, 1987 and the Russian/LTCM collapse of 1998 take their place in a familiar litany of recent financial upheavals alongside the currency and stock market collapses suffered by the 'tiger economies' of South-east Asia in 1997–8, the bursting of the new technology or 'dot-com' bubble in 2000 and, beginning in the summer of 2007, the shuddering 'crunch' in credit markets caused by the financial sector's overexposure to opaque instruments based on 'sub-prime' mortgages. As financial crisis has superseded nuclear war as the paradigmatic mode of global risk over this two-decade period, the evocative vocabulary of 'nukespeak' has migrated towards discourses surrounding market shocks and crashes. Most famously, in March 2003 the legendary American investment guru Warren Buffett, then the world's second richest man, described financial derivatives, whose market was valued at around 100 trillion dollars a year, as 'financial weapons of mass destruction, carrying dangers that, while now latent, are potentially lethal' (2003: 15).[2] The 'dangers' of derivatives would remain largely 'latent' for the next four years, but in the summer of 2007, as the US housing market began to contract, and 'sub-prime' mortgage-holders to default on their repayments, the vast trade in complex assets based on, or derived from, these mortgages unravelled, precipitating the 'credit crunch' in the global financial system. As this crisis deepened, Buffett's stark warning about the dangers of speculative excess in the derivatives markets was widely quoted. And it was echoed in the language of 'fallout', 'meltdown', 'holocaust', 'ground zero', 'toxic assets', 'nuclear winter' and 'financial Hiroshima' that pervaded the coverage of the crisis.

The ways in which anxieties concerning the fragility of the financial system have eclipsed nuclear paranoia in planetary consciousness, whilst at the same time absorbing the lexicon of radioactive catastrophe into their imaginings of market upheaval, have been increasing preoccupations for Paul Virilio over the last two decades. The first part of this chapter traces this strand of Virilio's work. I then turn to consider the particularly significant implications that his theorization of financial crises holds for the representation of such events in contemporary fictional narratives. In the final section, I compare the parallels between nuclear and financial dangers articulated by Virilio with those drawn by his fellow cultural theorist Jean Baudrillard, and assess the prospects for reform of the financial system that would take into account what Virilio calls the 'political economy of speed'.

From the atomic bomb to the information bomb

The invention and rapid proliferation of atomic, and later thermo-nuclear, weapons ushered in the age of what Virilio terms the 'integral', 'generalized' or 'global' accident. Whereas earlier technological accidents, such as shipwrecks, train derailments and aeroplane crashes, had been 'specific and localized' (Virilio 2000c: 40), the radioactive fallout from a nuclear explosion was uncontainable and could wreak devastation over vast expanses of territory, while a prolonged, intercontinental exchange of nuclear weapons had the potential to render the entire planet virtually uninhabitable. In the wake of the Cold War, as the threat of nuclear Armageddon has eased (without, of course, disappearing), a range of grave global dangers have risen to prominence, includ-ing, most notably, international terrorism, climate change and a variety of potentially pandemic diseases, such as HIV/AIDS and various virulent forms of influenza. Though he has by no means ignored these newly visible risks, Virilio has nonetheless consist-ently singled out the phenomenon of the global financial crash as the nearest contemporary equivalent to nuclear conflagration, for just as the horizons of existence were defined during the Cold War by the threat of the nuclear bomb, so are they defined today by the prospect of the 'information bomb', and the crash is its exemplary manifestation.

The information bomb, Virilio explains, is a form of global accident that 'is similar to the atomic bomb but only to the extent that it is a device based on energy. . . . Whereas the atom bomb was triggered by the energy of the atom, the information bomb is triggered by the energy of information and communication technologies' (2001a: 168). While the terminal, cataclysmic explosion of signs, images, and code posited by Virilio remains a hypothetical and indeed barely imaginable, scenario, he has repeatedly pointed to the financial crises of recent decades as the most significant signs of the imminent detonation of the information bomb. In his essay 'Speed and Information', for example, he outlines the idea of 'a bomb whereby real-time interaction would be to information what radioactivity is to energy' (1995: para. 13):

> After the globalization of telecommunications, one should expect a generalized kind of accident, a never-seen-before accident. . . . The stock-market collapse is merely a slight prefiguration of it. Nobody has seen this generalized accident yet. But then watch out as you hear talk about the 'financial bubble' in the economy: a very significant metaphor is used here, and it conjures up visions of some kind of cloud, reminding us of other clouds just as frightening as those of Chernobyl . . . (1995: para. 15)

The end of the Cold War was a decisive factor in establishing the capacity of the financial markets to generate paroxysms on the scale of those seen over the last two decades. Not only did the collapse of the Communist regimes in Eastern Europe transform the geopolitical scene, it also permitted the rapid penetration of finance capital into previously inaccessible regions, with often destabilizing results, and bequeathed the advanced information and telecommunications infrastructure that, as Virilio emphasizes, undergirds the global financial system. Ryan Bishop and Gregory Clancey elaborate on this latter point:

> As the Cold War itself has vanished from our collective screens, Cold War technology transfer to the private sector has spilled over into daily life with unintended consequences. The very same real-time technologies that allowed instantaneous data transfer for identifying military targets . . . [are] used to target global capital investments and pullouts. . . . Technologies designed to take snap-second decisions out

of human hands in military situations – taking the human element out
of the loop – function similarly with currency exchange markets and
other global investment strategies. (Bishop and Clancey 2004: 66)

Virilio has been a particularly forceful critic of the programme
trading systems alluded to by Bishop and Clancey here, which
are still widely used in stock exchanges around the world, despite
evidence of their role in the October 1987 crash in the United
States. He has repeatedly drawn direct parallels between radioactive fallout and the rapid ramification of market downturns via
programme trading. In an interview, for example, he identifies two
examples of the generalized or integral accident:

> the collapse of the stock exchange and radioactivity as [the] result of a
> nuclear conflict. These examples mean that when an event takes place
> somewhere today, the possibility arises that it might destroy every-
> thing. . . . Today's collapse of the stock exchange is a nice icon for
> the integral accident, in the sense that a very small occurrence changes
> everything, as the speed of quotations and programmed trading spreads
> and enhances any trend instantaneously. (2000c: 41)[3]

Virilio invokes nuclear disasters here and elsewhere in order
to emphasize the capacity of financial crises to radiate uncontain-
ably across global markets, as well as to draw attention to the
dangers inherent in delegating decision-making responsibilities to
machines, whether these be portfolio insurance schemes or missile
systems primed to automatically launch retaliatory strikes in the
event of a surprise attack. As McKenzie Wark writes in a strongly
Virilian analysis of the Black Monday crash of 1987, 'the scenario
Virilio fears with nuclear war – that the speed of the vectors of war
technology will become so fast that decisions pass out of the hands
of leaders and into the cold embrace of computers – is the scenario
that has already arrived within the immaterial economy' (1994:
211). Contemporary cultural representations of financial crises,
however, have largely refused to acknowledge the partial exclusion of the human from the functioning of the global financial
system. Novels have been particularly abundant and visible sources
of such representations, and exemplify this failure to confront the

delegation of agency from human to machine. It is to these works of contemporary fiction that I now turn.

Trade wars

One of the most striking characteristics of recent fictional depictions of financial crises is their almost universal insistence on attributing upheavals on the markets to deliberate acts of sabotage on the part of individuals or, at most, small groups. Evidence of this predisposition is particularly abundant in genre fiction, but only because this is where the preponderance of financial crash narratives have appeared in recent decades. It is also the default mode of 'literary' fiction, such as Sebastian Faulks' recent *A Week in December*. Though obtrusively schematic in its execution, Faulks' novel is evidently an attempt to paint a naturalistic panorama of metropolitan life in the incipient credit crunch days of late 2007, yet it quite inaccurately and implausibly ascribes responsibility for the collapse of a fictionalized Royal Bank of Scotland, and the destabilization of the wider British economy, to the machinations of a single City hedge fund manager. Even Don DeLillo, contemporary fiction's most sensitive chronicler of the decentred, impersonal networks that structure everyday life, uses the narrative of *Cosmopolis* to reimagine the bursting of the 'dot-com' bubble in the spring of 2000 as a consequence of the reckless trades of a loan, renegade speculator.[4] Not coincidentally, DeLillo's sociopathic protagonist reflects on several occasions over the course of the narrative's single-day duration on his ownership of a decommissioned Soviet nuclear bomber, as if his wilful destruction of market value were a displacement of his desire, frustrated by the US authorities, to fly this plane 'armed' (2003: 103).

As I have suggested, however, over the last several decades, depictions of financial crises have been largely confined to works of genre fiction. In these 'financial thrillers' the tendency to personalize the crash is reinforced by the demands of generic convention, which insist on the portrayal of world historical events as the outcomes of cat-and-mouse struggles between twinned pairs of independent, resourceful and tenacious antagonists. While forerunners of the form can be traced back to the early 1970s, the emergence of the financial thriller as a distinct sub-genre occurred as part of a post–Cold War situation in which a catastrophic crash on global markets came to be recognized as a more urgent threat than a military confrontation between the major nuclear powers. As Nicky Marsh remarks, 'these novels . . . [provide] fantasies in which global economic collapse [replaces] . . . Cold War fears of nuclear war . . . as the apocalyptic threat to the planet which the thriller [is] able to pose and defuse' (2007: 97).[5] The historical shift that propelled the financial thriller to prominence is underscored in an early example of the form, Joseph Finder's *The Zero Hour*, when the narrator observes that 'with the end of the Cold War we less and less often think about what might happen if an all-out nuclear war were to erupt', while a more pressing concern has become a financial disaster that 'would plunge America into a second Great Depression that would make the 1930s seem like a time of prosperity' (1996: 366).

Financial thrillers frequently converge with the parallel sub-genre of the 'techno-thriller' via their interest in the constitutive role played in contemporary capital markets by the technological infrastructure inherited from the geostrategic imperatives of the Cold War. They often place particular emphasis on how the speed and volume of electronic transactions exceed human comprehension. One of Finder's characters, for example, remarks, 'Today, five out of every six dollars in the economy isn't cash but – *vapor*. Streams of zeroes and ones zipping around through cyberspace. A *trillion* dollars a day now ricochet around the word by computer. A *trillion* – can you get your mind around that?' (1996: 302; emphasis in original). In Stephen Rhodes' aptly titled *The Velocity of Money*, the processing systems that transmit financial data around the planet are often more vividly and elaborately portrayed than the stock, one-dimensional characters who operate them, as in an ostentatiously technical four-page sequence recounting the light-speed 'binary discourse' conducted between a laptop, a geostationary satellite and supercomputers at the New York Stock Exchange and ten other sites across the United States (1999: 59–62). During the market collapse described in James Harland's *The Month of the Leopard*, it seems wholly futile for any one of the anonymous traders, stationed in massed ranks at identical computer terminals, to attempt to intervene in a crisis that gives every impression of possessing an impersonal logic of its own:

> Sweat [dripped] off the traders. The markets were plunging all around them, and they no longer had any idea whether they should be buying or selling. A stillness descended upon the office. . . . The men had lost all sense of direction, and were so confused some of them were refusing to trade. The financial equivalent of shell shock. (Harland 2002: 304)

Despite these gestures towards the capacity of financial systems to exclude human agency, however, the prevailing narrative momentum of these texts derives, as I have suggested, from active, strategic attempts on the part of individual investors to engineer catastrophic falls in asset prices. More specifically, financial thrillers tend to imagine the propulsion of markets to the brink of disaster as an alternative means of pursuing the strategic objectives of mid- to late twentieth-century geopolitics. As Marsh notes, such novels frequently depict rogue traders who persist 'with outdated twentieth-century ideological conflicts in attempting to use capitalism to destroy capitalism' (2007: 111). In David Schofield's *The Pegasus Forum*, for example, an insane Oxford economist plots to devastate the economy of Japan as revenge for the torture that he believes was inflicted on his mother in a Japanese prison camp during the Second World War. As the plan is put into action, the narrator describes the situation:

> The Japanese economic miracle, built from scratch after the American occupation, and the devastation of a ferocious war, had been levelled again. But this time it was an economic Hiroshima, in many respects a much more profoundly destructive explosion that its forebear, and one from which the fall-out would continue to settle for many years to come. . . . Not only had it destroyed the actual value of . . . institutions, it had destroyed the *belief* of the rest of the world in them. And that belief could not be reconstructed with bricks and mortar. (2001: 414; emphasis in original)

The ability to undermine investor confidence in this way is identified as 'the nuclear warhead in the financial warrior's arsenal' and the resulting crisis is likened to a 'mushrooming cloud' (2001: 25, 393). Stephen Rhodes and Martin Baker similarly figure the market positions adopted by their villains as if they were nuclear strikes targeted on enemy territory, describing the ensuing scenarios as 'a nuclear winter' (Rhodes 1999: 71, 486) and 'full-blown tactical nuclear warfare' (Baker 2008: 176). Rhodes even has an exasperated character complain about the ubiquity of this vocabulary: 'arrrgh. The old nuclear . . . analogy again' (1999: 312).

The narrative of James Harland's *The Month of the Leopard*, meanwhile, revolves around the discovery of secret bank accounts controlled by the Red Army before the fall of the Soviet Union. Together, the accounts constitute 'the greatest hidden fortune of the twentieth century. All the money that was looted from Europe after the war, all the German, Polish and Czech money, all the Tsar's money, all the money made from the labour camps, and all the gold and oil in Russia for seventy years' (2002: 318). This hoard, a kind of Pharaoh's tomb holding the appropriated plunder of the 'long war' of the twentieth century, is to be used to speculate against the economies of Eastern Europe so as to preserve what the villain describes as 'the Red Army's greatest achievement'. He explains:

> The capture of Eastern Europe and its absorption into the Russian Empire by the Red Army was, I suppose, the finest military achievement of the twentieth century. . . . The covenant was that all the money the Army had acquired over the century would be used to destroy Eastern Europe. . . . That is what this is all about. It is time for the money to be put to the use for which it was intended. (2002: 325)

Interestingly, the campaign by a plucky band of City professionals to prop up the markets and thereby foil this plot utilizes programme trading technology (2002: 298–301). Just like the dastardly plot to crash the markets itself, however, the dramatic impact on prices of this strategy is a consequence of the active intervention of a lone individual, who tinkers with the trading software so that it will do his bidding, rather than, as has typically been the case in reality, an effect of impersonal, systemic factors working themselves out at least semi-autonomously from human involvement.[6]

The financial thriller is primarily a novelistic sub-genre, but the formula established by texts like Schofield's and Harland's has recently made the transition to television. An episode of the popular BBC spy series *Spooks*, entitled 'On the Brink', which was broadcast in 2008, portrays a Czech Communist true believer posing as a financier to engineer a catastrophic collapse of the British economy as retribution for the West's ruthless post-Cold War imposition of free market capitalism on the vulnerable societies of Eastern Europe.

In these narratives, then, the predominant threat to global socio-economic stability in the contemporary moment – the financial crash – is presented as a revival of the military antagonisms of an earlier era. As Nicky Marsh suggests, one function of this strategy is to serve as a warning that the great ideological struggles of the twentieth century have not been safely consigned to history, but instead threaten to erupt again in the present (2007: 111). Another function, it would seem, is to lend familiar, emotive and readily intelligible form to a phenomenon that is otherwise too diffuse, anonymous, complex and abstract to be a viable subject for genre fiction. In 1984, Fredric Jameson drew attention to 'a whole mode of contemporary entertainment literature, which one is tempted to characterize as "high-tech paranoia" '. In these texts,

> the circuits and networks of some putative global computer hook-up are narratively mobilized by labyrinthine conspiracies of autonomous but deadly interlocking and competing information agencies in a complexity often beyond the capacity of the normal reading mind. Yet conspiracy theory (and its various garish narrative manifestations) must be seen as a degraded attempt – through the figuration of advanced technology – to think the impossible totality of the contemporary world system. (1984: 80)

While Jameson is willing to grant that these espionage narratives offer some, albeit oblique, insight into what he calls 'the whole new decentred global network of the third stage of capital itself' (1984: 80), the financial thrillers I have discussed, which ostensibly

take this global network as their primary object, in fact merely
re-inscribe it within the frame of geopolitical intrigue familiar
from that same older tradition of spy or conspiracy fiction. The
effect of the financial thriller is thus thoroughly mystificatory: in
these texts, there is no suggestion that massive financial crises are
endemic to the economic and technological organization of neoliberal capitalism; instead, they are reassuringly attributed to small,
marginal cabals of conspirators, who actively work to incite chaos
on the markets in the pursuit of anachronistic political objectives
and/or personal enrichment. Indeed, in a remarkable ideological
sleight of hand, *The Month of the Leopard* and the *Spooks* episode
'On the Brink' assign responsibility for these crises of capitalism
to embittered Communists, as if Communism's sins, well docu-
mented in these narratives, were not sufficient, and it must also
serve as the scapegoat for capitalism's structural failures. These
texts thus reflect the belief, widely held in and beyond the former
Communist nations of Eastern Europe, that, as Slavoj Žižek puts
it, 'we are not really in capitalism: we do not yet have true democracy but only its deceiving mask, the same dark forces still pull the
threads of power, a narrow sect of former Communists disguised as
new owners and managers – nothing's really changed, so we need
another purge, the revolution has to be repeated' (2009: para. 8).
As Virilio argues, however, democracy is most imperilled today
not by the danger that a shadowy band of would-be demagogues
(of whatever ideological persuasion) might attempt to arbitrarily
impose their will on the unsuspecting masses, but rather by the
emergence of technological systems from which the very possibility of the assertion of human will is excluded: 'In contemporary
societies decisions are made within incredibly short time limits. . . .
So today the question of democracy is not that it is threatened by
some tyrant but by the tyranny of technique.' Characteristically,
the 'exemplification' of this phenomenon is found in the financial
markets: 'What exactly is the automation of the quotations on Wall
Street? The installation of an automatic quotation system that functions without human assistance and in real time poses the problem
of decisions no longer being shared, since it is the machine that
decides' (2001c: 93).

Such a view of the financial markets has not been, and argu-

Image 9.1: Still from Aernout Mik, Middlemen, 2001, *video installation (carlier | gebauer).*

ably could not be, captured adequately in fictional narrative, whether narrowly generic or otherwise, because it is antithetical to the concern with human perception, motivation, deliberation and action that orientates and propels the plots of all but the most experimental fictional texts. Tellingly, one of the few contemporary works to do justice to the inhuman, machinic dynamics of the financial system is not only non-literary, but dispenses with narrative grammar almost entirely, even as it features recognizable human figures arrayed in space and time. *Middlemen*, a video installation by the Dutch artist Aernout Mik, appears to depict a stock exchange trading floor in the aftermath of a devastating crash.

The piece, which was included alongside footage of nuclear

explosions and other scenes of technological catastrophe in the
'Unknown Quantity' exhibition curated by Virilio in Paris in
2003, lacks any discernible plot development or significant events
(save the disaster that has, presumably, just occurred), presenting,
instead, traders immobilized in shock and confusion amidst a sea
of discarded computer print-outs and crumpled newspapers. The
effect of the video is well described in the catalogue for a more
recent exhibition, in which it also featured:

> Through the lens of the camera we get hold of a moment of shock and
> observe the spontaneous, uncontrolled reactions of individuals. The
> actors are stock brokers, middlemen, secretaries, but also furniture,
> computers, telephones, as the boundaries between subject and object,
> between human and thing seem suspended. . ... With these pictures
> Mik does not convey a view of human beings shaping actively the
> world – instead they seem to have become the objects of a process out
> of their control. ('Art, Price and Value', 2008)

Orbitalization and deterrence

The vision of dazed passivity in the face of financial disaster
offered by *Middlemen* is taken to an extreme in the writings of
Jean Baudrillard. Like Virilio, Baudrillard makes direct associations
between contemporary financial crises and twentieth-century
warfare. If the popular genre narratives I have discussed employ
these associations in order to unduly personalize and thereby
domesticate financial crashes, however, presenting them as the
wilfully malevolent acts of small groups of identifiable agents,
Baudrillard uses them in an alternative, but no less problematic,
manner, asserting the utter impersonality of the crash, its complete disconnection from the realm of human action, agency and
experience. In an article written in response to the Black Monday
stock market downturn of October 1987, Baudrillard argues that
crises of finance capital exist in the same virtual sphere as the
perpetually deferred threat of nuclear war: they are 'orbitalized',
cast adrift from the gravitational pull of the real economy or real

war, on which they can have no tangible impact. As Baudrillard puts it:

> Total, virtual war in orbit and multiple real wars on the ground . . . have neither the same dimensions nor the same rules, just as the virtual economy and the real economy do not have the same dimensions or the same rules. . . . There was, admittedly, a crisis in 1929, and an explosion at Hiroshima, and hence there was a moment when these two worlds explosively contaminated one another . . . but we should not be misled by this as to what was to follow. . . . What came after was quite different: it was the hyper-realization of big finance capital, the hyper-realization of overkill capacity, both orbitalized above our heads on a course quite beyond our grasp, and a course which is, fortunately, also beyond the grasp of reality itself. Hyper-realized war and hyper-realized money circulate in an inaccessible space, but in doing so they leave the world just as it is. In the end, the economies continue to produce, whereas the tiniest logical consequence of the fluctuations in the fictional economy would long ago have sufficed to wipe them out. . . . The world continues to exist, even though one thousandth of the available nuclear power would have been enough to annihilate it. (2002a: 23)[7]

Here, Baudrillard suggests that, because financial markets and nuclear weapons systems are pervaded by inhuman processes, their effects must be similarly remote from the everyday, human sphere. It is true that the impact of Black Monday was surprisingly contained, but as Baudrillard tacitly acknowledges through a reference to the Wall Street Crash of 1929, such an outcome can by no means be assured. The widespread impact of the credit crunch since 2007 would certainly give the lie to any notion of an absolute separation between the financial sector and the 'real economy' of labour and commodities. As Arthur and Marilouise Kroker remark with regard to Baudrillard's vision of a financial realm that 'long ago blasted off from material reality', 'when the meltdown suddenly happens, when that immense weight of over-indebtedness . . . plunge[s] back into the gravitational weight of real politics and real economy, we finally know what it is to live within trajectories of the catastrophic' (2008: para. 6). Similarly, nuclear war, in its actuality, may be receding towards the horizon of living memory, and its likelihood, on a mass scale at least, may have grown still more remote since Baudrillard wrote these words at the beginning of 1988, but it is complacent, at best, to assume that such events will never re-enter the atmosphere of reality.

As we have seen, Virilio identifies both nuclear weapons and a volatile financial system as very real threats to the ways of life of people around the globe. More than this, however, he argues that the architects of the information society and the virtual economy must learn the lesson of the nuclear age and act to put institutions, regulations and conventions in place that will curb the likelihood of the information bomb's catastrophic explosion:

> One may surmise that, just as the emergence of the atomic bomb made very quickly the elaboration of a policy of military dissuasion impera-tive in order to avoid a nuclear catastrophe, the information bomb will also need a new form of dissuasion adapted to the 21st century. This shall be a societal form of dissuasion to counter the damage caused by the explosion of unlimited information. (1995: para. 14)

Elsewhere, Virilio writes that the information bomb 'will very soon require the establishment of a new type of *deterrence* – in this case, a *societal* one, with "automatic circuit-breakers" put in place capable of avoiding the over-heating, if not indeed the fission, of the social cores of nations' (2000b: 108; emphasis in original). The reference here is to the 'circuit-breaker' or 'trading curb' systems imposed at the New York Stock Exchange and elsewhere in the wake of the 1987 crash, which automatically suspend trading during periods of extreme price volatility (see Virilio 2000b: 129). Circuit-breakers appear to have been only partially effective, though, and in 2007 the NYSE scaled back its system, abandoning provisions targeted specifically at programme trading.

In the wake of the 'credit crunch', however, the need for more far-reaching reform of the financial system has become starkly apparent. Speaking in October 2008, Virilio remarked that the ongoing crisis in credit markets 'incorporates the representation of all other accidents'. He pointed, in particular, to two post-Hiroshima moments when, to quote Baudrillard, the 'two worlds' of the nuclear and the human 'explosively contaminated one another':

> In 1979, at the time of the mishap at the Three Mile Island nuclear plant in the US, I did mention the occurrence of an 'original accident' – the kind of accident we bring forth ourselves. I said that our technical prowess was pregnant of catastrophic promises. In the past, accidents were local affairs. With Chernobyl, we have entered the era of global accidents, whose consequences are in the realm of the long term. The current crash represents the perfect 'integral accident'. (2008: paras 3–4)[8]

For Virilio, just as market crashes are not simply abstract, immaterial, ineffable phenomena, but causes of acutely felt hardship and dispossession, nuclear devastation is not – as it is for Baudrillard and many other contemporary commentators who apply nuclear rhetoric to financial crises – a sublime, cosmic, apocalyptic prospect, but – whether through industrial disaster or military testing – an all-too-real, terrestrial source of death and despoliation. The merger of nuclear catastrophe and financial upheaval in the discourse of the sublime is a profoundly conservative move because it serves to render invisible the untold victims – the oblivious 'downwinders', the duped 'sub-prime' mortgage-holders – for whom the results of nuclear contamination or market collapse could not be more palpable.

Alert to these material consequences, in the interview quoted above Virilio reasserts the idea that the architects of the financial system must take steps to limit the economic dangers they have brought into being, just as, since 1945, policy makers, scientists and engineers have been required to devise means of containing the destructive potential of atomic energy:

> For thirty years now, the phenomenon of History accelerating has been negated, together with the fact that this acceleration has been the prime cause of the proliferation of major accidents. . ... These accidents are not contingent occurrences. For the time being, the prevalent opinion is that researching the crash of the stock exchange as a political and economic issue and in terms of its social consequences is adequate

enough. But it is impossible to understand what is going on if one does not implement a policy based on the political economy of speed, the speed that technological progress engenders, and if one does not link this policy to the 'accidental' character of History. (2008: para. 5)

The mainstream response to the crisis – from politicians, appointed officials, financial professionals and economists – has included proposals to relate executive compensation more closely to companies' long-term performance; to restrict the leverage that financial institutions are permitted to assume; to reinstate divisions between commercial and investment banks; to regulate credit derivatives and ensure that they are traded on public exchanges rather than through private, 'over-the-counter' deals; and to break up institutions that have grown 'too large to fail' into smaller entities. As Virilio suggests, however, these proposals tend to treat market technologies as if they were the mere neutral means by which financial practices are enacted, rather than modes of mediation that actively shape how markets operate, and amplify their risks. One possible, and renewedly influential, measure that does take account of the 'political economy of speed' is a levy on financial transactions (usually dubbed a 'Tobin Tax' after the American economist James Tobin who first proposed it in the early 1970s), which would act as a 'brake' on the speculative behaviour and volatility encouraged by the capacity to send and execute orders instantaneously.

Other potential reforms proceed from the basis that, since advanced information and communications technologies have pushed the speed, volume and complexity of financial transactions beyond the threshold of adequate human oversight and regulation, the full resources of these same technologies must be utilized if zones of instability in the system are to be identified. Daniel Altman characterizes the views of the leading proponent of this school of thought, Andrew Lo of the Massachusetts Institute of Technology, in terms that resonate with the cosmological language employed by Baudrillard:

[Lo] sees the global financial system as the universe, where each financial center is a galaxy: a collection of stars, planets and other celestial objects held close to each other by their own gravity – in this case, the trades and contracts that tie them together. If you could chart the entire universe and measure all the forces connecting every object inside it, you would have what economists and other scientists call a network map. To Lo, fully understanding what's going on in the markets requires the entire map – . . . every major transaction that connects one entity to another, reported daily. (Altman 2009: para. 12)

The scrutiny of these 'maps' would be the joint responsibility of 'computers and human supervisors' (Altman 2009: para. 11). The ideas of Lo and others constitute genuine attempts to think through the 'the speed that technological progress engenders', but they remain open to the charge, repeatedly asserted by Virilio, that the response to the acceleration of technics beyond human limits is too often the surrender of yet more autonomy to machines, rather than a willingness to contemplate curbing or rerouting technological systems in ways that bring them back within the scope of human deliberation. Moreover, such mapping projects, which claim to offer 'stunningly new ways of collecting data about the global financial firmament, using all-seeing, all-knowing monitoring systems' (Altman 2009, para. 7), seem to hark back to a Cold War-era dream of anticipating and foreclosing all threats to the stability of the nation. In the 1980s, Virilio identified this impulse in the US military's 'Strategic Defense Initiative' (a.k.a. 'Star Wars'), characterizing it as the will 'to see all, to know all, at every moment, everywhere, the will to universalized illumination: a scientific permutation on the eye of God which would forever rule out the surprise, the accident, the irruption of the unforeseen' (1994: 70). As Virilio's work makes clear, however, no model of market surveillance, no matter how sophisticated, could contain a potential for crisis that is inscribed into the very fabric of the global financial system, just as a network of defence installations extending even into the heavens would not have guaranteed protection from nuclear attack. What we can be sure of, though, is that when the next crisis explodes across the world's markets, it will be bathed once more, in our imaginations at least, in the unearthly light of a nuclear flash.

196

Paul Crosthwaite

Notes

I am grateful to John Armitage, John Beck and members of the audience at the After the War: Post-War Structures of Feeling conference hosted by the Institute of English Studies, University of London in May 2009 for their invaluable comments on earlier versions of this essay. I also wish to thank Philipp Selzer of the carlier | gebauer gallery, Berlin for permission to reproduce a still from Aernout Mik's *Middlemen*.

1. For a detailed account and analysis of the role of portfolio insurance in the crash, see MacKenzie 2006: ch. 7. A highly readable, accessible treatment of similar material is Fox 2009: ch. 13.
2. Virilio quotes Buffett's remark in 2007: 108, n. 16.
3. Virilio also aligns programme trading with nuclear technology in 1999: 93 and 2001a: 172–3, and reflects more generally on the dangers posed by this element of the financial markets in 1998: 20–1; 2000a: 78; 2001b: 114; 2001c: 93; 2007: 10; and 2010: 153.
4. For a sustained analysis of *Cosmopolis* from the perspective of Virilio's social theory, see Crosthwaite, 2008.
5. For a comprehensive treatment of the financial thriller phenomenon, see Marsh, 2007: ch. 4. I approach financial thrillers from a different, psychoanalytic perspective in Crosthwaite, 2010.
6. A possible exception would be the events of 16 September 1992 ('Black Wednesday'), when a single investor, the Hungarian-American hedge fund manager George Soros, played an instrumental role in driving down the value of sterling, leading to the humiliating withdrawal of the pound from the European Exchange Rate Mechanism. Soros, dubbed 'the man who broke the Bank of England', is evidently, as Nicky Marsh notes, a model for the villains of several financial thrillers (Marsh 2007: 97–8). Even in this case, however, it is clear that Soros did not engineer the crisis, but rather simply had the skill, timing, resources and luck to capitalize on prevailing, systemic forces.
7. Baudrillard draws similar connections between financial and nuclear systems in 1983: 60 and 2002b: 135–6.
8. Arthur and Marilouise Kroker consider the status of the credit crisis as a Virilian 'global accident' in 2008: paras. 6–9.

References

Altman, D. (2009) 'The Network: How a Map Can Prevent the Next Financial Crisis', *New Republic*, 9 Oct. [www.tnr.com/article/economy/the-network?page=0,1].

'Art, Price and Value: Contemporary Art and the Market' (2008), Centre for Contemporary Culture Strozzina, Florence, Italy [www.strozzina.org/artpriceandvalue/index.html].

Baker, M. (2008) *Meltdown*. London: Macmillan.

Baudrillard, J. (1983) *Simulations*. New York: Semiotext(e).

— (2002a [1988]) 'In Praise of a Virtual Crash', in *Screened Out*. London: Verso.

— (2002b [1996]) 'World Debt and Parallel Universe', in *Screened Out*. London: Verso.

Bishop, R. and G. Clancey (2004) 'The City-as-Target, or Perpetuation and Death', in *Cities, War and Terrorism: Towards an Urban Geopolitics*, ed. S. Graham. Oxford: Blackwell.

Blustein, P. (2001) *The Chastening: Inside the Crisis That Rocked the Global Financial System*. New York: Public Affairs.

Buffett, W.E. (2003) *Berkshire Hathaway, Inc. 2002 Letter to Shareholders* [www.berkshirehathaway.com/letters/2002pdf.pdf].

Crosthwaite, P. (2008) 'Fiction in the Age of the Global Accident: Don DeLillo's *Cosmopolis*', *Static: Journal of the London Consortium*, 7 [http://static.londonconsortium.com/issue07/static07_crosthwaite.php].

— (2010) 'Blood on the Trading Floor: Waste, Sacrifice and Death in Financial Crises', *Angelaki: Journal of the Theoretical Humanities*, 15, 2: 3–18.

DeLillo, D. (2003) *Cosmopolis*. New York: Scribner.

Derrida, J. (1984) 'No Apocalypse, Not Now (full speed ahead, seven missiles, seven missives)', *Diacritics*, 14, 2: 20–32.

Faulks, S. (2009) *A Week in December*. London: Hutchinson.

Finder, J. (1996) *The Zero Hour*. London: Orion.

Fox, J. (2009) *The Myth of the Rational Market: A History of Risk, Reward and Delusion on Wall Street*. New York: HarperCollins.

Harland, J. (2002 [2001]) *The Month of the Leopard*. London: Simon and Schuster.

Jameson, F. (1984) 'Postmodernism, or, The Cultural Logic of Late Capitalism', *New Left Review*, 146: 53–92.

Kroker, A. and M. Kroker (2008) 'City of Transformation: Paul Virilio in Obama's America', *CTheory* [www.ctheory.net/articles. aspx?id=597].

MacKenzie, D. (2006) *An Engine, Not a Camera: How Financial Models Shape Markets*. Cambridge, MA: MIT Press.

Marsh, N. (2007) *Money, Speculation and Finance in Contemporary British Fiction*. London: Continuum.

Mik, A. (2001) *Middlemen*. Screen and moving-image loop (colour, silent). carlier | gebauer gallery, Berlin.

— 'On the Brink' (2008) *Spooks*, dir. E. Hall. Series 7, episode 5. BBC Three, 10 Nov.

Rhodes, S. (1999 [1997]) *The Velocity of Money*. London: Macmillan.

Schofield, D. (2001) *The Pegasus Forum*. London: Simon and Schuster.

Virilio, P. (1994 [1988]) *The Vision Machine*. London: BFI.

— (1995) 'Speed and Information: Cyberspace Alarm!', *CTheory* [www. ctheory.net/articles.aspx?id=72].

— (1998) 'Is the Author Dead?' (interview with J. Der Derian), in *The Virilio Reader*, ed. J. Der Derian. Oxford: Blackwell.

— (1999 [1996]) *Politics of the Very Worst* (interview with P. Petit). New York: Semiotext(e).

— (2000a [1990]) *Polar Inertia*. London: Sage.

— (2000b [1998]) *The Information Bomb*. London: Verso.

— (2000c) 'From Modernism to Hypermodernism and Beyond' (interview with J. Armitage), in *Paul Virilio: From Modernism to Hypermodernism and Beyond*, ed. J. Armitage. London: Sage.

— (2001a) 'The Kosovo W@r Did Take Place' (interview with J. Armitage), in *Virilio Live: Selected Interviews*, ed. J. Armitage. London: Sage.

— (2001b) Interview with J. Sans, in *Virilio Live: Selected Interviews*, ed. J. Armitage. London: Sage.

— (2001c) 'Perception, Politics and the Intellectual' (interview with N. Brügger), in *Virilio Live: Selected Interviews*, ed. J. Armitage. London: Sage.

— (2007 [2005]) *The Original Accident*. Cambridge: Polity.

— (2008) Interview with G. Courtois and M. Guerrin, *Le Monde*, 18 Oct. [www.lemonde.fr/opinions/article/2008/10/18/le-krachactuel-represente-l-accident-integral-par-excellence_1108473_3232. html]; English translation: [http://sites.google.com/site/radical perspectivesonthecrisis/news/paul-virilio-on-the-crisis].

— (2010 [2007]) *The University of Disaster*. Cambridge: Polity.

Wark, M. (1994) *Virtual Geography: Living with Global Media Events*. Bloomington: Indiana University Press.

Žižek, S. (2009) '20 Years of Collapse' *New York Times*, 9 Nov. [www. nytimes.com/2009/11/09/opinion/09zizek.html?pagewanted=1&_ r=3].

10

Virilio and Visual Culture: On the American Apocalyptic Sublime

Joy Garnett and John Armitage

Introduction

Paul Virilio, philosopher and cultural theorist, has long been engaged with questions of art, history and visual culture. A child of 1930s Paris, Virilio, remarkably, remains at the fore-front of French thought concerning contemporary conceptions of visuality and cultural studies. Yet, as is well known, Virilio's theoretical preoccupations are associated with ideas involving the visual culture of art and its histories as forms of knowledge that reveal themselves as pictorial representations. Drawing on the work of existential or phenomenological philosophers and artists as diverse as Albert Camus and Maurice Merleau-Ponty, Edmund Husserl, Maurice Blanchot and Guillaume Apollinaire, Virilio's influential theorization of visual culture nevertheless shares little in common with other vitally important French theorists of art, perception, and seeing in the present period, such as Roland Barthes and Jean Baudrillard, Jacques Derrida, Michel Foucault and Jean-François Lyotard. Focusing on the development of art and politics over the twentieth century, artists and their materials, Virilio's main work on visual culture in the twenty-first century is, arguably, his important text entitled *Art as Far as the Eye Can See* (2007).[1]

Rather than offer an extended theoretical narrative that explores Virilio's conceptual engagement with the entirety of contemporary visual culture, in the first section of this chapter we shall introduce and consider the main thrust of his endeavour to enhance the theoretical understanding of visual culture by way of a discussion of his *Art as Far as the Eye Can See*, a text that grapples with, amongst a myriad of other topics, new media's revolutionary impact upon art of the current era and its materials, information and communications technologies such as the Internet and the transformation of twenty-first century societies into societies predicated on the politics of speed.

Having briefly outlined Virilio's theoretical relationship to contemporary visual culture and his attempt to augment our knowledge of art's association with perception in the first section, in the second section, we critique Virilio's (2007: 2–3) supposition in *Art as Far as the Eye Can See* that real time absolutely outstrips the real space of important visual artworks. In addition, we do so with a view to enriching his and our own appreciation of art and looking under present-day conditions through a discussion of what we understand as a central yet absent theme regarding Virilio's comprehension of visual culture, namely, the absence of the vital concept of what we call the 'apocalyptic sublime', a 'Virilian'-like condition that 'may occur wherever there is a sharp discontinuity between what is expected and what is perceived' (Garnett and Armitage 2011: 59–78). Moreover, we suggest that a remarkable and significant added difficulty with Virilio's writings on visual culture today is a surprising lack of engagement with contemporary painters and especially painters of the apocalyptic sublime, as evidenced by their continued absence in both his own *Unknown Quantity* (2003b) exhibition and his and the French photojournalist and documentary filmmaker Raymond Depardon's *Native Land: Stop-Eject* joint exhibition at the *Fondation Cartier pour l'art contemporain* (Virilio and Depardon 2008).

What we are proposing, then, is that our conception of the apocalyptic sublime should be central to those current and as yet hypothetical theoretical perspectives in Virilio studies that are primarily involved with contemporary visual culture. To this end, in the third and final substantial section of this chapter, we offer a contribution to the embryonic sub-discipline of Virilian visual cultural studies by means of a discussion of three American painters whose work is especially concerned with what we label the 'American apocalyptic sublime'. We shall establish the parameters of this discussion by first focusing on a significant painting, *Untitled* (1983), by the late Canadian performance artist and filmmaker Jack Goldstein (1945–2003). Goldstein's important studies in the visual arts emerged from conceptualism and were, for example, included in Douglas Crimp's influential 'Pictures' exhibition at Artists Space in New York City in 1977 (Crimp 1979; Eklund 2009). Predominantly an appropriation artist, Goldstein is known for his use of found photographs, contemporary advertisements, television and other media-derived cultural materials to produce his striking images. Interrogating, dismantling and remediating such images, Goldstein's appropriated artworks appeared in various media that included film and photo-montage prior to his suicide (Isles 2003). It is, however, Goldstein's *Untitled* that we foreground below, first and foremost because of its significance regarding the affiliation between present-day visual art and vernacular or corporate-driven media narratives. Above all, Goldstein's painting resonates with our own idea of the American apocalyptic sublime. Goldstein's *Untitled* also forms the backdrop against which we will contemplate two other paintings, *Super Terrestrial* (2010) by Sarah Trigg (1973–) and *Tomorrow's Forecast: Strikingly Clear* (2008) by Marc Handelman (1975–). Both American painters of the apocalyptic sublime and working in New York City, Trigg is increasingly known for her abstract paintings and visual language developed from her own photographic research conducted over the course of several years whilst Handelman is recognized for his large-scale paintings, landscapes and abstract images that reflect important conceptual developments that have occurred in painting since Goldstein's death, specifically artistic strategies of media intervention, remediation and pictorial détournement. Goldstein, Trigg and Handelman are then painters for the twenty-first century whose works exhibit the American apocalyptic sublime and, as we shall demonstrate, cause difficulties for Virilio's declaration that real time has overtaken the real space of contemporary visual artworks.

We conclude with a critical evaluation of Virilio's and our own theoretical work on visual culture and an assessment of their likely impact on current theoretical perspectives in Virilio studies related to the contemporary visual culture of the American apocalyptic sublime. But let us begin with an introductory consideration of Virilio's theoretical understanding of visual culture in *Art as Far as the Eye Can See*.

Virilio and visual culture: *Art as Far as the Eye Can See*

Although clearly not one of the first philosophers or cultural theorists to use the concept of visual culture (see, for instance, the work of the art historian Michael Baxandall (1988) or, more recently, Nicholas Mirzoeff (2009)), Virilio has, nonetheless, been concerned with issues of art and its histories for many years. For Virilio, of course, as for many other French thinkers involved with contemporary ideas of visuality and cultural studies, the theoretical notion of visual culture, and especially in relation to art history, refers to the interrelated structures of knowledge and symbolic representation that have arisen since the Renaissance. More interested in the philosophy of art than in the sociology of art, Virilio's existential or phenomenologically derived perspective neverthe-less recognizes that not merely aesthetic but also socio-cultural factors mould new theoretical and visual abilities as well as those current methods entailing calculation and organization used in the visual arts such as the conventions of linear perspective. Still, Virilio's conception of visual culture is completely different from that of other significant French philosophers of art, perception and looking in the present-day, like Barthes (1992) and Baudrillard (2005), Derrida (1987), Foucault (2000) and Lyotard (1993). This is because Virilio's idea of visual culture has less to do with its use in advanced western societies per se and more to do with, first, its use in contemporary Western art and politics from the twentieth century onwards, and, secondly, its use in relation to artists and their materials. In its suggested and far-reaching inclusiveness of objects of study stretching a long way beyond the scope of things typically incorporated within the conventional categories of art history, Virilio's contemporary view of visual culture involves an essentially reworked twenty-first century explanation of the conceptions and techniques required to appreciate today's Western art, the place of politics, the twenty-first century behaviour of artists and the nature of their materials within the contemporary art world.

Virilio's theorization of visual culture is thus the designation for a new multifaceted conceptual engagement or field, a kind of speculative understanding or investigative synthesis centred on the examination of contemporary Western artworks. His account of contemporary visual culture and its goals are clearly evident in his *Art as Far as the Eye Can See*: anything but self-effacing or restrained, this is an uncompromising text that aims, in effect, to politicize contemporary art to its limits. At the same time, *Art as Far as the Eye Can See* is also a challenge to the subject of art history since, for Virilio, whilst art 'used to be an engagement between artist and materials', today, 'in our new media world, art has changed; its very materials have changed and have become technologized' (Virilio 2007: frontispiece). Given its radical form, Virilio's approach to visual culture brings together and considers these changes. Yet this transformation is for Virilio a sign of a wider socio-cultural and economic move towards 'chrono' or speed politics and what he describes as the crucial feature of the twenty-first century: the shift to an accelerated mass culture. From Virilio's perspective, contemporary students of visual culture should categorize and scrutinize those characteristics of mass culture that have been neglected by traditional art history, such as contemporary forms of panic. These traits of mass culture comprise films that provoke panic and television programmes that depend on panoptic or mediatized and technologized methods of seeing like *Big Brother*. Virilio's historical yet transformative concept of visual culture can therefore be appreciated not only as a new theoretical domain relating to the socio-cultural, economic and institutional investigation of present-day Western art but also to the cultural politics of that primary victim of induced panic and the new, panoptic technologies which, for Virilio, is the human reaction. Virilio's conception of visual culture thus develops out of an approach to film and cultural studies in particular that focuses on what 'we are losing' from 'the very human "art of seeing"', which is humanity's increasing inability to connect with itself or even with political and artistic events (Virilio 2007: frontispiece). In this uncompromising form, Virilio's idea of visual culture has started to consider issues that art history tends not to, such as the technologically induced demise of our feeling for the arts, or those it has no interest in bringing into its orbit, like terrorism.

In Virilio's radical description of visual culture, as evidenced, for example, in *Art as Far as the Eye Can See*'s 'Expect the Unexpected' (Virilio 2007: 1–33), he appears to want to confront art history, querying and refusing its established beliefs. In this questioning, it is not so much the technologies of the mass media as 'fear' that 'has become a dominant culture, if not an *art* – an art contemporary with mutually assured destruction' (Virilio 2007: 1–2; original emphasis). Here, the history of 'a mounting extremism' and 'war', 'escalation' and the 'balance of terror between East and West over the twentieth century' turn out to be the inducements for a reconsideration of our basic suppositions regarding notions of aesthetic value, not to mention our perceptions of peace and deterrence that, according to Virilio, are even now excluded from traditional art historical discourse concerning mass media culture (Virilio 2007: 2). Thus Virilio's approach to visual culture does not generally incorporate questions relating to conceptions of individual originality and physical skills, distinctive *objets d'art*, aesthetic styles and conventions recognized as consistent formal and themed objects, or the conviction that western standards in art are the absolute gauge and assurance of discrimination and aesthetic excellence. 'In fact', says Virilio:

> the postmodern period has seen a gradual shift away from an art once substantial, marked by architecture, music, sculpture, and painting, and towards a purely accidental art that the crisis in international architecture flagged at practically the same time as the crisis in symphonic music.

> This drift away from substantial art has been part and parcel of the
> boom in film and radio and, in particular, television, the medium that
> has ended up finally flattening all forms of representation, thanks to its
> abrupt use of presentation, whereby real time definitely outclasses the
> real space of major artworks, whether of literature or the visual arts.
> (Virilio 2007: 2–3)

Beyond film and radio, television and, naturally, the contemporary
art and insubstantial digital aesthetic imagery of the Internet, its
technological forms and networked systems, Virilio's bold reading
of visual culture in *Art as Far as the Eye Can See* aspires to redescribe the entire field of visuality under globalized socio-cultural
and economic conditions. However, his is not simply a discussion
of television's destruction of representation and sudden use of
presentation but also a deliberation on real time or the 'idée fixe
of the twentieth century', the 'acceleration of reality and not just
of history', together with the nature and significance of chronopolitics and the 'turbocapitalism of the Single Market', mass culture,
'ubiquitous media', and 'the power to move the enthralled hordes'
by way of this mass culture's stunning visuality as well as its characteristic visual, phenomenological, and ideological influence on
people who live in societies where this 'cold panic of which terrorism, in all its forms, is only ever one symptom among others'
(Virilio 2007: 3). Casting aside conventional discussions of, for
instance, advertising and hypertext if not of surveillance, reality
TV and conflict, Virilio's standpoint on visual culture is therefore unconventional in the sense that he approaches it from the
standpoint of fear and fright, from the 'programmed repetition' of
the 'population's disturbing panic attacks' and, perhaps to some,
a somewhat depressive understanding of everyday life (Virilio
2007: 4).

Critics, though, and particularly those from a conservative
intellectual and political position in art history, might doubt that
Virilio's openly socio-political texts will amount to anything other
than bewilderment if art and its histories are to be turned into the
study of 'cold panic', into the analysis of the 'expectation horizon
of collective anguish' where 'we strive to expect the unexpected
in a state of neurosis that saps all intersubjective vitality and leads

to a deadly state of CIVIL DETERRENCE that is the lamentable counterpart to MILITARY DETERRENCE between nations' (Virilio 2007: 4; original emphasis). Yet one window that is opened up by Virilio's contemporary conception of visual culture, we argue, is less one that is concerned with philosophical ideas of artistic worth, aesthetic intentions, or artistic intervention, and more one that is involved with theoretical ideas relating to art's association with a mode of creativity involving portents of widespread devastation and ultimate doom or the awe-inspiring condition we call the apocalyptic sublime.

The apocalyptic sublime

Now that we have summarized Virilio's theoretical associations with contemporary visual culture and his effort to supplement our understanding of art's connection to perception, in this second section, we question Virilio's (2007: 3) hypothesis in *Art as Far as the Eye Can See* that 'real time definitely outclasses the real space of major artworks . . . of the visual arts'. What is more, we do so with an eye to deepening his and our own grasp of art and looking in the present period by means of a deliberation on what we appreciate as a vital yet up to now absent theme concerning Virilio's insights into visual culture, specifically, the absence of the significant theme and concept of the apocalyptic sublime, a Virilian-like condition that, as noted, may occur wherever there is a sharp discontinuity between what is expected and what is perceived. In addition, we propose that a noteworthy and important further problem with Virilio's recent work on visual culture is a startling lack of concern with contemporary painters and particularly painters of the apocalyptic sublime, as shown by their sustained absence in Virilio's *Unknown Quantity* (2003b) exhibition and his and Raymond Depardon's *Native Land: Stop-Eject* joint exhibition (Virilio and Depardon 2008).

Our Virilian-inspired perspective on visual culture thus entails reflecting on art, perception and looking in terms of the apocalyptic sublime, in terms of the sharp discontinuity between what is

expected and what is perceived. Yet the concept of the apocalyptic
sublime is not a grand philosophy or cultural theory but simply a
hypothesis about contemporary visual culture that describes what
may arise in that vacuum between what is expected and what is
perceived. The work of those engaged with art history, we argue,
would benefit from a concern with the apocalyptic sublime, or, put
differently, with metaphysical states of combined awe and horror in
the face of immense natural or supernatural forces. Like Virilio, we
too are involved with questions of art history. But, unlike Virilio's
writings in the present period, we are interested in such issues from
the viewpoint of man-made or human-influenced events where
technology goes terribly awry. To embrace a Virilian theoretical
point of view on the apocalyptic sublime thus entails a contemporary conception of visuality and cultural studies, visual culture and
art history. However, the notion of the apocalyptic sublime also has
to do with a critical perspective on those organized configurations
of knowledge and pictorial representation that are surfacing today
within the advanced societies. Equally engrossed by the influence
of philosophy and photography on contemporary art as well as the
impact of the social life of the city on such art, our Virilian outlook
all the same acknowledges that not just the aesthetics of, for
example, landscape painting, but also socio-cultural developments
shape new theoretical and visual skills over and above those painterly techniques involving, for instance, an appreciation of how the
transcendental landscape paintings of the nineteenth and twentieth
centuries are succumbing to the twenty-first century encounter
with the apocalyptic sublime. Less concerned with measurement
and aesthetic ordering conventions than with, say, photography
and film stills, the apocalyptic sublime offers a visual art rooted
in a truly critical perspective on modern-day representations and
depictive media. Consequently, our contemporary idea of visual
culture is somewhat dissimilar to that of Virilio's philosophy of
art, perception and looking. Indeed, our conception of visual
culture is not simply about its application to extant Western art
and cultural politics from the twentieth century and beyond, artists
and their materials. Rather, in its projected radical incorporation
of objects of study continuing significantly beyond the variety of
items habitually included within even Virilio's non-traditional

categories of art history, our contemporary stance on visual culture implies a fundamentally revised twenty-first century account of the models and methods needed to understand art in relation to its own history, to film, and to the space of the politics and aesthetics that is the apocalyptic sublime, the twenty-first century activities of artists, and the character of their materials and use of paint and images pertaining to the destruction of all narrative unity in the realm of contemporary art.

Our Virilian theorization of visual culture is therefore the name for a new sub-discipline, of a kind of Virilian visual cultural studies, a sort of tentative knowledge or analytical synthesis focused on the investigation of contemporary artworks. However, and different from Virilio's explanation of contemporary visual culture and its ambitious objectives as set out in *Art as Far as the Eye Can See*, ours is a modest proposal relating to our idea of the apocalyptic sublime, a proposal that seeks, effectively, to further politicize contemporary art. Simultaneously, and reminiscent of Virilio's *Art as Far as the Eye Can See*, the apocalyptic sublime is also a challenge to the discipline of art history as, for Virilio and for us, whilst art once was a juncture between artist and materials, nowadays, in the era of 'new media in art' (Rush 2005), artists must engage the problem of technologized information as a subject and subtext of painting in particular. Art's actual materials have moved beyond purely optical and existential concerns and have become increasingly enmeshed within the culturally and socially significant implications of mediatized or technologized information. Hence our radical Virilian notion of visual culture draws together and studies this problem of mediatized or technologized information as a subject and subtext of painting. Nevertheless, in contrast to Virilio, this change is for us not only a symbol of a broader socio-cultural and economic turn towards chronopolitics and twenty-first century accelerated mass culture but also an indication of far-reaching political and technoscientific, experimental and perhaps even deadly turns towards as yet undreamt of technoscientific events and a wholly mediated mass culture.

Somewhere beyond Virilio's terminology, therefore, our analysis of visual culture aspires to classify and dissect those traits of contemporary mass culture that have been deserted by both conventional art history and Virilio, for instance extant varieties of enactment, observation and extreme experimentation with fleeting and precipitous landscapes. These features of mass culture include significant paintings and an aesthetics of the extreme that evoke the very real prospect of total annihilation and which count on the immense wonder of the physical universe or are intertwined and encapsulated in single photographic images or film clips. Our Virilian historical but original perception of visual culture can as a result be understood as a new conceptual spe-cialism concerned with picturing the enactment of beauty and horror, with contemporary art, with the post-Romantic tradi-tion of landscape painting, and with the cultural politics of the most important producers of the encounter with the apocalyptic sublime, an encounter that engenders new articulations of vision and other technologies of information, that, if not for Virilio, then for us, are the conflicted human responses to a rapidly developing moment. Our Virilian model of visual culture thus grows out of a perspective on painting above all that concentrates not on what humanity is losing from the human art of perception but on the re-absorption of new technologies in terms of the thoughts and predilections of earlier paradigms and media, a field that is flourishing today due to humanity's rising incapacity to relate to itself through new modes of image production and dis-tribution or to the changed political parameters of visual art and cultural production. In this modest guise, our Virilian-inflected appreciation of visual culture has begun to inhabit a territory that neither art history nor Virilio ever actually do, for example the terrain where all contemporary aesthetic media are chang-ing in response to the radical transformation in how we process technologized aesthetic information, or, in the case of Virilio, have no apparent interest in including in his own contemporary concerns, such as painting.

In Virilio's radical version of visual culture, as is made clear, for instance, in *Native Land: Stop-Eject*'s 'Conversation' between Depardon and Virilio (2008: 8–23), Virilio gives the impression of wishing to abandon art history. Discussing instead his well-known long-term work on speed and politics (Virilio 1986), Virilio ques-tions and rejects many of our founding principles concerning the shrinking of the world and temporality, supersonic transport, the acceleration of telecommunications, and the emerging world of instantaneity. In this interrogation, it is neither the electronic mass media nor the prevailing culture of fear or even art contemporary with mutually assured destruction as real time, the pollution of distances, and what Virilio calls 'the natural scale of things' that governs Depardon and Virilio's *Native Land* project (2008: 9). No longer concerned with the history of a rising fanaticism and conflict, intensification, or the balance of terror between East and West during the latter half of the twentieth century, Virilio's present-day inquiries are the stimulus for a reexamination of our key assumptions concerning conceptions of nostalgia and the magnitude of the world, of our awareness of scale and urbanism that, as indicated by Depardon and Virilio (2008: 9), add up not to problems relating to travel, country life, or a world in transit but to the following question: 'What is left of this world, of our native land, of the history of what so far is the only habitable planet?' Accordingly, we feel obliged to pose another question: what remains of Virilio's engagement with ideas of aesthetic appreciation or with conventional art historical discourse pertaining to mass media culture? A Virilian slant on visual culture does not, of course, normally include issues regarding notions of personal creativity and manual abilities, original works of art, artistic styles and practices understood as coherent formal and thematic objects, or the principle that western rules of art continue to be the unquestionable measure and warranty of discernment and artistic worth. Yet, we argue, any Virilian interpretation of the current era must not only face up to the slow movement away from an art formerly substantial but also to the preventative qualities of painting as a substantial art. Certainly, it must come to terms with paintings of calamities and catastrophes, with an art that contends with the crisis not just in the international style of modern architecture, symphonic music, sculpture and the drift towards insubstantial art but also in film, radio and television, as the digitization of all 'optical media' (Kittler 2010) continues to crush every traditional mode of representation. Against Virilio, however, and because of its sharp discontinuity between what is expected and what is perceived, we maintain that the apocalyptic sublime in the form of the real space of important paintings can, if not surpass, then, as a minimum, rupture and arrest for a moment the real time of presentation in the visual arts.

Far beyond the world of the mass media, the contemporary art and digital aesthetics and visuals of the Internet, its technological modes and complex arrangements, our Virilian yet moderate interpretation of visual culture as the apocalyptic sublime seeks to redefine an aspect of visuality with a focus on socio-cultural and economic conditions in the twenty-first century generally and landscape painting in particular. Nonetheless, ours is not a heroic attempt to reflect on the digitization of every aspect of optical media or on the obliteration of all customary forms of representation. More accurately, ours is a Virilian-inspired consideration of the character and meaning of various aesthetic experiments relating to the sharp discontinuity between what is expected and what is perceived, to the apocalyptic sublime. The apocalyptic sublime has less to do with the unexpected speeding up of contemporary presentation and real time, reality, history, politics and the economy, and more to do with the real yet apocalyptic forms and inspirational spaces of significant paintings that, we argue, are able to, if not outclass, then, at least, for a while, shatter and halt the real time of presentation in the contemporary visual arts. Within the context of a twenty-first century mass media culture of diffusion, driven by the emotional condition it incites in its spectators through dazzling visuality, phenomenological and discursive effects on the populace are not those of societies inundated by Virilio's cold panic – contemporary terrorism – but of societies swamped by the socio-cultural shifts triggered by new technological or mediated forms and their related symptoms. Ignoring traditional deliberations on paintings and conceptions of both the apocalypse and the sublime, our Virilian-derived position on visual culture is consequently sublime in that we consider it not from the point of view of terror and fear but from the point of view of representations themselves, of paintings forged in the contemporary city by artists sensitive not just to the future of the metropolis but also to intimations of obliteration, human displacement, paranoia, architectural replacement and alienation.

Resembling Virilio's, then, ours is a radical intellectual and political outlook on art history. Unlike Virilio's perspective, however, our sympathetic critique of his work does not so much mistrust his candidly socio-political texts like *Art as Far as the Eye Can See* as write from a viewpoint that can only be described as that of two slightly disorientated and unofficial art historians. We are, then, less interested in Virilio's analyses of cold panic than we are in contemporary artists' foraging for images online, less in the examination of expectation horizons and communal suffering than in twenty-first century landscape paintings based on photographs found on the Internet. For us, it is not a matter of struggling to anticipate the unforeseen in a condition of psychosis that weakens collective energies and brings about a lethal situation of civil deterrence that is the regrettable complement to military deterrence. Rather, it is an issue of critically considering depictions of various and often contemporaneous global incidents. So one clearing that is opened up by our Virilian view of visual culture, we contend, is less one that is broadly concerned with philosophical conceptions of art's connection with a form of imagination relating to omens of pervasive destruction and eventual disaster or the breathtaking state we call the apocalyptic sublime, and more one that is engaged with the practices over and above conceptions of contemporary art and its correlation with a kind of originality we call the American apocalyptic sublime.

On the American apocalyptic sublime

What we are suggesting therefore is that our idea of the apocalyptic sublime ought to be integral to those as yet hypothetical viewpoints on Virilio's analyses that are first and foremost engaged with contemporary visual culture. Consequently, in this last yet significant part of this chapter, we make a contribution to the nascent sub-field of contemporary Virilian visual cultural studies through various reflections on the American painters Jack Goldstein, Sarah Trigg, and Marc Handelman, whose work is particularly related to the American apocalyptic sublime. The limits of these considerations are determined initially by concentrating on Goldstein's important painting *Untitled* (1983), in the main because of its

significance concerning the relationship between his contemporary American visual art and his conceptual picture-making, the
aesthetic space of New York City, his appropriation art, films,
photo-montages and critical relationship with advertising, TV,
culture, mediated materials and imagery. Goldstein's *Untitled* also
creates the setting for our study of his own visual art and the critique
of the standardized language of business-driven media narratives,
all of which are crucial constituents of what we conceptualize as
the American apocalyptic sublime. Two other paintings, Trigg's
Super Terrestrial (2010) and Handelman's *Tomorrow's Forecast:
Strikingly Clear* (2008), are also considered here. American painters
of the apocalyptic sublime based in New York City, Trigg and
Handelman's very different paintings reveal, in the case of Trigg,
a move towards an almost purely abstract visual language derived
from her own long-term photographic investigations and which
is largely unconcerned with specific events or dates and, in the
example of Handelman, key practical developments that indicate theoretical advances that have transpired in painting since
Goldstein's suicide, in particular Handelman's aesthetic approach
to media intrusion, remediation and pictographic variations on
previous advertisements, where his artworks convey meanings that
are opposed to the original. Goldstein, Trigg and Handelman are
then painters for the present period whose works for us disclose
an American apocalyptic sublime whilst simultaneously producing
obstacles for Virilio's assertion that real time has left behind the real
space of contemporary visual artworks.

Jack Goldstein

Our Virilian-enthused perception of American visual culture
therefore involves thinking about Goldstein's painting, insights
and looking through the vocabulary of the American apocalyptic
sublime, through the visual language of the sharp discontinuity between what is expected in his appropriated photographic
images of natural, scientific and technoscientific events and what
is perceived in phenomena that approach or embody an American
apocalyptic and sublime state. However, the conceptual project

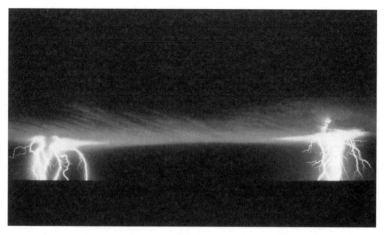

Image 10.1: Untitled, *1983, Acrylic on canvas (Jack Goldstein. From the collection of Mr. and Mrs. Michael Schwartz and The Estate of Jack Goldstein).*

of what we call the American apocalyptic sublime was not for Goldstein an all-inclusive attitude or aesthetic hypothesis but basically an assumption concerning American visual culture bound up with the recording of what he labeled the 'spectacular instant', a premise that explains what might happen within the context of a medium that breaches or overcomes the sentimental and realist norms of photographic narrative. In *Untitled* (Image 10.1), that vacuum between what is expected and what is perceived arrives in the shape of our confrontation with a black ground, reminiscent of the size and shape of a billboard.

The work of those connected with contemporary art history, as we shall demonstrate, can only profit from an involvement with Goldstein's American apocalyptic sublime, or, put another way, with his work on metaphysical, conceptual and aesthetic conditions concerned with the effects, ideas and peculiarities of cinema in particular. Hence, the shape of *Untitled* obviously alludes to the cinematic screen. Yet the painting's evocation of fear and dismay facing dark and huge physical and seemingly paranormal energies is punctuated on either end by two, irregular, dissimilar, and spectacular bundles of lightning, each touching down from the same height, illuminating in green and blue the otherwise static air around them, as well as the underside of the invisible, dark, ledge-like storm above. Similar to Virilio's and our own work here, Goldstein was also preoccupied with issues of art, history and, importantly, what Virilio (2009) calls the 'aesthetics of disappearance'. In *Untitled*, for instance, the bolts of lightning arrive at a non-existent place: there is no land and no horizon line, but simply a horizontal strip of pure black, behind which the blots of glowing light disappear, cut off by what resembles the lower edge of the wide-angle frame on a movie screen. Nonetheless, and distinct from Virilio's contemporary work on art, we want to pay attention here to similar questions to those posed by Goldstein and from the point of view of artificial or human-induced experiences. Consequently, as we engage in the contemplative role of viewers of Goldstein's painting, as expected, we are, it appears, also simultaneously positioned to fulfill the role of spectator or audience member, watching not a lightning storm in progress, captured on film, but a decontextualized and technologized film still, an instant on a screen. What we are seeing is a painting of a movie in which human inflected 'nature' has gone awfully wrong. To adopt a Virilian philosophical approach to Goldstein's American apocalyptic sublime as embodied in his *Untitled* is thus to contemplate Goldstein's contemporary notions regarding the functioning of the black horizontal strip which recalls other proscenium-like visual framing devices that pop up in many of his paintings. Clearly enthusiastically interested in American visual culture and art history, Goldstein's *Untitled* offers us borders of colour or darkness, which, by recalling abstract painting, scuttle the viewer's conventional desire for the 'transparent instant' as normally displayed through photography. Here, Goldstein's American apocalyptic sublime presents a visual analysis of those structured arrangements of knowledge and symbolic imagery that court the contemporary American social desire to buoy up a generations-long emersion in a culture of ever-expanding, naïve proliferation and consumption of photographs both amateur and professional. Just as absorbed by the effect of philosophy and photography on American art in addition to the influence of the communal existence of the American metropolis on his art, Goldstein's almost Virilian attitude and framing device ultimately dispels any doubts that what one is gazing at is indeed a painting, an artful and artificial construct wrought by the hand, despite the pristine, airbrushed, photograph-like rendering of the image depicted within the frame.

The aesthetics of *Untitled*, then, with its smooth, flawless surface reminiscent of other American landscape paintings, refracts and reflects, like them, available light, and calls attention to itself as both a contemporary object and as a representation of Goldstein's attempt at rendering seamless the representation of an event. *Untitled* therefore offers not a display of socio-cultural events but an image-instant as construct. Goldstein's painting is then a painting that is opposed to maintaining the powerful myth of truth that has fashioned old and new philosophies concerned with those visual abilities associated with photography. This is also why, instead of focusing on those contemporary painterly procedures relating to representations of the moment, our attention and awareness, are nothing like the attention and awareness focused on the tran-scendental American landscapes of the nineteenth and twentieth centuries', but are drawn to Goldstein's attempt itself, to the display of the death of narrative through the primacy of the instant, or, in other words, to our giving way to the contemporary encounter with the American apocalyptic sublime. Essentially unconcerned with measurement and aesthetic organizational practices than with, for instance, photographic and filmic depiction itself, with the depiction of an instant, as opposed to its embodiment, Goldstein's painterly treatment of his subject evokes the American apocalyptic sublime primarily because his visual art is based on a genuinely crit-ical viewpoint on everyday life and, especially, on how the instant is a representation of the very changes and conflicts that come to bear between the depictive media themselves, namely, painting, photography, and cinema. We see in *Untitled* the photographic medium itself euthanized, autopsied and on-display, corpse-like, through the lens of something-like its historic rival, painting.

As a result, our contemporary conception, description and, hopefully, accurate interpretation of American visual culture of which *Untitled* is a part, is rather divergent from that of Virilio's attitude to art, perception and looking, and particularly since Goldstein's paintings, indeed his entire endeavour, like our own, was in tune with the tragic and, crucially, open to the exploration of the resounding nihilism of our age. Certainly, our perception of American visual culture is not merely concerned with its function in an American art wrapped up with the cultural politics of artists and their materials. Instead, our understanding of Goldstein's interpretation of American visual culture is also fundamentally about its function in an American art gripped by the cultural politics and aesthetics of dehumanization, catastrophic events, material occurrences and reoccurrences and, in particular, his engagement with 'rationality' and ethical systems that have been delivered to us through narratives, creative and otherwise, and which, despite all the odds, continue to duplicate themselves whilst remaining somehow impervious to either explanation or sanction. In its anticipated radical inclusiveness of objects of study going appreciably beyond the diversity of things usually incorporated in even Virilio's avant-garde typology of art history, our perspective on Goldstein's place in American visual culture entails a basically reworked description of the paradigms and techniques required to appreciate his American art. Concerning the history of Goldstein's work from his films to his paintings, the sphere of their politics, aesthetics and their embodiment of the American apocalyptic sublime, it is critical to keep in mind his artistic behaviour, which was concerned with registering shock, awe and numbness in the face of the complete lack of cohesion between what one sees and what one knows or wants to know to be true. And it is here that the character of Goldstein's materials and their use in his paintings employ many previously leapt over details and images that can be seen as an attempt at the obliteration of all narrative cohesion in the field of contemporary art.

Our Virilian conjectures concerning contemporary American visual culture can then be described as a contribution to the sub-discipline of Virilian visual cultural studies, a contribution which is epitomized in part by our discussion of Goldstein's *Untitled*. For Goldstein's *Untitled* is itself a kind of speculation on the nature of knowledge, a speculation that, for instance, can disclose those 'instants' that can be stolen from the 'truth' of photography. It follows that, while Goldstein's *Untitled* cannot actually be represented as an exploratory fusion centred on the study of American artworks, it can be characterized as photography re-rendered in the very form and medium of painting that, at its best, reaches beyond the appearance of things to give us a sense, a picture, that insinuates all that which may be absent. On the other hand, and deviating from Virilio's elaborate and bold description of contemporary visual culture in *Art as Far as the Eye Can See*, our perhaps more straightforward if provisional narrative of Goldstein's *Untitled* regards it as the essence of the American apocalyptic sublime, as a painting that advances the politicization of American art by treading lightly on the borders of contemporary nihilism. Even so, and perhaps inadvertently suggestive of Virilio's *Art as Far as the Eye Can See*, Goldstein's *Untitled* does project a kind of cold tragicness if not cold panic as it walks us along the edges of the vast lacunae that continuously open up between meaning and salvation. Thus Goldstein's American apocalyptic sublime is something of a test for the subject of art history since, we argue, whilst American art previously signified the confluence of artist and materials, Goldstein's approach to new forms of media and art tussles with the question of technologized information both as subject matter and as the implicit meaning or theme of his paintings. Goldstein's art and often intangible materials therefore shifted outside of wholly ocular and experiential or empirical matters and became ever more entangled in the socio-culturally important repercussions of media and technologically derived information. There is therefore a sense in which our radical Virilian idea of American visual culture both organizes and scrutinizes this question of mediatized or technologized information as a topic and secondary theme of Goldstein's painting. This is revealed, for instance, by the way in which Goldstein's *Untitled* emits a similar sensation to that of Virilio's cold panic and related expectation horizon of collective anguish. Yet, counter to Virilio, this shift into cold panic is for us not just an emblem of a wide-ranging socio-cultural and economic move headed for some future chronopolitics or accelerated mass culture but also something that was perhaps anticipated by Goldstein's influential American contemporary art, by his politics, and, specifically, by his technoscientific experiments with paintings that co-opt potentially lethal yet sublime events, dismember and totally remediate mass cultural narratives of photography and cinema to clarify and render their helplessness in the face of cataclysmic realities.

Sarah Trigg

Faraway from Virilio's vocabulary, then, our contemporary examination of Goldstein's approach to American visual culture converges with numerous other American painters working to catalogue and explore specific features of American mass culture. These American painters and their investigations concentrate not so much on an American mass culture that has been abandoned as only lately been exposed. Sarah Trigg's recent collection of paintings, *Shape of a New Continent* (Image 10.2), for example, is distinctive for its aura of the American apocalyptic sublime and chiefly for the way that she applies the paint to her canvases.

Image 10.2: Super Terrestrial, *2010 Acrylic on canvas, 60 x 72 inches (Sarah Trigg).*

Very different from Trigg's (2009: 229–36) earlier *Daily Markings on the Face of the Earth* collection, the paint in her *Shape of a New Continent* series is poured on in paintings such as *Super Terrestrial*, with the occasionally exaggerated pull of gravity both defying Trigg's aesthetic predictions of or allusions to a successful outcome and adding a transcendent dimension. In *Super Terrestrial*, for example, the gravitational path is not at right angles to the horizon line, but leaning, which, disturbingly, means that this painting exhibits numerous gravitational directions simultaneously. Every so often pouring the paint with the canvas resting on the ground, Trigg's American apocalyptic sublime is thus concerned with how the paint pools and cracks to some extent, much like the surface of the Earth itself, above all in times of devastation, in times of drought or abnormally low rainfall, for instance, char- acterized, as we all know, but most of us only know from our TV screens, by the seemingly sinister forces that bring with them adversely affected growing and living conditions, prolonged short- ages, and dried mud for as far as victims' eyes can see. Trigg's individual paint marks are accordingly symbolic of the markings of humankind upon the Earth, with the canvas itself functioning as the Earth's surface. A fundamental idea emerging from *Shape of a New Continent* is that, like her previous *Daily Markings* series, the surface of the Earth is understood by Trigg as flesh that can be removed, examined and sampled as a tissue, taken from the living body of the Earth for diagnostic purposes. So, for Trigg, a central motif of the *Shape of a New Continent* series is that, as she put it and emphasized to the authors in a 2009 email conversation, '*thought is like matter that can shift, change, explode, and transform like geological processes*'.

In short, like Goldstein's, Trigg's work resides in a (perhaps gravitational) field of contemporary painting that seems to have escaped much of traditional art history and certainly Virilio. Choosing to situate herself in New York City, the United States' art market capital, to watch and to visually record America's and, at times, the world's excessive experiments with transitory and sheer landscapes, Trigg's encounters with the *Shape of a New Continent* alert us to an American apocalyptic sublime of flows, wrenches, and the natural force of attraction that is exerted by the Earth upon every object at or near its surface. Artists such as Trigg, who have chosen to remain living and practising through and beyond the events of 11 September 2001, in a New York City that, with uncanny resilience, continually overcomes and outruns its own peculiar, continuously renewed, condition of 'prime-target-fixation syndrome' (Vanderbilt 2002: 75) are accordingly uniquely positioned to appreciate the current state of American mass culture. Furthermore, Trigg's and countless other contemporary American artists' choice of painting as primary medium and mode of expression, despite (or perhaps, ironically, partly due to) their unflagging interest in and respective individual ease with an aesthetics of the extreme based on digital media technologies, also bring to mind the exceedingly genuine possibility of complete destruction. What we are putting forward here is the idea that artists which we associate with the American apocalyptic sublime are connected both by their similarly intense, if not obsessive, longstanding researches into the incalculable marvel that is planet Earth and by how this world becomes interlaced with the vernacular, summed up in single photographic images or, periodically, terror-inducing and frequently topical source materials, for example as film clips of September 11 or, more recently, TV images of the 2010 Deepwater Horizon oil spill in the Gulf of Mexico, which is the biggest marine oil spill in the history of both the US and the global oil industry. Our Virilian yet innovative historical view of this personal approach to and problematization of the visual culture of the American apocalyptic sublime can thus be grasped as a new theoretical area that centres on the work of artists such as Goldstein and Trigg. This conceptual arena is then one that is involved with Goldstein's, Trigg's, and others' paintings of the eruption of the splendour and revulsion witnessed not only in America but the world over in the present day.

Marc Handelman

Focusing on contemporary American art that is primarily influenced by the work of Goldstein, we now want to turn to the contemporary painting and cultural politics of one of the principal creators of the encounter with the American apocalyptic sublime, Marc Handelman. An encounter with Handelman's American apocalyptic sublime as discussed here is an encounter with a new post-Goldstein expression of vision, studies of military technology and reflections on corporate information, that, *pace* Virilio, for us, is symptomatic of the uneasy artistic reaction to an accelerated and emergent spectacular instant. Our Virilian strain of American visual culture as a consequence develops out of a perception of American painting in particular that focuses not on what artists like Goldstein, Trigg or Handelman lose from their art or awareness but on their re-incorporation of new technologies, on their ideas and preferences concerning previous models and media and on the limitations of human agency in the face of various products of our information-saturated media environment. These are subjects that are thriving at present owing not just to artists' mounting inability to fully involve themselves with or intervene in new technological forms of pictorial construction and dissemination, to the altered political strictures of American visual art and cultural production, but also to their increasing confusion when faced with the reification of dogmatic imagery and the fetishization of violence through its commodification. From this angle, therefore, our reworked Virilian understanding of the tropes, methods and processes of the visual culture of the American apocalyptic sublime has initiated a project that goes beyond both traditional art history and Virilio's conception of visual culture. In fact, it is an undertaking which simply assumes that every American aesthetic medium is presently altering in reaction to the radical changes taking shape in how we deal with technologized information. Hence, unlike Virilio, we have a strong interest in incorporating into our own contemporary concerns American painters such as Handelman.

In contrast to Virilio's radical account of visual culture, particularly as it is expressed in *Native Land: Stop-Eject*, we want to shift the discussion away not from art history as from Virilio's current and seemingly obsessive concern with chronopolitics, spatiality, temporality, air travel, telecommunications and instantaneity. Instead, we want to focus on Handelman's 2008 series of paintings, *Tomorrow's Forecast: Strikingly Clear*, chiefly because in this series Handelman explores the American apocalyptic sublime head-on

Image 10.3: Marc Handelman: Tomorrow's Forecast: Strikingly Clear.
2008. Oil on canvas. 74 x 58.25 inches (© Marc Handelman).

through the remodelling of nineteenth-century American landscape painting, focusing solely on the sky above the horizon rather
than the landscape as such. In this examination, it is not the mass
media, Virilio's rampant culture of terror or an art contemporary

with mutually assured destruction that concerns Handelman as the highly aestheticized and romanticized images produced by corporate, military, defence advertising campaigns. For Handelman's current paintings are based on spectacular images, on what might be called the appropriation of the sky as icon and as subject. Essentially undisturbed by Virilio's fixation on real time and spatiality, extremism, escalation, the balance of terror, if not war, Handelman's contemporary explorations are, rather, motivated by a desire to reconsider our basic suppositions involving the imagery offered in full-page newspaper advertisements by US defence contractors such as Northrop-Grumman, to reassess our consciousness of advertising's seductive landscapes that, as revealed in Handelman's *Tomorrow's Forecast: Strikingly Clear* (Image 10.3), come down not to Virilian quandaries regarding temporality and spatiality but, initially at least, to issues linked to advertising's use of block letters, in this case to spell out *TOMORROW'S FORECAST: STRIKINGLY CLEAR.*

What can we possibly say about Northrop-Grumman's world, except, perhaps, that it is a clever, if glib, evocation of weather control? Yet, in Handelman's world, in his contemporary art and history as encapsulated in one of his most eponymous paintings, we are presented instead with an uninhabitable planet, with a 'landscape' dominated by a central, white-hot ball, the sun, not setting or rising, but floating in a seeming moment of sublime stasis and, moreover, obscured by a device reminiscent of Goldstein's wide-screen edge and other proscenium-like elements. For these reasons, we think it important to consider a number of the issues that Handelman's painting raises. Indeed, and distinct from Virilio, we want to scrutinize Handelman's thoughts on aesthetics, art and alternative art historical theories and practices about America's mass media culture. Handelman's *Tomorrow's Forecast: Strikingly Clear*, for instance, includes a 'window' or layer to look through, a curtain-like encumbrance that appears and disappears throughout the picture plane in an all-over pattern, an obstruction through which we must peer while being blinded by the burning orb. Our Virilian take on American visual culture does not, obviously, typically involve questions on the topic of, for example, Handelman's individual vision and physical capabilities. However, we would like to draw the reader's attention to some of the original features of this work of art. Handelman's 'window', for instance, can be described as a 'pliage', as a folding that functions at once to partially obscure and to focus our gaze on the view beyond, as well as to call attention not to Handelman's artistic methods or practices *per se* but to the 'objectness' of the painting itself. And yet there is nothing here that could be considered coherent or formal since the thematic object, the image – and the message – to which our gaze is drawn, diverts and obstructs so as to become strikingly unclear. It is not that Handelman is questioning the principle that today American rules of art are the indisputable gauge and guarantee of taste and artistic value. Rather, we contend, any, perhaps post-Virilian, elucidation of Handelman's painting must not only accept the gradual transfer away from an art once substantial but also the preemptive character of his painting as a substantial art. For Handelman's painting is intended to rupture or arrest our view much the way in which the similar devices of Goldstein offer up not the fact of disaster but the 'fact' of 'depiction'. Handelman's art does not of course wrestle with Virilio's crises in modern architecture and music, sculpture, film, radio and television but, all the same, is a sort of reflection of the drift in the direction of insubstantial art, of a hovering between the ready-made digital image and the painting, between optical representation and mediated abstraction. But, more significant, as with all of his contemporary paintings, is Handelman's concentration not on Virilio's obsession with the compression of every form of representation but, instead, on the equivocal aspects of representation itself, on, in the present context, the genre of romanticized, corporate, military advertising photography. Almost in opposition to Virilio, therefore, and on account of the striking disparity between what is expected – between the 'real' message hinted at – and what is perceived even as it is romanticized in the source image itself, we insist that Handelman's American apocalyptic sublime in the form of the real space of his significant painting, *Tomorrow's Forecast: Strikingly Clear*, can, if not exceed, then, at least, break or block for an instant the real time of presentation in the American visual arts through an entity displayed on a canvas, an assertion that forms both the main thrust of our own work here and Handelman's artwork.

In a place still under development yet somewhere other than Goldstein's conception of the American mass media, other than his art and sense of futility, and other than his digitally mediated aesthetics founded on a lack of human agency and a visual project rooted in techno-nihilism and multifaceted remediations of the photographic and cinematic image, both our own and Handelman's post-Goldstein approach to American visual culture and its imagery as the American apocalyptic sublime aim to redescribe a facet of Goldstein's visuality with a concentration on Handelman's contemporary American socio-cultural and economic circumstances and on his landscape painting that, crucially, rejects Goldstein's annihilation or abstraction of the subject regarding the image. On the other hand, neither ours nor Handelman's are superhuman efforts to hypothesize the digitization of all optical mediums, the elimination of all traditional varieties of representation, or even Goldstein's ideas concerning our desire for technological imagery, media, or film bound up within various kinds of annihilation. To be more precise, both ours and Handelman's are a kind of post-Virilian inflected reconsideration of the nature and implications of artistic research involving the sharp discontinuity between what is expected and what is perceived, the American apocalyptic sublime, and, of course, Handelman's interpretation of Goldstein's fascination with banal images and objects that, for Goldstein himself, became after-images for destruction, war and conditions of alienation. Handelman's American apocalyptic sublime, unlike Goldstein's, thus has very little to do with the unforeseen acceleration of presentation and immediacy, truth, history, politics and the economy, and a lot to do with resisting real or false apocalyptic forms of alienation. Flying in the face of Virilio's cold panic and his now (in)famous descriptions of 'Delirious New York' (Virilio 2000: 18–23) as *Ground Zero* (Virilio 2002), Handelman's stimulating and crucial painting, we contend, reaches instead for his own renegotiation of the same territory, based not on Goldstein's glowing pristine surfaces and a seeming absence of the hand, but instead on a rupturing or halting of the real time of presentation in American visual art through a re-emphasis of the human scale and the body itself, and, hence, of the human origin of

picture-making. For even within the framework of a contemporary American mass media culture of transmission powered by the
force of the emotional state that it can rouse in its witnesses using
incredible imagery, the human body still has to negotiate and
renegotiate actual, tangible, paintings. As Handleman, in an email
discussion with the authors put it in April 2010:

> The reading of the image is never just at a level of signification and
> this perceptual dependency on the body, however, subtle, or retracted
> from, say, the movements of the body in Virilio's (Virilio and Parent
> 1996) 'oblique function' architectural scenarios is still an engaged
> perception.

Thus, for Handelman, the key questions concerning spectacular
imagery today are not about its phenomenological or discursive
impact on the general public as such as on the specificities of the
human body as a thinking entity. Here it is not contemporary
societies swamped with Virilian cold panic, terrorism, or even the
socio-cultural transformations activated by new information and
communications technologies, by new media and their associated
effects as how painting might yet still offer something to perception
that is currently being thoroughly reorganized by the perceptual
logics of digitized screens. In presenting this alternative consideration of Handelman's *Tomorrow's Forecast: Strikingly Clear* by way
of the concept of the American apocalyptic sublime, a post-Virilian
attitude towards American visual culture has emerged, one that is
less interested in the sublime as fear or dread but in the sublime
as an apocalyptic representation in the form of painting. Perhaps
what we have discovered is thus that New York City's artistic
population, particularly in the figures of Goldstein, Trigg and
Handelman, were and are at the same moment apprehensive and
passionate about the future of a city which, prior to 11 September
2001, was, unlike a lot of other cities around the world, innocent
of the destruction of its buildings from the air, of events that bring
in their wake individual dislocation and suspicion, architectural
substitution and estrangement.

In this final section our aim has been less concerned with making
a critique of Virilio and more concerned with exploring ways in

which we might develop his and our own radical intellectual and political position in art history. It is not a matter of rejecting Virilio's outspoken socio-political analysis in *Art as Far as the Eye Can See* as attempting to take it in new, perhaps oblique, directions and beyond the confines of traditional art history. We are not against Virilian studies of cold panic but feel that our contribution has involved a re-focusing not merely on contemporary artists but on contemporary American painters such as Goldstein, Trigg and Handelman. For these and many other American painters, whilst wholly content to scavenge for their source images online, point to and consider different expectation horizons and communities through their contemporary American landscape paintings than Virilio does when remarking on vision technologies. Like Virilio, Goldstein, Trigg and Handelman work hard to expect the unexpected. Distinct from Virilio, however, Trigg and Handelman, if not Goldstein, whilst recognizing the neurosis and deteriorating social dynamism all about them, refuse to surrender to such toxic circumstances or to the substitution of military deterrence by civil deterrence. Trigg and Handelman, above all, not only critically reflect on but also strive to represent what we have identified as the American apocalyptic sublime. And so, using Virilio's work as a springboard into a contemporary conception of American visual culture has, we argue, been productive in that the philosophy of art now has a new sub-concept, the American apocalyptic sublime, with which to engage the practices of diverse contemporary American artists and their unique concern with the aesthetics of disaster.

Conclusion

We want to end our thoughts on Virilio's links to visual culture with a critical appraisal of his and our own speculative writings on this important theme and appraise their theoretical value. What, for example, might the probable effect of our current perspective on Virilian studies concerned with the contemporary visual culture of the American apocalyptic sublime be? Let us bring this chapter to a close with a concluding reflection on Virilio's and our own philosophical appreciation of visual culture and the art of the American apocalyptic sublime.

To begin with, Virilio's philosophy and cultural theory regarding art, history and visual culture amount to an extraordinary *tour de force* of French thinking about visuality and cultural studies. His theorization of visual culture and contemporary art, history and imagery is second to none. Inspired primarily by Merleau-Ponty's existential philosophy and phenomenology of art, Virilio's influential viewpoint on visual culture is unique. Who else but Virilio could devise a theory of art, perception and seeing rooted in the belief that our eyes are presently wired shut and, moreover, are preparing our bodies to comply with the logic of panic? Who else but Virilio could ponder the contemporary development of aesthetics and politics, artists and their materials, and present a work on visual culture, *Art as Far as the Eye Can See*, devoted not to seeing as such but to a phenomenology of blindness, to a 'lapse of attention which lasted not for a minute but for a whole century' (Virilio 2007: 4)? Undeniably, few cultural theorists produce texts that are either as innovative or as significant as those created by Virilio.

Yet we have in this chapter been less involved with Virilio's theoretical ruminations on 'teleobjectivity', on his examination of blindness, or even with his abstract engagements with television. Instead, we have focused on Virilio's theoretical ideas about contemporary visual culture as articulated in his *Art as Far as the Eye Can See*. And, as we have established, for Virilio (2007: 4), new media's radical effect upon art and its materials is such that 'we no longer seek to see' in the era of the Internet, no longer seek 'to look around us' in our newly transformed societies founded on chronopolitics and, increasingly, blindness.

Even so, and as we have also ascertained, for us, Virilio's philosophical study of contemporary visual culture, whilst certainly imposing with respect to expanding our knowledge of art, perception and looking, is rather off beam in one respect, which is his (2007: 3) contention in *Art as Far as the Eye Can See* that 'real time definitely outclasses the real space of major artworks, whether of literature or the visual arts'. In this chapter, we have, then, questioned Virilio's line of reasoning on contemporary art whilst concurrently instituting and cultivating a key yet absent concept concerning his insights into visual culture: the important concept of the apocalyptic sublime. Akin to Virilio, we too are enormously preoccupied with expecting the unexpected, with visual environments relating to acute deficiencies in perceptual continuity, illogical perceptual sequences, processes, acts and faculties. But what is most extraordinary and which generates major obstacles for Virilio's recent work on visual culture is his notable lack of curiosity as regards contemporary painters. As we have argued and confirmed, one looks in vain, for instance, for painters of any sort, let alone painters of the apocalyptic sublime, in Virilio's recent art exhibitions.

Consequently, we employed our hypothesis concerning the apocalyptic sublime with the intention of nurturing current if so far conjectural premises in Virilio studies which are first and foremost engaged with contemporary visual culture. Our contribution is thus to the developing sub-discipline of Virilian visual cultural studies. Contemplating the work of Goldstein, Trigg and Handelman, three American painters of the apocalyptic sublime, we concentrated initially on Goldstein's important painting, *Untitled*, followed by Trigg's *Super Terrestrial* and Handelman's *Tomorrow's Forecast: Strikingly Clear*. For us, these painters and their works offer vital clues as to the appropriate techniques for researching the visual arts today, for investigating new conceptions of picture-making and aesthetic spaces. Either past or present residents of New York City, these appropriation and landscape artists exploit found photographs, advertising and TV imagery to create arresting paintings out of a progressively more dematerialized mass mediated American culture. Examining, questioning, taking apart and reworking media representations, these artists' principally appropriated artworks, paintings based on film, photo-montage and advertising, thus make a noteworthy contribution both to American visual art and, critically, to the critique of the everyday language of corporate media discourse. Illustrative of what we have identified as the American apocalyptic sublime, these paintings, these American landscapes and nonfigurative images, signal crucial theoretical events that have taken place in painting following

Goldstein's ground-breaking aestheticization of the American mass media. Goldstein, Trigg and Handelman, contemporary painters of the American apocalyptic sublime, we have been arguing, are not just important American painters in their own right but also, with respect to theoretical debates within art history and visual culture, emblematic of the problem that we have identified with Virilio's declaration that real time has left behind the real space of contemporary visual artworks.

Note

1. Art, politics and the contemporary history of aesthetics and technology are, needless to say, integral to all of Virilio's major writings, such as his *Art and Fear* (2003a). However, in engaging with his existing work on visual culture in this chapter, we have, mainly for reasons of space, chosen to focus on Virilio's current full-length text on art, perception, and looking, *Art as Far as the Eye Can See*.

References

Barthes, R. (1992) *The Responsibility of Forms: Critical Essays on Music, Art and Representation*. Los Angeles: University of California Press.

Baudrillard, J. (2005) *The Conspiracy of Art: Manifestos, Texts, Interviews*. Massachusetts: MIT Press.

Baxandall, M. (1988) *Painting and Experience in Fifteenth-Century Italy: A Primer in the Social History of Pictorial Style*. Oxford: Oxford University Press.

Crimp, D. (1979) 'Pictures', 8 *October*. 75–88.

Derrida, J. (1987) *The Truth in Painting*. Chicago: University of Chicago Press.

Eklund, D. (2009) *The Pictures Generation, 1974–1984*. New York: Metropolitan Museum of Art.

Foucault, M. (2000) *Aesthetics, Method, and Epistemology*, vol. 2: *Essential Works of Michel Foucault 1954–1984*. London: Routledge.

Garnett, J. and J. Armitage (2011) 'Apocalypse Now: An Interview with Joy Garnett', *Cultural Politics*, 7, 1: 59–78.

Handelman, M. (2009) 'Tomorrow's Forecast: Strikingly Clear', *ArtFagCity.com*, IMG MGMT series: www.artfagcity.com/2009/08/28/img-mgmt-tomorrows-forecast-strikingly-clear/

Isles, C. (2003) 'Vanishing Act: Chrissie Iles on Jack Goldstein – Passages – Obituary'. *ArtForum,* (May) 41, 9: 23–6.

Kittler, F. A. (2010) *Optical Media: Berlin Lectures, 1999.* Cambridge: Polity.

Lyotard, J.-F. (1993) *Lessons on the Analytic of the Sublime.* Stanford: Stanford University Press.

Mirzoeff, N. (2009) *An Introduction to Visual Culture.* London: Routledge.

Rush, M. (2005) *New Media in Art.* London: Thames and Hudson.

Vanderbilt, T. (2002) *Survival City: Adventures Among the Ruins of Atomic America.* Princeton: Princeton Architectural Press.

Trigg, S. (2009) 'Daily Marking on the Face of the Earth', *Cultural Politics*, 5, 2: 229–36.

Virilio, P. (1986) *Speed and Politics: An Essay on Dromology.* New York: Semiotext(e).

— (2000) 'Delirious New York', pp. 18–23 in his *Landscape of Events.* Princeton: Princeton Architectural Press.

— (2002) *Ground Zero.* London: Verso.

— (2003a) *Art and Fear.* London: Continuum.

— (2003b) *Unknown Quantity.* London: Thames and Hudson.

— (2007) *Art as Far as the Eye Can See.* Oxford: Berg.

— (2009) *The Aesthetics of Disappearance.* New York: Semiotext(e).

— with Raymond Depardon (2008) *Native Land: Stop-Eject.* Paris: Fondation Cartier pour l'art contemporain.

— with Claude Parent (1996) *The Function of the Oblique.* London: Architectural Association.

11

Impact Studies

Paul Virilio

Today, creating an event means above all turning your back on mimetism and engaging instead in the modelling of a propaganda that no longer speaks its name and is now without a doubt the most significant form of pollution there is.[1] This is ETHOLOGICAL pollution, this time, and it now goes hand-in-hand with the globalization of affects.

Whether we like it or not, creating an event means provoking an accident. In a time when the 'present' of this over-hyped *real time* dominates the 'past' as well as the 'future', the event is no longer innocent. This is where the *impact strategy* comes in, based on advertising but now underscoring the contemporary art and culture produced by the new political orthodoxy of the single brain in this era of globalization accomplished.

Already a few years back, a celebrated British critic described the artists of the rising generation as IMPACT MAKERS, thereby flagging the extreme importance of an 'art brut' where what counts is not so much the intrinsic quality as the intensity of the emotional state it provokes in its viewers; the artist in question seeking above all 'to capture the psychological intensity of onlookers' through the energy of a gesture – pictorial, sculptural or other – like that behind the sawn-up sculptures currently on show.

In these manifestations, so close in nature to the terrorism of the twenty-first century, the idea is not so much to link elements in a given space of time as to shake up the onlooker or the listener by means of an emotional impact strategy that involves the *surprising instant* more than the space-time of a finished work.

It also involves the sudden *lack of distinction between genres*, with the visual arts, the architecture of installations, the staging of exhibitions in museums, but also theatre, opera and the art of choreography, all the art forms and their specific morphology, abandoning themselves to this rhythmology in which provocation and intimidation sell so amazingly well that Anglo-Saxon advertising people have created the term SHOCK-VERTISING in reference to the commercial necessity of shocking to attract attention.

With this last form of anti-cultural incivility, we're no longer dealing with expressionism, or even with the 'neo-expressionism' of the figure-deforming avant-gardes of the twentieth century and their stereotyped representations. We are dealing with a sort of outrageous activism, whereby people are no longer content just to do away with *figuration*, but want to eliminate everything that makes an artistic genre intrinsically distinctive. Such confusion is perpetrated these days by what is known variously as a *spectacle vivant*, or 'live show', 'performance art' or even 'street theatre', which involves opera every bit as much as the circus, choral singing suddenly becoming a sort of background music for a kind of role-playing that is not so much about actors dressing up as the travesty of a *mise en scène* of jumbled-up genres.

At Salzburg, for instance, over the summer of 2006, the music of Mozart, according to the music critics, 'fulfilled the function of a comforting balm relieving the tension arising from a sound-track of superimposed and amplified voices, visions of suffering à la Pina Bausch and gesture worthy of hip-hop'.[2]

With Joachim Schlomer's *Rex. Tremendus*, the final part of his trilogy on the music of Mozart, morphing takes over from the unforgettable *morphology* of Mozart's œuvre. Far from complementing each other, visual and sound sensations blur in this MAGMA where rhythms win out over forms and their limits, dragged down as these are into illusionism, the indistinction of an ART WITHOUT END, with neither head nor tail, in which audio-visuality achieves the chaos of all the images' EVOLVING-INTO-MUSIC.

There is no 'ARTFUL DECONSTRUCTION' here, but only the DEREALISATION of the art of perceiving, a fatal confusion of the perceptible, analogous to the confusion of a Babelian language, where everything melds in the indifference and passivity of a subject completely at sea.

Over that summer of 2006, we also learned that the former head of the Italian government, Silvio Berlusconi, had regaled guests with a fake earthquake and a simulated volcanic eruption in the vast park attached to his property. The illusion was so perfect, they say, that next-door neighbours called the fire brigade, thinking there was a fire.[3]

Now, there's a good example for you of this 'accident', this catastrophe, that tends to renew 'the event' (artistic or other), with the musical evening and bel canto making way for the 'special effects' of an impact strategy in which the exemplary œuvre completely disappears, replaced by a spectacular terror. The *assault on decency* of the Surrealists or the Expressionists bows out once and for all before *the assault on emotional value* of a 'neo-terrorism' that spurns aesthetics, just as the commando spurns politics, with the *indiscriminate attack* now massacring anonymous victims instead of declared adversaries. The morphology of military action gradually loses its aims, its objectives, in aid of a transpolitical chaos no one seems to benefit from.

On another note, this one purely festive, we are seeing the general spread of a kind of *spectacle vivant* that never misses an opportunity to mix street arts with film festivals, books or contemporary visual arts. This is not to leave out this year's première, a politics festival, which brought together the speaker of the Scottish Parliament, George Reid, and 'James Bond', alias Sean Connery. Let's hope that next time they stage it, the Edinburgh Fringe doesn't forget to invite the 'Terminator', Arnold Schwarzenegger, governor of California.

Avignon, Salzburg, Edinburgh 2006: the *event accident* is on a roll and the confusion of genres at an all-time high, with the major risk that *construction* and its deconstructions, even *form* and its singular morphologies, will be swept away in its raging torrents – in the wake of the *figure* and its successive figurations.

To try and understand the panic behind 'postmodern' represen-tations a bit better, let's go back a moment to a single word, that Anglo-American word MORPHING, so popular in current par-lance. Morphing refers to the continuous, animated transformation of one image into another and so participates in the KINEMATIC and its now very particular energy, with the added importance of media audio-visibility.

Whether we acknowledge it or not, what we're dealing with here is a metamorphosis of the space of representations – of all representations, aesthetic, political or other – that is to say, of the formation of the perceptible and the pertinent, whereby the *acceleration of reality* today extends the acceleration of history that modernity was already a portent of, the obvious patrimonial trace.

This explains the catastrophic substitution of the event for cultural action and its perennity, promoting instead the shock of images to the detriment of the weight of forms and words. TELEREALITY wins out over objective REALITY in a sort of blindness, a teleobjective blinkering that far outstrips (and how!) all reason, all political thought, every bit as much as artistic thought, through its hallucinatory conditioning power over the masses as over individuals, since the *real space* of forms yields its aesthetic obviousness to the *real time* of the 'transformism' of facts. The only thing that gains by this is the optical illusion provided by stage and screen, the *spectacle vivant* never being anything more than another term (this one French) for an Anglo-Saxon term: LIVE COVERAGE.

Ultimately, everything will be played out in the political arena of democracy, as on the theatre stage of contemporary art, over the choice between two words: LIFE or LIVE.

With that last word signalling the telepresence of a broad-cast recorded *as it happens*, the first word loses its objective pre-eminence and, in sum, its *presence as fact*, in the face of the tyranny of the real time of an instantaneity now gearing up to replace the famous spontaneity of the revolutionaries of yore, with the RAVE PARTY suddenly becoming the model of membership, wherever the community of emotion dominates the community of interest of the old political parties.

October 2006

Translated by Julie Rose

Notes

1. 'Impact Studies' is published here with the permission of Paul Virilio and the Maison des Cultures du Monde. It was originally published in 2007 as 'Etudes d'impact' in *Internationale de L'imaginaire*, n.s. 22, *Événementiel Vs Action Culturelle*, published by Maison des Cultures du Monde, Babel, pp. 74–80.
2. See the article by Eric Dahan in *Libération*, 11 August 2006.
3. See note headed 'Les idées explosives de Berlusconi' in *Sud-Ouest*, 18 August 2006.

Index

Note: page numbers in italics denote illustrations